THE MAKING OF A TORY HUMANIST

William Wordsworth and the Idea of Community

THE MAKING OF A TORY HUMANIST

William Wordsworth and the Idea of Community

Michael H. Friedman

New York · · COLUMBIA UNIVERSITY PRESS · · 1979

The Andrew W. Mellon Foundation, through a special grant, has assisted the Press in publishing this volume.

Library of Congress Cataloging in Publication Data

Friedman, Michael H   1945–
    The making of a Tory humanist.

    Bibliography: p.
    Includes index.
    1. Wordsworth, William, 1770–1850—Political and social views.   2. Community life in literature.
I. Title.
PR5892.P64F7   821'.7   79-10968
ISBN 0-231-04668-5

Columbia University Press
New York   Guildford, Surrey

For my parents and my wife, Mary

CONTENTS

ACKNOWLEDGMENTS

IT was my privilege to study with and learn from the late Lionel Trilling of Columbia University. It was he who first taught me to appreciate and read Wordsworth. More than that, I learned from him that the study of all great literature is, in part, the study of the moral and the social life.

My debt to Carl Woodring and Steven Marcus of Columbia University is very great, indeed. They read my manuscript through its many stages of development and were generous with their wise counsel and encouragement.

I would also like to thank Karl Kroeber of Columbia University, David Ferry of Wellesley College, and Rudolf Storch of Tufts University, with whom I discussed Wordsworth, with great profit to myself, while I was writing this book.

Abbreviations Used in the Text and Notes

P.W. William Wordsworth, *The Poetical Works*, 5 vols. Ernest de Selincourt and Helen Darbishire, eds. (Oxford: Clarendon, 1940–1949).

Prel. William Wordsworth, *The Prelude*. Ernest de Selincourt and Helen Darbishire, eds. (Oxford: Clarendon, 1959). All references are to the 1805 text.

Prose William Wordsworth, *The Prose Works*, 3 vols. W. J. B. Owen and Jane Worthington Smyser, eds. (Oxford: Clarendon, 1974).

E.L. Ernest de Selincourt, ed.; rev. by Chester Shaver, *The Letters of William and Dorothy Wordsworth: The Early Years, 1787–1805* (Oxford: Clarendon, 1967).

M.L. Ernest de Selincourt, ed.; rev. by Mary Moorman, *The Letters of William and Dorothy Wordsworth: The Middle Years, 1806–1811* (Oxford: Clarendon, 1969).

D.W.J. Mary Moorman, ed., *The Journals of Dorothy Wordsworth* (Oxford: Oxford: Clarendon, 1969).

Lakes C. M. L. Bouch and C. P. Jones, *A Short Economic and Social History of the Lake Counties: 1500–1830* (Manchester: Manchester University Press, 1961).

ONE

THE NEED FOR COMMUNITY

GENIUS is not a thing to be limited, circumscribed or easily defined. "Bring out," says Blake, "number weight & measure in a year of dearth."[1] The advent of genius resists explanation and must be taken as a given, as must its disappearance. No attempt, then, will be made to explain, simply or totally, the decline of William Wordsworth's powers of creation. But it should be possible to examine usefully such a decline without claiming to have fully understood it.

It was the fate of Wordsworth's genius to be intimately involved with the stability of England's social and economic structures at a time when patriarchal political economy was disintegrating and England was being propelled into developed industrial capitalism. The forces changing English society were beyond the powers of any one man, even one of genius, to control. These forces eventually destroyed the England in which Wordsworth's greatest work was created. Indeed, Wordsworth's England was being destroyed even as he wrote his major works. Wordsworth's creativity seemed to have been linked to a strong need for a sense of an enclosing, supporting community. At first, to be sure, it seems odd, perhaps incongruous, to say this of the poet who did so much to make solitude and introspection the very stuff of poetry, but the oddity will disappear, I hope, as we examine the conflicts out of which Wordsworth's best poetry emerged. Wordsworth was

1

not an exception to Aristotle's bland but powerful observation; he was neither less than fully human nor a god.[2]

But if Wordsworth was neither beast nor deity, it did not follow that he was to enter the polis simply or directly. Rather Wordsworth was driven with many turnings and vicissitudes down a path which would, paradoxically, lead to community as a haven from himself. The Wordsworth who wrote the poetry of his great decade, 1797 to 1807, did not possess a secure or fully developed sense of identity. Instead, his ego was torn between two opposite but causally related senses of self, two different modes of perceiving the self in relation to the outside world. He described himself as

> Having two natures in me, joy the one
> The other melancholy. . . .
> *(Prel.* x, 869–870)

The joyous nature of which Wordsworth writes was one that was confident, proud, exultant, even imperious. This nature I shall call the princely sense of self. In the "Intimations Ode" Wordsworth speaks of the child's essential princely nature as having been wrongfully appropriated from him:

> The homely nurse does all she can
> To make her Foster-child, her Inmate Man,
> Forget the glories he hath known,
> And that imperial palace whence he came.
> *(P.W.* 4:281)

The melancholy nature corresponded with an opposite sense of self, a self that lived fearfully and abjectly, a self in which he was, to quote an early letter of Wordsworth's to his siter Dorothy, "a contracted spirit" *(E.L.* 32), fearing either diminution or absolute dissolution of the boundaries of perceived personal existence. This was the self that, according to one of the reminiscences about his poetry that Isabela Fenwick recorded verbatim in the years 1842 and 1843, was forced "while going to school" to grasp "at a wall or a tree to recall myself from this abyss of idealism" *(P.W.* 4:463). This self contracted upon itself, withdrawing all affect from the outside world, leaving the phenomenal world terrifyingly dead and unreal thereby creating what Wordsworth called an abyss. This sense of self I shall refer to, borrowing from Wordsworth's letter, as the contracted self. It was Wordsworth's fate to oscillate painfully between these radically opposite senses of self. It was to alleviate this problem that he came to need a stabilizing and enclosing social community.

In examining this proposed duality I shall be using a number of analytic concepts and devices developed by Marx and Freud respectively. As a result, some of my readings of Wordsworth will conflict with traditional interpretations of his poetry. The resulting readings will often appear heterodox. To some, no doubt, they will appear perverse. But my readings are not the result of a desire to be iconoclastic or eccentric. It is my belief that the methodological and analytic structures erected by Marx and Freud provide a framework for a more comprehensive explanation of certain details in Wordsworth's life and writings than other structures of thought have been able to supply.

In using psychoanalytic methodology, I shall avoid, wherever possible, using obtrusive psychoanalytic terminology. But it is my use of Marxist historical materialist methodology that, for an American reader, requires some explanation. If there is any assumption that is fundamental to my understanding and reading of Wordsworth, it is that he was, above all else, a moralist. In attempting to trace the development of his Tory humanism, I am examining the social and political aspects of his moral vision and these aspects of his vision are closely connected to the social and political processes at work during Wordsworth's lifetime. Karl Marx, writing forty and more years after Wordsworth, could see more clearly than could Wordsworth the spirit, the laws of development, and the internal contradictions of capitalism as capitalism had manifested itself in England up to Marx's time. Marx's vision penetrated the ideological obfuscations generated by capitalism itself, and reached its essential rather than phenomenal reality. Marx was the first to see capitalism steadily and see it whole. It is Marx the analyst and historian of capitalist society up until his own time who I believe can help elucidate Wordsworth's attempts to find a stable place for his painfully riven self within a rapidly changing social structure. So it is not the teleological Marx who believed that he had found absolute laws of capitalism, nor Marx, the outraged moralist, denouncing the oppression of the proletariat, who I shall use in studying Wordsworth, though the careful reader will find me in sympathy with Marx, the moralist. I do not, however, hereby disclaim my belief in these other aspects of Marxism.

England's changing social and economic structures affected Wordsworth and pained him. If Marx can help Wordsworth's reader understand the essential, rather than the phenomenal nature of these changes, then Marx can, I hope, help the reader understand Wordsworth in the context of Wordsworth's own time. I have tried to use Marx only, on the one hand, when his analysis of social reality corresponds with Wordsworth's perception (thereby further validating Wordsworth's perceptions), or, on the other hand, when Marx's analyses seem to illuminate, retrospectively, social processes that seemed confused and dark to Wordsworth. By using Marx to clarify what was dark to Wordsworth, I shall attempt to show that Wordsworth's confusions were historically conditioned and could not easily be avoided until later developments made the true nature of events clear. If, for example, Wordsworth states his love for the traditional order, I shall quote a passage from Marx in which Marx describes how and why the process of capitalist development weakens and then destroys the traditional order.

But I fear that, despite all that I have just said, I shall seem to most American students of literature foolish, if not ill-bred, for bringing Marx to bear on the study of literature, despite the brilliant work of Georg Lukács, Walter Benjamin, Jean-Paul Sartre, Lucien Goldmann, Raymond Williams, and Stefan Morawski. We are once again being asked to believe that literature is entirely self-referential, having to do with nothing else in life but itself and other literature.

Having said this, I shall summarize briefly what I take to be this study's major argument. I shall then return to the matter of the princely and contracted selves. This study will attempt to trace how Wordsworth's egoistic childhood strivings, or oedipal impulses, to use the technical terminology, joined with the immense social and historical forces partially set in motion by the French

Revolution to turn him into an ardent revolutionary, rebelling consciously against traditional social forms and unconsciously against his father. Further, it will attempt to show how his individual assault upon tradition and the father collapsed when the internalized father in him proved too strong, how he reacted against the egoistic struggle he had participated in and, significantly, against the social and historical forms in which it seemed to be embodied. This oppositional reaction would seem to have been decisive for it meant that he set his energies against the new developments in the long history of capitalism. He was to oppose industrialism and the movement to complete the rationalization of England's political economy. He was, that is to say, to set himself against England's future. In conclusion, I shall explore the possibility that the strain of opposing what was not to be successfully opposed helped to weaken him as a poet by distracting him from his true poetic subject, being, to a subject he was ill suited for, the preservation of a way of being.

That Wordsworth's mind was riven and perplexed by two opposing senses of himself, one princely, the other contracted, is an assertion at once too momentous and too intricate to be left as mere assertion. It is necessary, before proceeding further, to examine this proposition in detail, and I propose to begin by examining the princely sense of self and the psychic dynamics that shaped it. It is clear that, at least in some moods, Wordsworth thought of himself in grandiose, imperious terms. Keats immortalized this aspect of Wordsworth's being by categorizing it as the egotistical sublime. Evidence of this sublime egotism is scattered throughout Wordsworth's work. One might do well to begin by looking at the poem, "There is an eminence, of these our hills," written in 1800 (P.W. 2:115). This eminence, Stone-Arthur, Wordsworth informs us in the Fenwick note (P.W. 2:488), is called after William by members of the Grasmere household. The poem tells us why. This eminence holds privileged discourse with the sun. It is "The last that parleys with the setting sun." It has beneficent healing powers for the small human figures beneath it, for it "often seems to send/Its own deep quiet to restore our hearts." One might infer that he who possesses so much power might possess the power to blight as well as to restore. And finally, "The star of Jove" doubles its beauty upon approaching this peak. Even Jove is a beneficiary of this power. Heady stuff, this!

In Book I of *The Prelude* he tells us that Nature took special and meticulous care in nurturing him because he was "A favor'd Being" (*Prel.* I, 364) and later, in Book XIII he numbers himself among those whose "minds are truly from the Deity,/For they are Powers . . ." (*Prel.* XIII, 106–107). Earlier, remembering his childhood, he records:

> . . . An auxiliar light
> Came from my mind which on the setting sun
> Bestow'd new splendor. . . .
> (*Prel.* II, 387–389)

Not only did Wordsworth feel himself possessed of a princely, moral grandeur, but he evidently was capable of appearing as a powerfully radiant, moral beacon to those who knew him. Judging from Wordsworth's replies to his friend William Mathews, particularly those of September 23, 1791 and May 13, 1792 (*E.L.* 57–59, 75–78), Mathews appears to have turned to the equally young Wordsworth for moral authority. The same was true of Basil Montagu and later, in a less simple and less one-sided way, of Samuel Taylor Coleridge. Certainly Raisley Calvert must have felt some kind of awe and reverence for Wordsworth, a conviction of his greatness that could not have been solely a response to poetic works of genius, in order to have left him a legacy to enable him to pursue a poet's life free from want.

What seed time had this imperial soul? How did it come to have a sense of itself as being so special, so large, so powerful? The answer to these questions might well be found, paradoxically enough, in a small child's psychic sense of his vastness and omnipotence. Wordsworth's sense of self, as has been proposed, was peculiarly developed. From childhood on, its boundary with the outside world could be extremely fluid. This boundary could dissolve, allowing the self to expand and incorporate the outside world, nature, into an ego that did not distinguish between self and other, creating a sense of bliss and of oneness with creation that Romain Rolland called "oceanic feeling,"[3] and that

Wordsworth called the sentiment of being, a "bliss ineffable" (*Prel*. II, 419). More often this expansion of the sense of self or being was incomplete, but incorporated aspects of the phenomenal world while altering them in such a way as to create feelings of mastery and power.

>   . . . A plastic power
> Abode with me, a forming hand, at times
> Rebellious, acting in a devious mood . . .
> The gentle breezes, fountains that ran on,
> Murmuring so sweetly in themselves,
>   obey'd
> A like dominion. . . .
>   (*Prel*. II, 381–392)

As a result of these incorporations, which in turn led to further feelings of mastery, and to the unitive moments of the sentiment of being, Wordsworth experienced on such occasions exaltation and a sense of grandeur that gave rise to fantasies of princely power. These fantasies emanated from the feelings of omnipotence that Freud ascribed to the childhood phenomenon he called "primary narcissism."[4]

But in itself this explanation of the dynamics of the princely self merely raises another question: Upon what historical, that is to say biographical, experience is this masterful, princely, unitive sense of self based? Wordsworth knew the answer and in Book II of *The Prelude* he tells us, although not referring specifically or consciously to himself alone:

> Bless'd the infant Babe,
> (For with my best conjectures I would trace
> The progress of our being) blest the Babe,
> Nurs'd in his Mother's arms, the Babe who sleeps
> Upon his Mother's breast. . . .

This infant:

> Doth gather passion from his Mother's eye!
> Such feelings pass into his torpid life
> Like an awakening breeze. . . .
>   (*Prel*. II, 237–245)

And here in this "awakening breeze" is the original and prototype of the "corresponding mild creative breeze" (*Prel.* I, 43), the Romantic metaphor for the creative imagination.[5] Significantly, without the mother the infant's life is "torpid." But the maternal glance animates the torpor; it creates relationship. Crucially, it creates between mother and child a unitive field of pleasure in which subject and object unite in identification, and a unitive field of force, the force of imagination. From this experience the imagination develops. This loving relationship is the model for all other relationships the infant mind establishes, and will ever establish, between itself and the outer phenomenal world:

> . . . and hence his mind
> Even [in the first trial of its powers]
> Is prompt and watchful, eager to combine
> In one appearance, all the elements
> And parts of the same object, else detached
> And loath to coalesce.

From his mother, that

> . . . beloved Presence, there exists
> A virtue that irradiates and exalts
> All objects through all intercourse
>   of sense.
>   (*Prel.* II, 245–260)

Here with this "beloved Presence" we are close to "a presence that disturbs me with the joy/Of elevated thoughts," a presence "interfused" with the light of setting suns, with the ocean, air, sky and "mind of man."

> A motion and spirit, that impels
> All thinking things, all objects of all thought,
> And rolls through all things.
>   (*P.W.* 2:261–262)

In "Michael" there is confirmation of the suggestion that the force of love and that of the imagination are fundamentally one. For Michael there emanates from his beloved Luke "things which were/Light to the sun and music to the wind" (*P.W.* 2:87). That is to say that the affective power of love is capable of performing the same transformations as the plastic power of the creative imagination. But the power of love, of imagination, has its origin, as we have seen, in the love the mother first bestows on the child. And it is from this love, as well as from the fragile boundaries of the infantile ego, that Wordsworth derives his princely sense of self.

Let us briefly return to the passage in *The Prelude* describing the relationship between mother and babe. The babe, we find, is not simply given love; rather he is "Subjected to the discipline of love" (*Prel.* II, 251) that quickens his faculties and connects him with the world. The line is slightly disturbing. One could easily misread it to mean that in the process of loving her babe the mother must chastise him for his own good. Parents, however loving, in fact often do this. But the line resists this easy reading. Nor may it be dismissed simply as an oxymoron. It insists on a radical assertion, so radical and uncomfortable that Wordsworth, in revising the text, may even have removed this line out of feelings of discomfort not unlike those the reader may feel. To love, to treat with tender affection, is to subject the infant self to a stern discipline. Yet this is so. Wordsworth's perception is profound and correct. For a self at rest will remain solipsistically at rest unless acted upon by a socializing, acculturating outside force. Love pleasantly forces the self to reach beyond itself, outside itself. Wordsworth grieves for Bonaparte because Bonaparte, unsubjected to the discipline of love, is locked in the sterile cave of his own being.

> The tenderest mood
> Of that Man's mind—what can it be? What food
> Fed his first hopes? . . .

Bonaparte could not learn that which a good ruler must learn, for "Wisdom doth live with children round her knees" (*P.W.* 3:110).

Much of what makes infant life significant comes from the mother. For Wordsworth, there is not simply a human form divine but also a female form divine. And when he first saw a morally deteriorated representative of his mother's class of being when he was seventeen, his moral world was convulsed. He was traveling two hundred miles south of his "pastoral hills" when first he heard "The voice of Woman utter blasphemy." It was the first time he had seen a prostitute. He "shudder'd" and

> . . . a barrier seem'd at once
> Thrown in, that from humanity divorced
> The human Form, splitting the race of Man
> In twain, yet leaving the same outward shape.
> (*Prel.* vii:412–426)

As all images of women were shaped and colored by the first woman in his life, and as any woman could be imagined as being mothering, let us tentatively suspend possible disbelief, and assume that this woman, merely by being a woman, was psychologically linked in Wordsworth's mind to his mother. If this is so, then for Wordsworth to see this woman, utterly in contrast with the moral ideal of womanhood that he had established in reverence for his mother, was enough temporarily to drain his moral world of meaning.

Not only is the mother capable of helping to establish in the blessed babe the beginnings of a significant moral world, but by penetrating his torpor with her love, she creates security and community for the child and establishes the prototype for all subsequent experience of affective community. Such a loved creature is no alienated, anomic being. Quite the contrary.

> No outcast he, bewildered and depress'd;
> Along his infant veins are interfus'd
> The gravitation and the filial bond
> Of nature, that connects him with the world.
> (*Prel.* ii, 261–264)

To anticipate somewhat, Wordsworth's experience of his mother's love was, as he later remembered and reconstructed it, largely one of joy and communion. Such love precluded his becoming a bewildered depressed outcast. In the future, only forms of social community that created this sense of affective communion, as opposed, for example, to the anomic London of Book vii of *The Prelude*, could win his allegiance and provide him with the sense of security and stability that he required.

But if with his mother's love he was not an outcast, without her love, certainly after her death when he was eight, he was just such an outcast. The glorious period of his life during which he received her love did in retrospect seem indeed princely. He would be haunted all his life by a sense of a golden age of childhood that was lost to him forever, however often and assertively he denied that loss. His mother's love seems to have constituted this golden age. Without her love and in communities without sufficient affective relations he was a solitary whose very solidity of being was threatened.

But at this time, modern capitalism was eroding traditional affective relations. These patriarchal, feudal relations were, however, more persistent in Westmoreland and Cumberland than elsewhere in England. Heriot, a feudal duty or tribute due, under English law, to a lord upon the death of a tenant, lasted there into the first quarter of the nineteenth century (*Lakes* 230). These traditional relations at least had claimed to be based upon mutual responsibilities and human need rather than upon economic calculation. The new social formations of modern capitalism were replacing these traditional social relations with the stark competitive relations of the marketplace, transforming what had been use-values into commodities. Industrial and rural capitalism and the new bourgeois order would come to be viewed with horror by Wordsworth and others, as a threat to their personal senses of being.

In his essay "The Capacity to be Alone,"[6] Donald Winnicott proposes that this capacity, as opposed to the inability to be alone, on the one hand, or the inability to enter into and sustain social relations, on the other, might be regarded as the crucial gauge of maturation. According to him, the ability to be alone bespeaks a successful internalization by the infant of his mother's presence. After such internalization, introjection, if one would prefer, the infant can remain calm and secure even while his mother leaves him to pursue tasks in other parts of the house, for example. Such a child will develop a secure and stable sense of self, and will, in Winnicott's terminology, successfully complete the maturational process. But what of the children who fail in this essential task? They will not develop a secure sense of self; they will not go on to finish this maturational process. From the perspective of Winnicott's essay, Wordsworth's dual sense of self appears in a new light. In his mother's presence, his experience of being was truly glorious, allowing him the possibility of princely power. Without her presence, or that of one of her surrogates, such as Nature may be said to have been, his sense of self could shift alarmingly from that of prince to that of outcast, with his very sense of being threatened. This was the contracted self. There may well have been, then, a fundamental instability in Wordsworth's sense of his own being that had its origin in an intense dependence on his mother. Though most infants exhibit a similar intense dependence on their mothers, this does not universally result in sharply opposing senses of self. Why Wordsworth did not successfully complete this maturational process and develop a stable inner sense of his mother's presence is more a matter of speculation than of useful investigation. It is likely that the constitutional or environmental factors that caused this failure will never be isolated. We shall return to the problem of the genesis of this hypothesized dual sense of self.

In his princely identity Wordsworth possessed powers of mastery over those portions of the physical universe that his ego would incorporate and alter to suit his desire. These powers could bestow "auxiliary light" upon "the setting sun." "The midnight storm/Grew darker in the presence of my eye." Power is the key to this experience, willed control over the world of eye and ear. He was a god, the bestower of life.

> To every natural form, rock, fruit or flower,
> Even the loose stones that cover the high-way,
> I gave a moral life. . . .
> *(Prel.* iii, 124–126)

This projected power achieves its most compelling and most perplexing form in the well-known passages describing the "spots of time," moments possessing a "vivifying Virtue" that derives from their ability to remind the self of a time when

> . . . the mind
> Is lord and master, and that outward sense
> Is but the obedient servant of her will.
> *(Prel.* xi, 258–273)

The mind then is "nourished and invisibly repair'd" by reference back to moments when the enormous power of the external world is overcome by the mind's desire to recreate the world to suit its own psychic needs. At such moments the powerful principle of reality may be said to have yielded to the principle of pleasure. Yet both of the moments or spots of time that Wordsworth chooses to represent, and from which sustaining power is drawn, startle the reader, so little connected do they seem with joy. Both involve some form of loss and both involve dreary, and apparently depressing landscapes. How can such moments be sources of joy? Here the reader is halted, and not necessarily without a struggle to break through. A possible way to get through this difficulty may lie in treating these two memories as psychic structures similar to dreams, in viewing the morbid dreariness that invests both memories as a displacement of emotional emphasis designed to disguise the actual source of pleasure. The recollection of being lost at the Penrith Beacon seems to support the conjecture that these "spots of time" are complex mental structures or constructions rather than simple and unelaborated memories.

The five-year-old Wordsworth has been taken riding by James, a family retainer. Wordsworth becomes separated from his guardian and wanders inadvertently to the spot where a convicted murderer had been hanged. All that now remains is the moldering gibbet and the letters of the murderer's name engraved in the turf, and kept legible by succeeding generations of local inhabitants. From there, the young boy climbs up to the Penrith Beacon and sees a lone wind-tossed woman bearing a pitcher on her head. His mind invests the scene of the woman and the beacon with a heightened dreariness.

This episode seems to show evidence of having been altered and developed in years following the actual experience. Is it likely that a childish spectator, "not yet six years old," would understand the deathly significance of an already moldering gibbet post or that the engraved letters of the murderer's name would hold any significance to a probably preliterate child (*Prel.* xi, 279–302)? If the child could not understand the significance of either the decayed gibbet or the lettering in the turf, and it is most likely that he could not, what could be the source of the preternatural dreariness? The answer is that the sense of dreariness may have been the result of a displacement of affect. It was probably a construction unconsciously added to the memory at a later time.

If the source of pleasure of these moments has been hidden from Wordsworth's conscious mind, where is the pleasure in these peculiar memories to be found? With my best conjecture I would trace the source back to the forbidden area of a childhood sexuality. For if, as I shall suggest, the oceanic moments of the sentiment of being are intensely sexual, then these recollections of psychically mastering the outside world may be sexually tinged as well. For the process in which the outside world is invested with and colored by the self is related to the even more intense experience of the sentiment of being in which the boundary containing the self utterly dissolves and the ego merges with the world outside it.

These pleasurable moments of the sentiment of being and of mastering the outside world originated, in Wordsworth's phychic history, at a time early in infancy before a coherent ego had developed. At such a time, there was as yet no sharply delineated self. Pleasurable sensations coming from inside the infant were not clearly distinguished from those coming from the outside world. It is easy, at such a primitive stage of the self's development, to feel a continuity between the as yet ill-defined self and the outside world. For an infant at this stage, the outside world would appear to share the infant's affective states.

In the terminology of psychoanalysis, this stage of development is known as the oral stage since during it the dominant organs of sensual pleasure are the mouth, lips and tongue. Typically this stage of child development extends through the first year and a half of life.[7] More than metaphorically the infant may be said to drink in pleasure, a process technically known as oral incorporation. This cannot fail to remind the close reader of Wordsworth of the especially Wordsworthian metaphor of drinking or tasting beautiful landscapes. These lines from Book I of *The Prelude* are exemplary:

> Yes, I remember, when the changeful earth,
> And twice five seasons on my mind had stamp'd
> The faces of the moving year, even then,

A Child, I held unconscious intercourse
With the eternal Beauty, drinking in
A pure organic pleasure from the lines
Of curling mist, or from the level plain
Or waters color'd by the steady clouds.

(Prel. i, 586–593)

Wordsworth, sharing the common condition of humanity, also experienced egoistic childhood strivings for his mother, which being forbidden, were seen as meriting punishment by the same father who stood in the way of the young boy's egoistic desire to be sole recipient of his mother's attention. These strivings and the fear of paternal retribution belong to a later period of Wordsworth's psychic history than do the origins of the sentiment of being and the feelings of mastery over the outside world. These egoistic strivings and fears probably date to approximately Wordsworth's fourth year. It is impossible to know for how long the princely feelings of an expanded, powerful self and the terrified feelings of a self fearing contraction or dissolution existed side by side as unrelated psychic entities, forming no polar opposition. But eventually the two senses of self were brought together as opposing poles of the same emotional structure, for it is the aim of the ego to seek to synthesize and integrate all that falls within its limited power.

Now that the general areas of Wordsworth's childhood sexuality relevant to the two opposing senses of self, their separate origins and later synthesis, have been touched upon, it is time to return to an examination of the "spots of time" passages. Hidden in these "spots of time" are pleasurable recollections of his early sexuality.

The spot of time associated with the Penrith Beacon seems to record a victorious encounter with the punitive paternal authority. This authority, carrying with it the threat of murderous retaliation and annihilation, is represented in the recollection by the moldered gibbet-mast, executor of judgment against him who would defy moral authority. The boy sees this post with its implied threat of retributive punishment, but, undaunted, goes on to exercise his pleasurable impulse to master the outer world, an impulse characteristic of the princely self, by making the outward sense the servant to the mind's will. He imposes over everything he sees a uniform tone. All outside him, in obedience to his will, takes on a "visionary dreariness." Despite the gibbet, which threatens egoistic impulses, he succeeds in exercising mastery. This impulse in self-assertion is masked behind "the visionary dreariness" that the mind's eye finds everywhere, but the sexual aim of that impulse to control is at least suggested by the cluster of images that are insistently associated with the spot of time. The passage containing these suggestive images follows:

> . . . forthwith I left the spot
> And, reascending to the Common, saw
> A naked Pool that lay beneath the hills,
> The Beacon on the summit, and more near,
> A Girl who bore a Pitcher on her head
> And seem'd with difficult steps to force her way
> Against the blowing wind. It was, in truth,
> An ordinary sight; but I would need
> Colours and words that are unknown to man
> To paint the visionary dreariness
> Which, while I look'd all around for my lost Guide,
> Did at that time invest the naked Pool,
> The Beacon on the lonely Eminence,
> The Woman, and her garments vex'd and toss'd
> By the strong wind.
>
> (*Prel.* xi, 302–316)

The nakedness of the pool is twice insisted upon; beside the pool is seen, beneath a phallic "lonely Eminence," also twice referred to, a woman whose garments are "vex'd and tossed/By the strong wind" once more doubly cited. That the tossing of the woman's garments does have sexual significance is made less improbable when, in the next line, Wordsworth invokes "those two dear Ones, to my heart so dear" (*Prel.* xi, 317). The dear ones are Mary Hutchinson and Dorothy Wordsworth, the first his wife-to-be, the second his sister with whom he lived and to whom he may well have been attached by strong, albeit unconscious, incestuous ties, as F. W. Bateson has suggested.[8] Wordsworth refers to walks that he took with Dorothy and Mary in the summers of 1788 and 1789. At that time Mary, whom he married on October 4, 1802, was not yet engaged to him.

The second spot of time is even more puzzling. Now a schoolboy living away from home, the young Wordsworth is eagerly awaiting the arrival of horses that are to carry his brother and himself to their father's home for the Christmas holidays. Unable to control his impatience, Wordsworth climbs a nearby hill the better to catch sight of the approaching horses. There he sits.

> . . . half-shelter'd by a naked wall;
> Upon my right hand was a single sheep,
> A whistling hawthorn on my left. . . .
> (*Prel.* xi, 358–360)

During the anxiously awaited holiday, Wordsworth's father dies, leaving young William an orphan at the age of thirteen. Afterwards, he writes, he would mentally "repair" to the hill where he had awaited the horses and "drink,/As at a fountain." Why should his mind repair to a dreary windblown scene of a "single sheep," "one blasted tree" and an "old stone wall" to drink "As at a fountain" when this same scene is intimately involved in his own mind with his father's death and the dispersal of his remaining household? The obvious answer provokes disbelief. Surely Wordsworth cannot be experiencing the pleasure of victory in his childhood strivings against his father. One would expect that such triumphant feelings could not be experienced consciously, or if experienced consciously, not in such a direct and undistorted connection to his father's death. But Wordsworth does appear to derive pleasure from a memory directly associated with his father's death. To be sure, the pleasure is displaced backward in time so that it stems not from a recollection of the death itself, but instead from a moment prior to the death. The pleasure stems from recalling the episode of waiting expectantly for the horses.

> And afterwards, the wind and sleety rain
> And all the business of the elements,
> The single sheep, and the one blasted tree,
> And the bleak music of that old stone wall,
> The noise of wood and water, and the mist
> Which on the line of each of those two Roads
> Advanced in such indisputable shapes,
> All these were spectacles and sounds to which

I often would repair and thence would drink,
As at a fountain. . . .

(*Prel.* XI, 376–385)

This moment is doubly eligible to be the site of the displaced pleasure. First, as in the other spot of time, the "visionary dreariness" serves to disguise the positive elation. But second and more significantly, the moment of waiting eagerly for the horses is a moment of waiting eagerly to be taken home to his father and is therefore a moment of an intense expression of the love that coexisted with feelings of hostile rivalry in making up an intense ambivalence toward the father.

It should be noted that self-mastery, freedom from the father, is present in the first spot of time, and may help to explain why the experience at Penrith Beacon resonates for so long in Wordsworth's memory. The child Wordsworth has been guided by the family servant James, who in the screen memory may represent Wordsworth's powerful father. It is only when he becomes free of James, that is free of the father, that the experience becomes deeply significant for Wordsworth. Then he is free to exercise mastery over the world around him by projecting onto it a visionary dreariness. Later in life his mind repairs to this memory for restoration, a memory of early freedom from paternal restraint, that may symbolize the wished for, but forbidden vanquishing of the father in the oedipal drama of the family romance.

It has been suggested above that the experience of psychically mastering the outer world of eye and ear was a less intense, less developed experience, than the princely experience of the sentiment of being. The experience of the sentiment of being in which there is no longer a felt distinction between self as subject and outer world as object appears to recapitulate the union of mother and suckling infant in an intense mutual field of pleasure. At such moments the light of sense would go out. For what function do the sensory organs perform but to present to a coherent ego indications of the world outside the self? The received gratification of the experience of the sentiment of being was intense. When all his thoughts "Were steep'd in feeling" he

                    . . . was only then
Contented when with bliss ineffable

I felt the sentiment of Being spread
O'er all that moves, and all that seemeth still, . . .
                    Wonder not
If such my transports were; for in all things
I saw one life, and felt that it was joy.
                              (*Prel.* II, 415–430)

Is it any wonder that a being granted access to such transport felt himself a privileged and special creature? Common parlance when referring to some special treat describes it as being fit for a king. And such usage may not, in so stating things, be far from Wordsworth's felt experience. Surely he was Nature's darling, her special child. The experience of mastery over the world of outer sense and the experience of the sentiment of being created for Wordsworth a privileged sense of self, the princely self I have been referring to. Nature served him, literally fed him sensual pleasure. Even as a child he held unconscious intercourse

With the eternal Beauty, drinking in
A pure organic pleasure from the lines
Of curling mist. . . .
                    (*Prel.* I, 590–593)

Elsewhere he speaks of drinking "visionary power" (*Prel.* II, 330).

Lionel Trilling emphasizes that Wordsworth is a poet who insists on examining being, that he is an ontological poet.[9] Trilling's insights undoubtedly penetrate to the core of what is essential to Wordsworth's vision and contribution to culture. But he does not fully examine why Wordsworth should also be driven to examine, as he does, idiot boys, mad mothers and decrepit men "bent double, feet and head" (*P.W.* 2:237) for demonstrations of their being. What is the pressure that drives Wordsworth to reassure himself that mankind on the very margins of existence possesses being? The answer lies in part, I think, in the fact that being, in Wordsworth's most powerful experience of it, his most powerful sentiment of it, was highly charged with generalized sexual pleasure. Truly to be was to have access to this pleasure; and all being, no matter how apparently minimal, was not without this pleasure. Wordsworth is also capable of finding joy in passive being, in "wise passiveness" (*P.W.* 4:56), for to a developed sensibility being is rich in and of itself.

But here when we have seen how deeply interfused for Wordsworth are the intense experience of being and the princely sense of self, we are brought up hard and abruptly against the dialectically implied opposite sense of self, the contracted self, for, as Freud insisted, each psychological formation implies an opposite, perhaps unconscious, formation. For what if, not Lucy, but Wordsworth should cease to be? What if his soul could not only expand beyond the self into nature but contract into itself, become, as the soul in "The Poet's Epitaph," "ever-dwindling" (P.W. 4:66)? Then he would be deprived of power and intense pleasure. This would be a terrible loss, and he feared such loss greatly.

If, as has been postulated, Wordsworth had a peculiarly developed sense of self so that the self could expand and incorporate the outside world, then the boundaries of this unstable self could also contract, leaving the outer world seemingly drained of life and of reality.

Wordsworth wrote a Fenwick note to the "Intimations Ode" of great importance to the student of his poetry. In the portion of the note that I shall quote, Wordsworth is attempting to explain the lines:

> But for those obstinate questionings
> Of sense and outward things,
> Fallings from us, vanishings;
> Blank misgivings of a Creature
> Moving about in worlds not realized. . . .
>
> (P.W. 4:283)

He writes in the note "I was often unable to think of external things as having external existence, and I communed with all that I saw as something not apart from, but inherent in, my own immaterial nature" (P.W. 4:463). Here it would seem that Wordsworth was writing about the sentiment of being, the oceanic experience characterized in all of Wordsworth's recollections as being intensely pleasurable. These lines from the note might well be read as a gloss for the opening lines of the poem:

> There was time when meadow, grove, and stream,
> The earth, and every common sight,

To me did seem
Apparelled in celestial light,
The glory and the freshness of a dream.
(P.W. 4:279)

But these are not the lines specifically referred to in the note. Following the part of the note already quoted, Wordsworth goes on to write: "Many times while going to school have I grasped at wall or a tree to recall myself from this abyss of idealism to the reality" (P.W. 4:463).

This passage describes a state very different from the joyous union of the sentiment of being. It describes an opposite experience, one of contraction into the self rather than an expansion beyond the self. Yet Wordsworth, in his adult attempts to understand his childhood, conflated the two processes for reasons that I shall try to suggest. Wordsworth criticism has, understandably, taken the poet at his word and has seen one process by which the young Wordsworth related subject to object rather than two processes. Whose word, it would seem, could be more authoritative on this subject than that of Wordsworth himself? A reexamination of the note will, I believe, reveal a heretofore hidden complexity.

Wordsworth tells us that often while on the way to school he had to clutch at hard material objects such as walls and trees to recall himself from the "abyss of idealism." Wordsworth appears in this passgage to portray himself as having had an experience describable in terms of idealist philosophy. But surely the young school-bound boy did not clutch desperately at wall or tree to free himself from the influence of Berkeleian philosophy. This was not the mature Samuel Johnson kicking a stone in refutation. Even if it were possible for us to miss the note of terror in Wordsworth's recollection, he goes on to tell us that as a child he had been terrified. "At that time," he writes, "I was afraid of such processes" (P.W. 4:463). Wordsworth here is clearly far from the child who remembers drinking in pure organic pleasure. If Wordsworth later came to identify the experience of the abyss of idealism with the experience of the princely self, that later identification was an adult revision of a childhood experience.

How did Wordsworth come to make such a revision? In order

to answer this question one must first ask, what reality did the child attempt to secure in this grasping? Ultimately, I believe, the secure reality of his own being. If the outer world, the walls and trees, began to seem unreal, falling from him, vanishing, it was because he was contracting into solipsism, into a self devoid of relation to anything outside the self. Wordsworth felt himself to be in a world in which all objects were unreal and dead. Later, as an adult attempting to understand this childhood circumstance, Wordsworth used the vocabulary of idealist philosophy to explain the state he remembered fearing. Such a philosophy supplied, at the time, the only available vocabulary to explain a state in which the material world seemed unreal. It is likely that conversations with Coleridge, a convert to philosophical idealism, would make this choice of terminology even more nearly inevitable. An abyss of idealism suggests a realm filled either with the subject's spirit or with some transcendent spirit. But the world the terrified youngster contemplated, far from being filled with spirit, was drained of it, was void.

Wordsworth's self, as it had come to develop by the time he was nine, was, like other developed selves, filled with affect. In normal states the affect would be distributed between himself and the world around him. Now, in the moments of the sentiment of being, which, as I have suggested, originated prior to the establishment of a coherent ego, affect would pour from him, saturating the world around him with what seemed to be vitality. But in the moments described in the Fenwick note, misleadingly described as moments verging on the abyss of idealism, all his affect would be withdrawn from the world. It would contract into himself, leaving the outside world not filled with spirit as in the oceanic moments, or filled with the spirit the word idealism would imply, but leaving a world devoid of affect, of vitality. This contraction, when compared to the gradiose expansion of the self into all that moves and all that seemeth still, must have been painful as well as fearful.

Yet these apparently opposite states possess dialectically common features. It was these shared features plus his dependence on idealist terminology that led to Wordsworth's conflation of the two opposite states. Both states were highly subjective; both resulted in the outer world's taking on appearances far from the mundane;

both were looked back upon by the older poet as experiences that shared in the task of bringing him to his mature poetic vocation; both seemed to testify to his privileged relation to nature; and both were felt to be numinous.

There is a further factor, too, that contributed to making Wordsworth identify two radically opposite states, an identification, as has been seen, that has contributed to a certain misunderstanding. In neither state does the self exist relationally to an outer world beyond the self, for a developed, coherent ego can only exist securely when the self can establish a stable identity in relation to what is not the self. In the glorious moment of the sentiment of being all thinking things, all objects of all thought are incorporated within the self. To the degree that the expansiveness of the princely state of being denied the objective reality of the outside world, it might well have precipitated these contractions that may have begun in order to allow room for an object world free of itself, in order to reintroduce relationship. It is even possible that at times these contractions, if violent enough, or sudden enough, may have gained such momentum that the self contracted implosively in upon itself withdrawing all affect from the outer world. But the self contracted in upon itself, surrounded by a world devoid of real, as opposed to ideal, objects also could not exist relationally. The sharp, often abrupt, alteration between two opposing senses of himself could cause such painful contractions. The question of how to establish a stable identity was Wordsworth's dilemma of self, to solve which a steadying external social community had to be sought as one of the means for dealing with this dilemma.

If the expanded self was experienced as fully realized being, sexually gratifying, the implosion of self might well be experienced as a received punishment. The self, in expanding beyond its previous boundaries, incorporated what may have been felt as being forbidden, for the sought-for union with nature recapitulated the union with the mother. In the strivings of childish egoism the father stood as a Blakean "Thou shalt not." The pain-filled contraction away from incorporation, which had attained the meaning of attempted appropriation, may have been felt as retributive paternal power, forcing Wordsworth in upon himself, possibly from fullest being to dreaded non-being. The father then would be feared as threatening annihilation in return for Wordsworth's princely activities and pleasures.

The episode of stealing the boat in Book 1 of *The Prelude* (*Prel*. 1, 372–427) offers the clearest example of felt paternal retribution for childish egoistic desire, desire, in part, for the mother. Wordsworth must have been at least nine years old when he stole the boat, because he is already a student at Hawkshead. The episode describes an attempt to possess and master the boat, that here symbolizes at least in part the now absent mother. The boat, for instance, is hollow and can contain and enclose him.

First the theft of the boat itself is described in terms that appear to have sexual connotations. After leaving shore, he describes his oarsmanship:

> I dipp'd my oars into the silent lake
> And, as I rose upon the stroke, my Boat
> Went heaving through the water. . . .

It is only then that a mighty force rises like the principle of phallic power to oppose and chastise him:

> . . . a huge Cliff,
> As if with voluntary power instinct,
> Uprear'd its head. . . .
> And, growing still in stature, the huge Cliff
> Rose up between me and the stars. . . .

So impressed is the young Wordsworth with the self-levitating mountain which opposes his "act of stealth/And troubled pleasure" that he returns the boat filled with "serious thoughts." But the most consequential result of this encounter with the admonishing cliff is the effect on the young thief's mind. He is punished by thoughts that drive him away from relationship, from the possibility of enlarging the self by imaginative incorporation. He is driven as punishment into a diminished isolated state. In his thoughts "There was a darkness, called it solitude. . . ." The word solitude, so rich in Wordsworthian association, is invoked as part of a punishment for an act of egoism and self-aggrandizement. The punishing paternal force is the "Wisdom and spirit of the universe" that "giv'st to forms and images a breath/And everlasting motion" (*Prel*. 1, 428–430).

"Hart-Leap Well" (*P.W.* 2:249–254) is another poem that shows acquisitive egoism and sexuality punished, here by having the emblem of egoism blasted and withered. The lesson Nature teaches in this poem is,

> "Never to blend our pleasure or our pride
> With sorrow of the meanest thing that feels."

Because Sir Walter does not abide by this rule, the pleasure house to which he "led his wondering Paramour" has turned to dust. All around Hart-Leap Well, the fountain memorial of the hart Sir Walter so relentlessly drove to its death, is barren waste. The fountain is blighted by the power in Nature that punishes pride and egotism.

In attempting to explain Wordsworth's apparent division between two opposite senses of self, reference was made to Winnicott's essay on the capacity to be alone. The division can be partly explained in Winnicott's terms by Wordsworth's inability to incorporate an enduring sense of his mother's love and presence. On the one hand, the triumphant, princely sense of self corresponds to the infant bathed in his mother's love, but now the relationship between these psychologically antithetical affective states becomes asymmetrical. The contracted sense of self threatened with dissolution was the result, not of maternal loss, but of paternal retribution. Is this not a contradiction? Not if one considers that in the economy of the mind psychic events are overdetermined, and that different stages of development leave different and often contradictory deposits behind them. Fears of both maternal loss and paternal retribution may function simultaneously to bring about the contracted self. Nevertheless, it remains true that Wordsworth regularly represents these two opposed yet related senses of himself. It would be appropriate at this point to marshal certain examples of Wordsworth's being threatened with contraction, dissolution and annihilation.

We need not depend solely on the Fenwick note to the "Ode" and the line from "The Poet's Epitaph" for evidence that suggests that the soul might be fated to be "ever-dwindling." There is, for example, a striking incident related in Dorothy Wordsworth's *Grasmere Journal* that has not received the attention it deserves.

On Tuesday, November 24, 1801, Dorothy makes the following entry about William:

> —he had been surprised and terrified by a sudden rushing of winds which seemed to bring earth sky and lake together, as if the whole were to enclose him in—he was glad he was in a high Road. (D.W.J. 62)

In other words, a thirty-one-year-old man had been reduced to terror by a belief that all the elements, save fire, drew together to engulf and annihilate him, and he ascribed his survival to the good chance of his being on a high road safe from the tumult. This is a man to whom the possibility of annihilation was both ready and real.

The threatened self is a major element of one of Wordsworth's principal themes—the ravaged solitary. But I hope the reader will not be impatient if I postpone examination of this important subject. There is a passage in Book VIII of *The Prelude* that bears strikingly upon the Fenwick note to the "Ode." Wordsworth is comparing his childhood to Coleridge's London school days and notes how much more salubrious was childhood in the Lake Counties, how, because of the mountains, "the fit," whatever shape the fit might take, was less threatening to the stability of his being.

> . . . I had forms distinct
> To steady me; these thoughts did oft revolve
> About some centre palpable, which at once
> Incited them to motion, and control'd
> And whatever shape the fit might take
> And whencesoever it might come, I still
> At all times had a real solid world
> Of images about me. . . .
> (*Prel*. VIII, 598–605)

Wordsworth does not identify the emotional malady referred to as the "fit" though the counter-reference to a steadying, solid world of images suggests the abyss of contraction that he had fought off by grasping a wall or tree. The steadying effect of the solid world is to the "fit," which was liable to come upon him at any time, what the "wall or tree" are to "the abyss of idealism." Nature's concrete forms acted to stabilize a self threatened with contraction into solipsism. In this stabilizing capacity of the landscape, we find hinted at one of the reasons Wordsworth gathered eidetic images of landscape and hoarded them, squirrellike, for future use. A vividly recalled image might work against contraction, "in lonely rooms, and 'mid the din/Of towns and cities" (P.W. 2:260) when the fit was upon him.

Perhaps the most keen lament over impending annihilation is found in the opening of Book v of *The Prelude*. Here the vision of absolute destruction, of complete termination, may be expressed so clearly because the terror has been displaced from Wordsworth, the subject, to the loved object he participates in creating, culture. Should the earth be withered by "fire sent from afar," though all life be extinguished and "Old Ocean in his bed" be left "sing'd and bare/Yet would the living Presence still subsist."

> But all the meditations of mankind,
> Yea, all the adamantine holds of truth,
> By reason built, or passion, which itself
> Is highest reason in a soul sublime;
> The consecrated works of Bard and Sage . . .
> Where would they be?
>
> (*Prel.* v, 28–49)

Wordsworth painfully contemplates the destruction of mankind's most impressive creations. The passage bears witness to a brooding contemplation of the possibility of annihilation and may owe much of its passionate intensity to a displacement from the self to that which emanates from the self. In this case, culture would function metonymically as both the self and what the self creates as object.

On a smaller and less impressive scale, Wordsworth wrote several short poems that deal with the changeful duality of the princely and annihilated selves. Wordsworth's conscious and didactic purpose in writing these poems was to make his reader beware of being so vain or inconsiderate as to undervalue shy creatures of modest means. To undervalue such creatures is to lose contact with significant aspects of nature and therefore with what these aspects have to teach. The belittler of the daisy or the eglantine would not learn to recognize the beauty and worth of humility and humbleness of station. Nor would such a belittler learn that modest, unobtrusive creatures affirm both the inner strength and the need for external protection of the humble. But if Wordsworth wrote the following three poems with a definite didactic purpose, there is no reason to suppose that these poems do not, at the same time, help to illustrate what I have suggested is Wordsworth's divided sense of identity.

In an almost playful manner, "The Waterfall and the Eglantine" (*P.W.* 2:128–130) presents a dialogue between the powerful forces of contraction and the threatened self. The waterfall opens the exchange speaking to the briar-rose that "was living, as a child might know,/In an unhappy home," explicitly likening the threatened briar to a wretched, helpless child. The waterfall roars,

> "Dost thou presume my course to block?
> Off, off! or puny Thing!
> I'll hurl thee headlong with the rock
> To which thy fibers cling."

In vain the briar appeals to a past shared life. Equally vain, but especially important if Wordsworth's voice resonates with the briar's, is the briar's appeal to its own ability to create beauty.

> "When spring came on with bud and bell,
> Among these rocks did I
> Before you hang my wreaths to tell
> That gentle days were nigh!
> And in the sultry summer hours
> I sheltered you with leaves and
>   flowers. . . ."

In the poem "The Oak and the Broom" (*P.W.* 2:130–134), written and published as was the previous poem in 1800 and immediately following it in the "Poems of Fancy," Wordsworth shows the threatened self, the broom, enduring while the more powerful and boastful oak perishes, thereby giving verse form to a fantasy that may have provided solace to Wordsworth's fragile sense of continued being. The oak boasts of its superior power to maintain its hold on life. The broom simply replies that since "Disasters, do the best we can,/Will reach both great and small;" it will live stoically without fear. Needless to say, the oak is struck by a storm and whirled far away while "The little careless broom was left to live for many a day."

"To the Same Flower" (P.W. 2:138–139), the second poem to the daisy, uses the daisy to play with two opposed senses of self. Wordsworth explicitly casts his lot with the daisy, asking that his heart be given "a share/Of thy meek nature!" Employing a stanza form taken over from Robert Burns, Wordsworth alternately sees the daisy as a humble, contracted creature or as a powerful and glorious one. Under the guise of play, that is, he writes out permutations of each of the divisions within himself. On the one hand, the daisy is an "unassuming Common-place/Of nature with that homely face" and "A starveling in a scanty vest." On the other hand, the daisy is "A little Cyclops . . . Staring to threaten and defy" or possessed of "A silver shield with boss of gold."

It is doubtful that anyone would place the second daisy poem in the first rank of Wordsworth's poetry, but the poem serves as a useful introduction to a far more significant manifestation of the effect of Wordsworth's riven sense of self upon his poetry. The daisy as starveling confronts the daisy as the powerful, defiant cyclops as do opposing doubles, one clinging to the margin of biological being, the other possessing a giant's power. Here, in the juxtaposition of two conceits descriptive of a single flower, is shadowed forth the Wordsworthian experience of the encounter with the ravaged solitary.

The list of such solitaries is long; these figures seem to be connected with many of Wordsworth's greatest poems and passages. Some, like Simon Lee, the leech gatherer, the old man traveling, or the Cumberland beggar, are so old that they are all but, in Milton's words, "Devoid of sense and motion." [10] Others, like the discharged soldier or the blind beggar, are wasted by bodily infirmity. What is there about this, the encounter with someone made almost marginal to being, that accounts for its perseverance in Wordsworth's work and the greatness he so frequently achieves with it? In part, to be sure, Lionel Trilling is correct. The frequent appearance of such characters bespeaks Wordsworth's concern for being, even in circumstances that seem almost the negation of being, but I believe that part of the answer is to be found in the postulated dual sense of self within the poet.

"Simon Lee" (*P.W.* 4:60–64) allows us to take a first look into this possibility. Simon himself seems to be as decrepit as anyone can and yet still be said to be:

> And he is lean and he is sick;
> His body, dwindled and awry,
> Rests upon ankles swoln and thick;
> His legs are thin and dry.

Simon, it is true, has a wife, Ruth, but at the moment in which the poet encounters him, Simon is typically alone. Old Simon is feebly and vainly attempting to remove "A stump of rotten wood" with his mattock. The speaker offers to aid the "overtasked" old man. He strikes "and with a single blow/The tangled root I severed." While I was contemplating this passage, the Homeric formula ". . . in the pride of his strength" came with seeming inevitability to my mind. And it was fitting that this be so. It is possible that in meetings such as the one with Simon Lee, Wordsworth's dual sense of self receives dual representation, as in dreams in which the dreamer appears simultaneously as two distinct individuals. This narrative structure, repeated again and again in Wordsworth's poetry, would then function as a wish. The powerful, vital, princely young poet Wordsworth, who in the pride of his strength splits the root that overtasks Simon Lee, separates himself from the helpless, ravaged other Wordsworth who struggles against dissolution, by projecting the ravaged self outside onto another. Further, in the psychic economy of this narrative structure, the wish to continue living would be gratified by the perception that such figures as Simon, or the leech gatherer, however diminished they may be by the forces of contraction, still continue to be. They affirm the possibility of being even where being seems about to turn into non-being. Simply, they are.

Such an egoistic wish to survive even at someone else's expense, to be sure, must be punished, for it is perceived by part of the ego as being evil. This part of the ego perceives the part of the ego that strains for survival, not as self, but as other. Consequently it punishes the egoistic other. Simon's gratitude leaves the speaker not merely grieving but "mourning," a word which, being the last in the poem, carries heavy emphasis. The speaker mourns because it is painful for him to contemplate situations in which the human condition can so reduce a man that he will shed tears of thanks, as Simon does, for a seemingly small favor. But if the speaker must pay with pain he has still made a good bargain. In "Resolution and Independence" (P.W. 2:235–240), the satisfaction, in the form of renewed fortitude and strength, is allowed to appear undeflected, but one suspects that this direct expression of satisfaction rather than grief is made possible because the speaker's suffering has been displaced to a point in time just before the encounter with the leech gatherer. Before the meeting, the poem was sunk in melancholy, a functional equivalent of the speaker's mourning in "Simon Lee."

Perhaps the suggestion that these encounters between Wordsworth's speakers and solitaries represent a wish can be further illustrated and regarded from a different point of view if we examine the episode of the discharged soldier in *The Prelude* (*Prel*. IV, 363–495). Here the division of the ego is expressed by the juxtaposition of two opposing meanings of the word "solitude." Both Wordsworth, who renders aid, and the soldier who needs it are described as being solitaries. The passage opens with Wordsworth declaring that

> A favorite pleasure hath it been with me,
> From time of earliest youth, to walk alone. . . .

So he walks on this evening more alone in the public road than amid "pathless solitudes." While he is walking thus, the beautiful evening helps restore him. It is then that he sees the ghastly discharged soldier.

> . . . He was alone,
> Had no attendant, neither Dog, nor Staff,
> Nor knapsack; in his very dress appear'd
> A desolation, a simplicity
> That seem'd akin to solitude.

As he slouches against the mile-post he utters "Groans scarcely audible." No two human beings could be more different, one pursuing a favored pleasure while "drinking in/A restoration like the calm of sleep," the other pitifully reduced by hunger and fatigue. Yet both are bound together by the fact that each in his own way participates in solitude.

It is clear that, as Wordsworth uses the term, there is a radical ambivalence in the word "solitude." Someone who becomes solitary in order to pursue a "favorite pleasure" "alone/Along the public Way" is seeking in some way and for some reason to be free of social constraints. But society is itself double. Just as it can be a constraint, so it can also be a support. A social constraint may be, and indeed often is, simultaneously a social support. If the young Wordsworth is momentarily without constraint, the discharged soldier certainly lacks support. Literally, he cannot stand. This passage is exemplary. For what Wordsworth has done here, and what he does less manifestly in his encounters with other ravaged solitaries, is to preserve for himself the removal of constraint and project onto or into the double the removal of support. This is another way of seeing the wish embodied in the narrative structure of the poetry of encounter.

Having pressed this much from the narrative structure of encounter, it is tempting, and perhaps it would be discreet, to let the matter rest there; but if one has gotten this far, one can try to take another step forward. Among the male solitaries, there exists a further striking quality. Often just when the speaker is prepared to find only weakness and decrepitude, he finds instead stoic power and fortitude. This is so of the discharged soldier, of the old man traveling (particularly in the original, uncut version of the poem), of the old Cumberland beggar, of the fisherman in "A narrow Girdle of rough stones and crags" and, of course, of the leech gatherer. It has been suggested that part of the wish fulfilled in the narrative structure we have been examining is the wish to be reassured that even the self acted upon by the powers of contraction can still continue to be. In the instances just referred to, the wish may be present in a more positive form—namely, that these figures not only be, but be heroic. This can be taken as a manifestation of Wordsworth's wish to feel himself heroic, to maintain his princely nature even after having been diminished by the forces of contraction, having been made to appear less than princely by forces that oppress him. The fantasy of being princely but of being unrecognized may well be universal. It is the situation of Odysseus scorned and despised in his own palace while disguised as a beggar. It is, of course, the story of the family romance as well, in displaced form again. In the family romance the child in fantasy and in desire, replaces the parent of the same sex.

I hope that by now I have established the conception of Wordsworth's two dialectically opposed senses of self, at least as a working hypothesis. At this point in the argument, I would like to examine a poem, a great one, in which it is possible to follow Wordsworth's movement from the unitary sentiment of being to the abyss of "idealism" and then back to an intermediate position. I propose to read "Resolution and Independence" with reference to this particular argument, because in "Resolution and Independence" it is possible to make out a causal link between the imperial and contracted selves. The imperial self is only hinted at in stanzas II and III in the poem. The main body of the poem shows why the experience of expansion is unstable and how the opposed experience of contraction may be precipitated by expansion.

In stanzas II and III the speaker is filled with joy. "The pleasant season did my heart employ. . . ." Wordsworth does not say or believe that he has projected the joy upon the landscape in an expansive, emotional gesture; he describes the landscape as filled with joy, but as the phenomenal world is emotionally neutral, so, upon analysis, the emotion must be seen to emanate from him. It is not humanly possible to determine whether or not a hare is experiencing mirth. It is possible to see a mirthful hare only if one unconsciously projects mirth onto the hare, and then perceives one's own projection:

> All things that love the sun are out of doors;
> The sky rejoices in the morning's birth;
> The grass is bright with rain drops;— on the moors
> The hare is running races in her mirth. . . .

By implication in stanza III he has experienced a joyful expansion in creating this joyous world, so complete, that the light of sense goes out or at least flickers.

> I heard the woods and distant waters roar;
> Or heard them not. . . .

"Or heard them not." This is a crucial moment. The self, as subject, has expanded until there is nothing outside as object.

What follows is a theoretical reconstruction of what I take to be the emotional process that brings the speaker from joy to dejection. The self is one with the objects it has penetrated. In oneness, as Parmenides observed, there can be no activity,[11] so that, in the oceanic experience, the self seems passive, itself almost an object. The blissful but relatively helpless state of the suckling infant has been recreated. Since the perceptual system of consciousness supplies the stream of stimuli from the outside world in order to help locate and define the ego's relation to the outside world, this perceptual system is no longer needed when the boundary between self and other has dissolved. As a result the light of sense goes out. No longer can there be a definite assertion made as to whether or not the roar of woods and distant waters is heard.

But at this point something important happens. The sentiment of being is not allowed to continue or gradually to abate. It terminates abruptly. This may be caused by the inability of the self to merge fully with the world outside it. Whatever self, whatever coherent ego remained would realize itself to be in a helpless, passive and dependent condition. This could trigger intense anxiety as a signal that the self was in a vulnerable, potentially dangerous situation. The expansion has therefore reached its furthest limit.

> But, as it sometimes chanceth, from the might
> Of joy in minds that can no further go. . . .

Anxiety becomes too pressing, causing not only an end to the joyous expansion but also an implosive contraction of affect into an isolated and troubled self:

> And fears and fancies thick upon me came;
> Dim sadness—and blind thoughts, I knew not, nor could name.

He broods upon "Solitude, pain of heart, distress, and poverty," and contemplates an end in which the forces of contraction will have reduced him after he had started with hope and promise:

> We Poets in our youth begin in gladness;
> But thereof come in the end despondency and madness.

For him to be contemplating such a despondent future, his being in the present must have already contracted. His self has been detached from the world it had penetrated. The affect that had saturated the outside world has ebbed back into the ego, leaving the ego at least coherent. He is again subject and the world object, but he is a troubled subject threatened by the forces of contraction and annihilation. It is at this point that he encounters, observes and questions the leech gatherer.

But his contraction has been too precipitous. The movement from union of subject and object back to troubled subject has gained momentum. The result is an implosion of self into itself, into solipsism—the threatened abyss of "idealism." The outside world becomes so unreal that the threat exists that there is nothing real and solid for him to exist in. If the objective world dissolves, the self cannot establish relationship with anything. The old man, even while he is speaking, begins to dissolve for the poet. A wall or tree must be grasped.

> The old Man still stood talking by my side;
> But now his voice to me was like a stream
> Scarce heard; nor word from word could I divide,
> And the whole body of the Man did seem
> Like one whom I had met with in a dream. . . .

But there is a wall or tree. It is the leech gatherer himself. Not only does he allow the poet to escape the abyss of "idealism" but the old man's hardness, his perdurability, gives the poet something so solid that its very memory may be invoked to act as wall or tree in any future necessity.

> . . . and, when he ended,
> I could have laughed myself to scorn to find
> In that decrepit Man so firm a mind.
> 'God,' said I, 'be my help and stay secure;
> I'll think of the Leech-gatherer on the lonely moor.'

"Resolution and Independence" helps us see some further relationships between the princely self and the sentiment of being, on the one hand, and the contracted self and the abyss of "idealism," on the other. This reading is not an attempt to explain the poem's richness, though I hope some aspects of the poem have been illuminated.

There is a sonnet first published in 1807 which so parallels "Resolution and Independence" that it merits quotation. Again the outward movement of the self precipitates a contraction of the self. Though the fear that causes him to leap from "the delicious stream" is treated fancifully, I believe that the original experience was similar to the one described in the longer, greater poem. Perhaps in another mood he was drawn again to a painful subject in the attempt to master a traumatic source of pain by treating it lightly.

> How sweet it is, when mother Fancy rocks
> The wayward brain, to saunter through a wood!
> An old place, full of many a lovely brood,
> Tall trees, green arbours, and ground flowers in flocks;
> And wild rose tip-toe upon hawthorn stocks,
> Like a bold Girl, who plays her agile pranks
> At Wakes and Fairs with wandering Mountebanks,—
> When she stands cresting the Clown's head, and mocks
> The crowd beneath her. Verily I think,
> Such place to me is sometimes like a dream
> Or map of the whole world: thoughts, link by link,
> Enter through ears and eyesight, with such gleam
> Of all things, that at last in fear I shrink,
> And leap at once from the delicious stream.
>
> (P.W. 3:21)

"Resolution and Independence" bears heavily upon two aspects of Wordsworth's way of thinking that grow out of his dual sense of self and become decisive in shaping his social and political ideas. The first is a peculiar sense of his own history. To himself he exists in a present traveling away with each heart beat from the Golden Age of the princely self that is located in an ever-receding past. In the future there awaits the troubled, frightful world of the contracted self, "Cold, pain, and labour, and all fleshly ills."

> We Poets in our youth begin in gladness;
> But thereof come in the end despondency and madness.

The second aspect of his thinking flows from the first. What is in question is the nature of his almost obsessive fears of the annihilated future. The predominant terror is that which would reduce a gentleman to labor—impoverishment. In his anxiety Wordsworth mixes together both the fear of being declassed and the fear of actual physical want and suffering.

> My former thoughts returned: the fear that kills;
> And hope that is unwilling to be fed;
> Cold, pain, and labor, and all fleshly ills;
> And mighty Poets in their misery dead.

Fears of financial reverses and povery haunt him. In Stanza VI of the poem, he realizes that he has paid little heed to insuring himself against future reverses. The last line of the previous stanza had listed the possible ill-fortune of another day. The line and stanza climax in the word "poverty."

> But there may come another day to me—
> Solitude, pain of heart, distress, and poverty.

The fear of impending poverty can be traced in Wordsworth's letters from his college days to his old age, as his 1845 sonnet, "To the Pennsylvanians," may attest. These two themes, Wordsworth's unique sense of personal history and his fear of impending poverty, must be dealt with before it is possible to bring this chapter to a close.

Wordsworth viewed himself as suspended between a golden past and an annihilated future. This was how his inner duality was refracted when he projected it through the prism of time. He was not unique in viewing his personal relation to history in this way. Raymond Williams, in his study, *The Country and the City*, discusses what he calls the writer's "negative identification."

> . . . the exposure and suffering of the writer, in his own social situation, are identified with the facts of a social history that is beyond him. It is not that he cannot see the real social history; he is often especially sensitive to it, as a present fact. But the identification between his own suffering and that of a social group beyond him is inevitably negative, in the end. The present is accurately and powerfully seen, but its real relations, to past and fu-

ture, are inaccessible, because the governing development is that of the writer himself. . . .[12]

As early as Wordsworth's first large work, "An Evening Walk," composed between 1787 and 1789, we find a hint of a lost past more rich than the present. The observation that "twilight glens endear my Esthwaite's shore" precedes "And memory of departed pleasures, more" (P.W. 1:4).

It would be tiresome to catalogue all of Wordsworth's poetic tributes to the glorious age of childhood. It will suffice to cite his "Ode: Intimations of Immortality" (P.W. 4:279–285). It is not to the point here to enter the controversy as to whether or not "the faith that looks through death," "the philosophic mind," brings adequate recompense for the losses suffered with growth and age. The point is that the poem raises the question of the value of adult life as compared with that of a "Child, yet glorious in the might/Of heaven-born freedom." Starkly and directly the poem asks:

> Whither is fled the visionary gleam?
> Where is it now, the glory and the dream?

Childhood is the lost world of glory, dream and visionary gleam. The child, of course, enters the world "trailing clouds of glory." He is the "best Philosopher" and "Seer blest!" The examination of possible personal loss gives force and direction to the "Ode."

The Prelude is filled with luminescent memories such as the recollection of ice skating in a winter dusk, or of hearing the flute one evening in a boat on Windermere. But in Book XI he says:

> . . . The days gone by
> Come back upon me from the dawn almost
> Of life: the hiding-places of my power
> Seem open; I approach, and then they close;
> I see by glimpses now; when age comes on,
> May scarcely see at all. . . .
> (*Prel.* XI, 334–339)

Time may well bring its compensations, but it does bring loss. In "Residence in London" Wordsworth recalls the image of a beautiful infant boy, the son of a prostitute. The image of the infant boy recurs to Wordsworth through the years, but the child is:

> . . . as if embalm'd
> By Nature; through some special privilege,
> Stopp'd at the growth he had. . . .

This "foster child of silence and slow time" is then spared. He is:

> . . . no partner in the years
> That bear us forward to distress and guilt,
> Pain and abasement. . . .
> (*Prel*. VII, 398–405)

Though Wordsworth is, so to speak, lost in the adult world of guilt and distress, the vanished world of innocence and joy is still present in his mind, almost as a kind of encapsulated consciousness. Speaking of the period of his "infantine desire" Wordsworth writes:

> . . . so wide appears
> The vacancy between me and those days,
> Which yet have such self-presence in my mind
> That, sometimes, when I think of them, I seem
> Two consciousness, conscious of myself
> And of some other Being.
> (*Prel*. II, 28–33)

Whether the guilt-free past were vanished or encapsulated, Wordsworth habitually looked to the future with ominous dread. Sometimes the dangers that seemed to loom so threateningly before him were so slight as to be invisible to others. Mary and Dorothy poked fun at poor William, anxiously contemplating a future that saw him withering in Newgate where he would be committed for seditious libel as a result of his Cintra pamphlet (*M.L.* 336–337).

The problem of why the annihilated future so often took the form of destitution still remains to be examined. It would be possible, of course, to invoke the psychoanalytic formulations whereby fear of financial loss is a symptom of obsessional neurosis, or is a symbol of abandonment and, indeed, Wordsworth was left

abandoned when his mother died when he was eight and again
when his father died when the boy was thirteen. While it would
not be wise to ignore such connections, these notions raise more
questions than they solve, and such solutions are not free from the
imputation of having begged the question, of having put a label on
the problem.

No matter what the radical content of an anxiety, be it the
classical fear of castration or any other, it can only reach consciousness in the form of an anxiety that is historically possible. It
must attach itself to a signifier available in the world that present
history offers to the conscious psyche. In this way, that which is
most intensely intrapsychic can become, if in some form it succeeds in escaping repression, profoundly connected with social and
historical processes. Thus, Wordsworth's fears of future annihilation could not take the form of a fear of being sold into slavery,
though such a fear was an historically available possibility to the
Joseph of *Genesis*. More obviously, Wordsworth's fear of future
annihilation could not manifest itself as a morbid fear of airplanes
or elevators. Freud himself could not have had his famous dream
of Irma's injection any time before the historical possibility existed
of administering an injection.

But Wordsworth lived in a world, as to some extent do we, in
which it was possible for a man who had a financial competence
or a great capacity and willingness to work, or both for that matter,
to end his days destitute and faced with starvation. In such a world
fear of economic destitution was an historically available signifier
for Wordsworth's personal fear of contraction. As long as the kind
of capitalism that we are historically familiar with exists as a means
of ordering the social forces of production and distribution, poverty
of the sort Wordsworth feared will remain a possible fate to be
feared both in itself and as a vehicle for unconscious terrors and
anxieties.

Wordsworth lived at a time of central importance in the long
and complex development of capitalism as a social and economic
system. Wordsworth's dates, 1770 to 1850, correspond roughly
with the first phase of the world's first industrial revolution. What
yet remained of the traditional affective ties that bound men to one
another—and these endured longer in the Lake counties than else-

where in England—was being replaced by a system of relations determined by rationalistic, self-seeking and utilitarian calculation. This social conflict between opposing sets of values had begun long before Wordsworth's birth, and even as a youth his sympathy was aroused by the displaced rural poor. He was drawn especially to figures who presented themselves as solitaries because, perhaps, even as a youth he may have seen in them, in horror, his own possible and often contemplated fate.

There was a rapid increase of visible rural suffering and pauperization following the accelerated rate of enclosure in the eighteenth century and the General Act of Enclosure of 1801, on the one hand, and the demoralizing Speenhamland method of administering the poor rates of 1795 on the other. Although Speenhamland was less corrosive in the Lake counties than elsewhere (*Lakes* 306), there was ample opportunity for Wordsworth to observe men, once independent, driven both off the land and into poverty. That this was a process that had been going on continuously although not uniformly for hundreds of years and could have been seen by earlier observers did not lessen the effect such observations had on Wordsworth. Unquestionably, pauperization was a readily enough available social fact to become for Wordsworth the conscious symbol for an inner and personal terror. In the 1797 version of "The Ruined Cottage" he writes that because of "Two blighting seasons" "A happy land was stricken to the heart." As a result,

> . . . Many rich
> Sunk down as in a dream among the poor,
> And of the poor did many cease to be. . . .[13]

This passage is important because it seems to establish two things: first that the fear of sinking down into the poor, of being declassed, was so real among those considered rich, that it could enter their psyches and be used as a symbol that expressed profound anxieties of every kind; and second that the feared consequence of poverty was dissolution, that is, literally, ceasing to be. It is true that countless earlier generations had almost certainly dreamed anxiously of poverty. What is important, however, is the fact that at this moment in time a poet should find this aspect of dream life, an aspect not previously rendered in verse, literally remarkable, so remarkable that he made use of it in creating a simile. Indeed, poverty can be, or seem to be, the cause of the isolation that brings one to the margin of nonbeing. When Wordsworth and Michel Beaupuy encounter the "hunger-bitten Girl" languidly leading her heifer to browse, she is described as being "in a heartless mood/Of solitude" (*Prel.* IX, 510–517).

One of the original *Lyrical Ballads*, "The Last of the Flock" (*P.W.* 2:43–46), allows the reader to follow the process of gradual, but relentless, impoverishment and traces its emotional effects on the victim. Wordsworth's conscious polemical purposes in "The Last of the Flock" were to show that Godwin had underrated the importance of private property in maintaining wholesome human affections; and further that even the affections within a family could be strengthened by the preservation of a modest property. Finally the poem attacks the poor laws to the extent that they work against the maintenance of such a modest property. But the fact that Wordsworth had conscious polemical purposes in regard to the value of private property does not exclude the possibility that "The Last of the Flock" may be read as a document that reveals certain hidden psychological meanings that the accumulation and dissipation of property held for Wordsworth. The speaker in the poem is a well-traveled man, but he sees something unexpected, especially on English soil—a solitary man weeping "in the public roads, alone." The man is carrying a lamb which, it turns out, is the last survivor of a once large and prosperous flock of fifty sheep, enough sheep to make him "rich/As he could wish to be." He has had to sell this flock one by one until it has diminished to the lamb he is now carrying to the painful final sale. The speaker sees him now impoverished, reduced to tears, a vestige of the man he was when he was seemingly secure with property. The process of impoverishment has adversely affected his character. As he sold sheep after sheep,

> "To wicked deeds I was inclined,
> And wicked fancies crossed my mind. . ."

The process also destroys his affective capacity and wholeness. As the forced sale continues, he comes to realize that "I loved my children less." The wholeness and integrity of his being diminished proportionally to his diminishing wealth. Security of being is linked to security of property. An unstable and contracted being is thus linked to loss of property.

The poem reveals an especially important further relationship.

> "Sir, 'twas a precious flock to me,
> As dear as my own children be;
> For daily with my growing store
> I loved my children more and more.
> Alas! it was an evil time;
> God cursed me in my sore distress;
> I prayed, yet every day I thought
> I loved my children less;
> And every week, and every day,
> My flock it seemed to melt away."

There is a clear link between the forces that build up personal strength and property, on the one hand, and the power and capacity to give love, on the other. The larger his flock grows the more he loves his children. Reciprocally, there is a link between the forces that contract the self and diminish property and the inability to give love. The smaller his flock becomes, the less he is able to love his children.

A link has been established between certain forces that help build up the self and the ability to give love. If the nature of the forces that build up or diminish the self can be discovered, this insight may be extended. Whom does the shepherd blame for the terrible diminution of his flock? God! It is God who cursed him even in the time of his sore distress. Implicitly God had previously been responsible for the growth of his flock from one ewe to fifty sheep. The Lord giveth and the Lord taketh away. God is the Father in his most exalted sublimation—the father who can lovingly protect or who can punish, with contraction and other forms of punishment, forbidden childhood strivings. The state of being tearfully isolated and reduced to poverty may also be understood on one level of the unconscious as paternal punishment.

It is now that the connection between the forces that build up the self and the ability to give love can be extended. If enrichment and strength increase the capacity to love, then correlatively, the father's protective and supportive love, even in the symbolic form of God's love, increase the very security and stability of the self and the ability of the self to give love. On the other hand, if the father in his anger withdraws love, revealing punitive wrath, then the self is rendered helpless and vulnerable. Not only is it unable to love, it is unable to be loved by the father. To be loved by the father is to be allowed truly to be. To have the father's love withdrawn is to threaten the security and continuity of being. In this reading of "The Last of the Flock," a poem whose surface meaning records the decline of a single shepherd's fortunes, wealth of property has been emotionally connected to the father's love for his son and ultimately with the son's capacity to be and to love.

The division of Wordsworth's psyche, which I have posited, between the princely self and the annihilated self, has at least one formal implication. It is possible to study the formal structure of some of Wordsworth's poems and show that in some of the poems, particularly in the first person meditations, the formal structure recapitulates and recreates his own psychic structure. This is the case in "Tintern Abbey" (P.W. 2:259–263).

In a note to the 1800 edition of *Lyrical Ballads* Wordsworth wrote of "Tintern Abbey":

> I have not ventured to call this Poem an Ode; but it is written with a hope that in the transitions and the impassioned music of the versification, would be found the principal requisites of that species of composition. (P.W. 2:517)

The first aspect of "Tintern Abbey" that leads Wordsworth to liken it to the ode is the poem's "transitions." The poem is filled with them, filled with transitions between a voice that speaks of all it has lost and yet may lose, and a voice that speaks of present recompense and of expansive intensely pleasurable moments of the sentiment of being. These transitions are transitions between Wordsworth speaking as the annihilated self and Wordsworth speaking as the princely self. The alternation between these selves creates the transitions, the turns and counterturns, that are a major formal element of the ode. It is in this way that the formal structure of the poem recreates the structure of its creator's divided self. The poem opens on the note of loss:

> Five years have past; five summers, with the length
> Of five long winters!

The passing of and loss of five years of life is twice insisted upon, the second time with sense of the abrasion of being that passage through time entails. Behind the enumerated long winters there may be an echo of the *ubi sunt* motif. But immediately there is a turn. Time has brought restoration—"again I hear," and "Once again/Do I behold . . . ," followed by a descriptive passage containing at least one significant transition. The "secluded scene" before the poet impresses upon him "Thoughts of more deep seclusion. . . ." The thoughts of seclusion are followed by the rest of the description of the scene, but the scene ends as the contracted voice, still brooding on the theme of seclusion, enters again, with the evocation of a "Hermit's cave, where by his fire/The Hermit sits alone." Significantly, the word "alone" ends the first verse paragraph.

The second verse paragraph starts with the poet clinging to the eidetic image of the Wye amid the forces of contraction, "in lonely rooms, and 'mid the din/Of towns and cities. . . ." But the power of the image of the Wye allows the princely self, in another turn, to speak of the special and intense pleasures that save the princely self from forces of contraction embodied in "the heavy and the weary weight/Of all this unintelligible world. . . ." The verse paragraph ends with the princely selfrebounding from such weary weight and expanding beyond the limits of the body, beyond the confines of selfhood, to

> . . . —that serene and blessed mood,
> In which the affections gently lead us on,—
> Until, the breath of this corporeal frame
> And even the motion of our human blood
> Almost suspended, we are laid asleep
> In body, and become a living soul:
> While with an eye made quiet by the power
> Of harmony, and the deep power of joy,
> We see into the life of things

"We see into the life of things." There could be, it seems, no assertion more assured, more unqualified than this claim of potency made in behalf of the princely sense of self, but it is the very potency, the actual reality of the force of the expanded sense of self, that is immediately called into question in a sudden loss of faith and confidence. "If this/Be but a vain belief," writes Wordsworth of the description of the achieved sentiment of being, that had seemed so positive. Wordsworth has led his reader to exhaltation only to question it. What had seemed achieved experience is now but a doubtful possibility. "If this/Be but a vain belief?" "Do I wake or sleep?"

Now Wordsworth's spirit plummets as the contracted self iterates a catalogue of loss. The beauteous forms, which have not been to him as is a landscape to a blind man's eye, have begun to decay, though still present,

> And now, with gleams of half-extinguished thought,
> With many recognitions dim and faint,
> And somewhat of a sad perplexity,
> The picture of the mind revives again. . . .

The present scene may provide "Food/For future years," but this he only dares "to hope." He recalls the passionate intensity and joy of his intense relationship with nature, described in terms of sexual passion. But "That time is passed/And all its aching joys are no more,/And all its dizzy raptures." All is changed, changed utterly, but at this moment of loss a terrible beauty is born, a terrible beauty in harmony with "The still, sad music of humanity. . . ." This music sounds in the poem at a moment of peripety. Aching joys and dizzying raptures have been lost, but in return for them the poet has received "Abundant recompense." And now when the poet has suffered painful loss, limitation, and contraction, his other voice, his princely voice answers, almost antiphonally. Again the limits of selfhood are broken as the self expands blissfully in a grand epiphany of the princely self. If number, weight, and measure are to be brought out in times of dearth, there is no way the losses already catalogued can be measured against the bountiful abundance of this recompense.

And I have felt
A presence that disturbs me with the joy
Of elevated thoughts; a sense sublime
Of something far more deeply interfused,
Whose dwelling is the light of setting suns,
And the round ocean and the living air,
And the blue sky, and in the mind of man:
A motion and a spirit, that impels
All thinking things, all objects of all thought,
And rolls through all things.

With these lines, these elevated thoughts, the poem has reached such epiphanic intensity that the turn and counterturn of the ode form can be maintained only with the greatest difficulty. The form of the poem alters from that of ode to that of direct address. The poet makes one more significant turn—not a turn from the princely voice to the contracted voice, but a turn from meditation toward his sister, Dorothy. Significantly, however, as he addresses her and contemplates her future, he envisions her future as alternately exalted and contracted. In her he sees his former passionate self:

. . . in thy voice I catch
The language of my former heart, and read
My former pleasures in the shooting lights
Of thy wild eyes.

From this passionate intensity there is a transition. The poet prays that nature will protect his sister, that she will not be harmed by

. . . evil tongues,
Rash judgments, nor the sneers of selfish men,
Nor greetings where no kindness is, nor all
The dreary intercourse of daily life. . . .

He blesses the "sober pleasure" that will replace in her "these wild ecstasies." Then if the full violence of the forces of contraction should fall upon her, she should think of him and this moment, much as he, in lonely rooms, had thought of the Wye:

If solitude, or fear, or pain, or grief,
Should be thy portion, with what healing thoughts

Of tender joy wilt thou remember me,
And these my exhortations!

And then his contracted self speaks one final time as he imagines his own death, in terms of some absolute future inability to hear or see his sister. But in the final turn of the poem these forebodings are surmounted as he imagines his sister, restored by her memory of him. In this way, I believe, does the form of "Tintern Abbey" recapitulate the form of its creator's divided ego.

This chapter has examined a posited duality in Wordsworth's sense of self. Certain implications of this duality have been explored. It may be useful to conclude with an examination of another aspect of this duality that bears upon something essential to Wordsworth's poetry. In *Sincerity and Authenticity* Lionel Trilling characterizes an essential aspect of Wordsworth's poetry as being epiphanic. He carefully distinguishes between two types of epiphanies:

> In one, spirit shows forth from nature; the sudden revelation communicates to the poet a transcendent message which bears upon the comprehension of human existence or upon the direction his own life should take. . . . The other . . . has as its locus and agent some unlikely person . . . who, without intention, by something said or done, or not done, suddenly manifests the quality of his own particular being and thus implies the wonder of being in general.[14]

I would like to identify the former experience as the epiphay of expansion and the latter experience as the epiphany of contraction. I shall use the apostrophe to the imagination following Wordsworth's crossing the Alps as an example of the epiphany of expansion, and the blind beggar episode as an instance of the epiphany of contraction.

Wordsworth and his companion Robert Jones have, in Book VI of *The Prelude*, just been informed that they have unknowingly already crossed the Alps (*Prel.* VI, 501–548). They have been disappointed in their expectation, perhaps highly excessive, of the sublime experience of knowing that they had reached the physical summit of their journey. They are met instead by flat anticlimax. Wordsworth says of the bewilderment he then experienced, "I was

lost as in a cloud,/Halted, without a struggle to break through."
Now, retrospectively, he realizes that his bewilderment was due to
a misapplication, perhaps even a profanation, of the power of
imagination. He had made the mistake of trying to derive imaginative fulfillment from a finite predetermined moment at a finite
predetermined place. Now, looking back upon his life with the
increased wisdom of maturity, he realizes that imagination is to be
found in such moments as when at seventeen he felt "the sentiment of Being" (*Prel.* II, 405–434). Imagination is to be found in
such moments as those described in "Tintern Abbey":

> In which the burthen of the mystery,
> In which the heavy and the weary weight
> Of all the unintelligible world,
> Is lightened:—that serene and blessed mood,
> In which the affections gently lead us on,—
> Until, the breath of this corporeal frame
> And even the motion of our human blood
> Almost suspended, we are laid asleep
> In body, and become a living soul:
> While with an eye made quiet by the power
> Of harmony, and the deep power of joy,
> We see into the life of things.
>   (*P.W.* 2:260)

Now, enlightened as to the true domain of imagination,
Wordsworth corrects his youthful error. When he sought and saw
the visible world he was blind to the invisible world of the infinite.
Now he realizes that imagination is to be found only in a realm
not bounded by time and space, a realm revealed only in intermit-
tent "flashes."

>   . . . in such visitings
> Of awful promise, when the light of sense
> Goes out in flashes that have shewn to us
> The invisible world, doth Greatness make abode.
>   (*Prel.* VI, 533–536)

This passage is rich in meaning and in suggestion. Notice, again,
how in these transcendent moments the sense of self as a distinct
subject seems to be obliterated, as the self merges with a world

larger than itself, so that the physical senses that locate the self within the finite sensuous world are not needed. They go out, as in "Tintern Abbey" where we are "laid asleep/In body, and become a living soul." The passage now stresses the experience of expansiveness, of being larger than the quotidian self:

> . . . our home
> Is with infinitude, and only there;
> With hope it is, hope that can never die,
> Effort, and expectation, and desire,
> And something evermore about to be.
>   (*Prel.* vi, 538–542)

Solipsism has been left behind; the limits of selfhood have been shed. Home is with infinitude, spatial in connotation. Temporal bounds have been abadoned. We are part of a process that stretches to eternity, part of a chain of events "evermore about to be." This epiphanic moment has brought the poet into contact with the infinite. The pedestrian limits of the getting and spending have been left behind. The "Imagination" passage is an example of an epiphany of expansion.

The epiphany of contraction is every bit as meaningful as that of expansion but, as may be inferred from the word contraction, it is not filled with joy. It may well be painful and terrifying. Wordsworth experiences such an epiphany in "Resolution and Independence" as I have read it. In "Resolution and Independence" this contraction is followed by a gradual reopening. The epiphany of contraction I shall examine now is his encounter with the blind beggar in *The Prelude*'s "Residence in London." It has been chosen because I believe this epiphany of contraction is deliberately opposed, in the structure of *The Prelude*, to the just-examined epiphany of the apostrophe to imagination, which occurs in the book just preceding "Residence in London." Also, the blind beggar episode bears heavily on the need for community that will be examined in later chapters. For Wordsworth was going to make an attempt to escape from his centripetal duality by, among other means, uniting himself with some form of community.

Wordsworth opens the passage by noting that though "foolishness, and madness in parade" are most prominent in urban life, they are neither unique to life in the city, nor are they what makes city life unique. What does make the city unique is the peculiar experience of which he gives one of the earliest and one of the greatest expressions. It is the experience of anomie, of rootlessness:

> How often in the overflowing Streets,
> Have I gone forward with the Crowd, and said
> Unto myself, the face of every one
> That passes by me is a mystery.
> Thus have I look'd, nor ceas'd to look, oppress'd
> By thoughts of what, and whither, when and how,
> Until the shapes before my eyes became
> A second-sight procession, such as glides
> Over still mountains, or appears in dreams;
> And all the ballast of familiar life,
> The present, and the past; hope, fear; all stays,
> All laws of acting, thinking, speaking man
> Went from me, neither knowing me, nor known.
> *(Prel.* VII, 587–606)

Later, in the beginning of Book IX, Wordsworth refers less forcefully to the same rootless feeling that London induced:

> . . . in the midst of things, it seem'd,
> Looking as from a distance on the world
> That mov'd about me. . .
> *(Prel.* IX, 23–25)

Referring to the longer, more penetrating passage, Raymond Williams analyzes the social and psychological processes at work.

Wordsworth saw strangeness, a loss of connection, not at first in social but in perceptual ways; a failure of identity in the crowd of others which worked back to a loss of identity in the self, and then, in these ways, a loss of society in itself, its overcoming and replacement by a procession of images. . . .[15]

But if we are to come to a full understanding of this episode and of the phenomenon of the epiphany of contraction, we must extend and push beyond Williams' analysis.

Wordsworth observes that the face of everyone he meets is filled not with meaning, not with recognition, not with reference, but with mystery. There is no available community in which and by which he may establish or confirm his identity by pressing against it as he had against a wall or tree. He desires knowledge of others. He wishes to penetrate the mystery of the masked face. But it is no Faustian quest for transcendent knowledge that motivates him. If he cannot break through the anomic, unintelligible masks he is threatened with a painful contraction into nothingness. The world he inhabits will become dead, an unreal "second-sight procession" such as "appears in dreams."

The mysterious faces are unknown to him. They are not penetrated with his projected being. They cannot, therefore, reflect his being back to him. They are, for him, lifeless. When Wordsworth's affections were detached from a person or object, that person or object would become that much less coherent, real and significant to him. Writing of the politics of revolutionary France when he knew no more about them than what was contained in "the master Pamphlets of the day," he said:

> . . . all things were to me
> Loose and disjointed, and the affections left
> Without a vital interest.
>
> (*Prel.* ix, 96–107)

London was filled with mysterious faces, which, unable to contain or reflect his affections, threatened to become loose and disjointed. All things threatened to relapse into chaos and become without form and void—all things including Wordsworth himself.

London was very different from the kind of community he compares it with in the opening of Book viii, with its description of an innocent country fair. The rural community was an affective community held together by emotional ties. Such ties were subjective. In this context none of the faces would be a mystery to him. All the faces would have absorbed his being and would contain it. He could reaffirm his existence in and through them. Further, he would have absorbed and contained their being in a subjective reciprocity.

Here is at least a partial answer to the secret of Wordsworth's obstinate questionings of strangers such as the leech gatherer. When confronted by a stranger, his conscious thought might be,

"The face of him I meet is a mystery." But beneath this mysterious surface might lie another hidden and more insistent thought. "To this being I am a mystery. I have no real existence for him. Without his capacity to enhance reflexively my being, my existence is that much more precarious and threatened. I must enter into relationship with him." Next, Wordsworth finds himself saying, "This morning gives us promise of a glorious day" (P.W. 2:238).

But in the passage we are examining, Wordsworth is adrift in a nonreflexive and anonymous society. He is driven "By thoughts of what, and whither, when and how." But the questions remain unuttered. And contracting into himself in his psychic chaos the reality of other beings begins to dissolve. The people who fill the street become part of

> A second-sight procession, such as glides
> Over still mountains, or appears in dreams. . . .

They become parts of the abyss of "idealism," parts of his mental life devoid of their own significance. All "the ballast of familiar life . . . all stays" went from him, as he sank into the timeless abyss of "idealism," devoid of "The present, and the past." This collapse into solipsism is very similar to that in "Resolution and Independence." There, while he listens to the old man tell of his labor, the leech gatherer's words become to the withdrawing listener "like a stream" (P.W. 2:239). Here in *The Prelude* the procession of humanity becomes streamlike; it "glides/Over still mountains."

Suddenly on one occasion when he was "far-travell'd in such mood" (*Prel*. VII, 607–622), that is of withdrawal into himself, he is "smitten with the view/Of a blind Beggar." The blind beggar was, to the best of our knowledge, a formidable type. According to E. P. Thompson, he was the " 'aristocrat' of the vagrant fraternity, with whom the sighted and able-bodied sought to travel in order to share his takings." [16] Because of his blindness the beggar is, like the leech gatherer, not fully sentient. Only half the world of eye and ear is open to him (in Wordsworth's valuation, less than half). As with the leech gatherer, Wordsworth uses physical immobility as a symbol of insentience. He is an "unmoving man" with a "fixèd face" who is "propp'd against a Wall."

As the leech gatherer is "like a man from some far region

sent" to administer "human strength, by apt admonishment" (*P.W.* 2:239), so Wordsworth by seeing the blind beggar is turned round "As with the might of waters" and is brought back from the feared abyss of "idealism." As with the leech gatherer, Wordsworth's being is again saved from devastation by the fact that such a being as the beggar, however maimed and ravaged, truly *is*. Being is again affirmed. And again, as with the leech gatherer and Simon Lee, Wordsworth's being is preserved by using the opportunity afforded by the encounter with a ravaged solitary to project the maimed, contracted self onto another, a double, leaving the healthy, princely self secure and intact. Yet it is clear that even if these mechanisms function as they do when Wordsworth encounters other solitaries, much in the encounter with the blind beggar remains to be explained. The incident has a density and specificity that demand further examination.

The beggar is blind. He cannot see, cannot, that is, in the terms employed above, absorb others into himself. The best he can do is to attempt to project himself upon others by means of his meager written identification. He wears "a written paper, to explain/The story of the Man and who he was" (*Prel.* VII, 613–614). In "Resolution and Independence" Wordsworth asks questions of the stranger. Here, though inclined to ask questions of what, whither, when and how, he is, rather, told without asking. The spectacle smites him and turns him around perhaps because it answers the questions which, if asked, would have prevented him from withdrawing from reality. With the questions answered he returns to reality. But he does not simply return. He is propelled by a jarring force, the force of insight of the epiphany of contraction.

> My mind did at this spectacle turn round
> As with the might of waters. . . .
>
> (*Prel.* VII, 615–617)

What he sees is deeply shocking. He does not see merely a written sign. He sees a type. It seemed to him that "in this label was a type." With the word "type" we are brought back to the preceding book, to the passage immediately following the apostrophe to the imagination:

The unfetter'd clouds, and region of the Heavens,
Tumult and peace, the darkness and the light
Were all like workings of one mind, the features
Of the same face, blossoms upon one tree,
Characters of the great Apocalypse,
The types and symbols of Eternity,
Of first and last, and midst, and without end.

(Prel. vi, 566–572)

In Book vi the "types" are of eternity and infinitude. The apostrophe to the imagination is an epiphany of expansion. It relates to the living universe and is transcendent. The meeting with the blind beggar, on the other hand, is an epiphany of contraction. It relates to the world of man and to finitude. Its mode of transcendence is that of tragedy, of suffering and limitation endured. The label the blind man wears bears a message of seemingly confining limitation:

>   . . . this Label was a type,
> Or emblem, of the utmost that we know,
> Both of ourselves and of the universe. . . .

(Prel. vii, 617–619)

Upon seeing this type of finitude Wordsworth is chastened "As if admonish'd from another world" (*Prel*. vii, 622). He had been seeking answers "of what, and whither, when and how" and in response he has literally seen a sign. He has been asking for an affirmation of his being in and through other hitherto mysterious people in society. He finds that affirmation but in a terribly limited form. He is shown that identity must always, within the human realm, remain identity. There can be no transcendence beyond the self into others. "Points have all of us within our souls,/Where all stand single" (*Prel*. iii, 186–187). There is an ultimate failure of human connection. Only within circumscribed limits may we know others or they us. Relations in this world, so necessary in establishing a secure sense of self, must always be finite, limited, and incomplete. His grand attempts to achieve the high degree of insight and understanding that he believes belongs to a true poet are rebuked. He is "admonished as if from another world."

The two opposing kinds of epiphanies are juxtaposed in order to indicate that the riddle of the self cannot be solved completely in and through this world, but only in moments of transcendence when the self and identity cease and we become one with the universe. That is, paradoxically, the self can be saved from contraction and the fear of contraction only in moments when the light of sense goes out, and it ceases to be, in any ordinary sense, a self.

But if, as the epiphany of the blind beggar teaches, what we know of ourselves and of the universe is limited, this is not to say that the self can do no better than exist in a world in which the face of every person met is a mystery. Implicitly, one should seek and/or create a society in which the unbridgeable gulf of ignorance and identity that separates people from one another is reduced to a bearable limit or minimum. Identity can survive if we create a truly human community, bound together by mutually strengthening ties, a community in which everyone attempts to know, love and support his fellow man. One must struggle against the divisive society of competing integers that was being established by the developing capitalist and industrial social relations. This capitalist world was based not on affectivity but on utility and abstract calculation. Raymond Williams writes:

> Wordsworth saw that when we become uncertain in a world of apparent strangers who yet, decisively, have a common effect on us, and when forces that will alter our lives are moving all around us in apparently external and unrecognizable forms, we can retreat, for security, into a deep subjectivity, or we can look around us for social pictures, social signs, social messages, to which, characteristically, we try to relate as individuals but so as to discover, in some form, community.[17]

And it was precisely community that Wordsworth sought to discover—a supportive community for his riven self, a community in which the faces of those he met would be filled with meaning, recognition and reference, not with mystery.

The duality of the princely and contracted selves lay at the core of Wordsworth's being. Such seed time had his soul. Riven by a wound to his being, he sought relief from his emotional difficulty in a surrounding community. No attempt will be made here to assert that a secure social community would have been a sufficient remedy for Wordsworth's difficulties. It is, indeed, overwhelmingly likely that his psychic economy would use many mechanisms to deal with such a source of pain. Perhaps the act of poetic creation itself helped him to deal with his problem of identity. And it is likely that his intense bonds with Dorothy and Coleridge, and later with Mary and his children, with all those who made up the little household world that revolved around him, helped to stabilize and solace him. But to examine fully all the methods Wordsworth employed to heal the pain of an insecure sense of identity would be an ambitious task, and would, if indeed it could be done at all, require a book-length study of its own.

Yet to assert that Wordsworth, living at the time he did, would be likely to seek relief from an inner conflict in external social arrangements would be an understatement. Wordsworth lived through a time of enormous, even millennial social expectations. Of these times he was later to write:

> Bliss was it in that dawn to be alive,
> But to be young was very heaven. . . .
> (Prel. x, 693–694)

Dawn supplied one of the most common metaphors for the French Revolution in the republican pamphlets of the time. The rising sun of the new day is Blake's emblem of the creative Los at his anvil. Wordsworth was but one of many of his generation to seek, consciously or unconsciously, release from inner pain in the new possibilities seemingly opened up by the French Revolution.

TWO

THE SEARCH FOR COMMUNITY

WORDSWORTH responded to the social possibilities that the French Revolution seemed to hold out, in part because Wordsworth by himself could not heal the rent in his divided psyche. As I have suggested in the previous chapter he sought to confirm himself in, through and by participation in a social community larger than himself. The word "confirm" is particularly apt here, deriving as it does from the Latin verb *confirmare*, to make firm. From a community larger than himself he could obtain a firmness, a perdurability that his painfully changeable sense of self could not obtain in solitude. Certainly Wordsworth sought to enter a social community for many reasons other than unconscious emotional need. Many of his reasons were undoubtedly conscious and quite rational. But to say that participation in community was a partial solution to one of Wordsworth's perplexities is to beg a significant question. What kind of community would satisfy Wordsworth's particular emotional needs? Was Wordsworth's selective, or would any form of community suffice? Did, that is to say, Wordsworth's instability of identity bring into being a corresponding set of particular political ideas?

The careful reader may have already found a seeming inconsistency regarding Wordsworth and community as I have discussed it in the first chapter. In the analysis of the blind beggar passage of *The Prelude*, I suggested that Wordsworth could escape the anomic ravages of London only in a particular kind of traditional rural community, bound together by affective ties. Wordsworth describes such a community in the account of the country fair that follows and is deliberately set off against his description of London. Yet in concluding the first chapter, I also said that Wordsworth, like others of his generation, was to seek release from inner distress in the possibility of revolutionary social change apparently made available by the French Revolution.

There is no question of contradiction or inconsistency in Wordsworth, in his search for a stabilizing form of community. He was to find such a community in Grasmere as he idealized it into a stable reflexive and affective world. To Grasmere he was to add "the gleam . . . that never was, on sea or land" (P.W. 4:259). No, not contradiction or inconsistency, but development, for before Wordsworth could find his home at Grasmere he had to pass through the "fiery furnace" (Prel. VII, 398–400) of the French Revolution. Nor was he to be "embalmed" by Nature "through some special privilege" as he passed through the ordeal. Unlike his fantasy image of the beautiful infant son of the London prostitute, he was to change. The ordeal of the French Revolution would alter him, as it altered many others. In Blakean, as well as in geographical terms, Grasmere lay west of France. It was Wordsworth's task:

> To find the Western path
> Right thro the Gates of Wrath. . . .[1]

Before retracing the steps that led Wordsworth through this Blakean gate of experience, it is appropriate to raise the question of whether or not a terminology adequate to describe one aspect of Wordsworth's emotional life, when Wordsworth is examined as an isolated individual, is also sufficiently elastic to describe Wordsworth once he has passed through the wrathful gate and become a participant in the turbulent history of the French Revolution. I have postulated a duality that divides Wordsworth's identity between a princely sense of self and a contracted sense of self. The terms princely self and contracted self have seemed useful to me, and I have used them as tools with which to examine certain aspects of both the poet and his poetry. But the dichotomy between the princely self and the contracted self, though it still seems valid, is too absolute to accommodate the extensive range of experience, hope, and fear that a student of Wordsworth must deal with when he expands the scope of his investigation to include not only the troubled emotional life of a great poet, but that same emotional life and its interaction with society at a time of dramatic social change.

For the events of the French Revolution were certainly felt to be dramatic by all those who lived through them. Even today, if one gives oneself imaginatively to the events set in motion by the summoning of the Estates General in 1789 one may well be struck by the awesomeness of what seemed to be the opening of a brave new world of human history, as well as what seemed to many, such as Edmund Burke, the foreseeable end of civilization as it was possible to conceive of it at that point in time. It is not merely that Wordsworth found himself to be young and alive in a dramatic epoch. It was not merely the best of times and the worst of times. The events set in motion by the French Revolution were more than colorful. They were complex and contradictory as well. At the same time that France was the center of European, if not world, turmoil, the capitalist social order in England, developing and changing for hundreds of years, was entering a period of dramatic expansion, now regarded as the first phase of the Industrial Revolution. Both Revolutions were to make contemporary observers aware that something momentous, rapid, and perhaps uncontrollable was taking place.

In light of this drama and complexity I have chosen to supplement the terms princely self and contracted self with two terms descriptive of two of the possible types of human power, effective power and affective power. To have effective power is to have the actual material power to influence and change events and people in the real world. To lack effective power is to be helpless in the real world and unable to exert any influence outside oneself. To have affective power is to have what Wordsworth called imagination or highest reason. It is to have the power of the sympathetic imagination, the ability to respond intuitively, emotionally to the world, to perceive organic relationship and unity. It is, as well, the power to alter the world not by changing it physically, but by projecting emotional colorations outward onto the world. Wordsworth speaks of this:

We have had deepest feeling that the mind
Is lord and master, and that outward sense
Is but the obedient servant of her will.
                    (*Prel.* xi, 271–273)

To lack affective power is to lack imagination, to live in a world
that is meaningless and dead, devoid of significant relationship and
unity. It is to live in a hard material world unresponsive to human
needs and wishes. It is to inhabit what William Blake called Ulro.

The princely self would correspond to the self who possessed
both effective and affective power. Such a self would inhabit and
control a meaningful and beautiful world. The contracted self
would correspond to the self utterly devoid of both effective and affective power. Such a self would be shrunken, mean, and helpless,
pushed to the very border of nonbeing, of dissolution.

It is obvious that there are two more possible permutations:
the self with effective power but devoid of affective power and the
self possessed of affective power but without significant effective
power. These two states will play their respective roles in
Wordsworth's emotional history. I hope that by opening the possibility of equating the princely self with a being possessed of both
powers and the contracted self with a being stripped of both, I have
created, by reason of the two as yet unused permutations, a more
supple and useful theoretical model.

Before following Wordsworth's development from his admission to Cambridge to his recovery from his spiritual crisis following
his loss of faith in revolutionary politics, it may be useful to preface this account of a poet's search for a stabilizing community
with Wordsworth's account of his unconscious dedication to some
morally worthy end. Wordsworth, at the age of eighteen, is walking home from a night of dancing, in a dawn "More glorious than
I ever had beheld." He describes the scene and follows his description with these words:

> My heart was full; I made no vows, but vows
> Were then made for me; bond unknown to me
> Was given, that I should be, else sinning greatly,
> A dedicated Spirit. On I walk'd
> In blessedness, which even yet remains.
>   (*Prel.* iv, 332–345)

Wordsworth has been marked, has been dedicated, as Samuel had been dedicated by Samuel's mother, Hannah.[2] Unless Wordsworth is to sin greatly, he has been bound to abstain from all the common uses of the world. Presumably, a life dedicated to seeking pleasure or self-advancement or self-aggrandizement is forbidden him. His must be a life above getting and spending, above common egoistic pursuits. But the picture of a dedicated, bonded spirit, however specially sanctified, seems to be that of a young man limited to the choices he may make in life, withdrawn from the shock and strife of the world in order to free his soul from that which would contaminate him and thereby render him unfit for his sacred task.

During his Cambridge years, however, Wordsworth the dedicated spirit contained another self, a more assertive self. As an old man remembering the period he had spent at Cambridge, Wordsworth recalled an ambition he had entertained that had had seductive power. Having studied military history and strategy, he wished for a career in the army, because he thought he had had "a talent for command."[3] This is the authentic voice of the princely self. It is not likely that Coleridge's sordid adventure with the dragoons was the result of a personal belief in a talent for command.

There may well have been a continual tension in Wordsworth, during his Cambridge years, between the Wordsworth who felt himself to be a dedicated spirit and the Wordsworth who felt that he possessed a talent for command. Wordsworth's involvement with and advocacy of the French Revolution was to release such tension and liberate, for a time, the Wordsworth who strove not only for power over the real world, but for a full and wide-ranging emotional life as well.

It is now my intention to follow Wordsworth's life sequentially, starting with his tuition at Cambridge, following with his conversion to the principles of the French Revolution, his crisis of spirit that resulted from this conversion, and his subsequent recovery from this crisis. And it is precisely at this point that I must deal with a vexing methodological problem. Wordsworth's inner life during the period of his conversion to revolutionary politics, his despondent crisis of faith and his subsequent spiritual rebirth, is little recorded—outside *The Prelude*. There are some illuminating personal letters, his "Letter to Bishop Llandaff," and *The Bor-*

derers. But these are inadequate to the task of recreating Wordsworth's state of mind at this time. The critic is left with two choices. Either he must avoid investigating this crucial period in Wordsworth's life, or he must turn to *The Prelude* for help. I have chosen to read *The Prelude* in hope of finding clues to Wordsworth's development. Whenever possible I have searched for supporting material elsewhere. Where I have been unable to find such supporting material I must be skeptical about my own hypothesis.

The problem is, of course, that *The Prelude* is not an autobiography, but a work of art, an imaginative work based upon, but not faithfully recording, Wordsworth's own experience. Writing as a poet, Wordsworth had to be more concerned with the imaginative and spiritual truth of what he was creating than with mere biographical fact. And even when he attempted, with the best will in the world, to record what he took to be his state of mind in, say, 1792 or 1795, he was recording this as late as 1805. Inevitably he revised his experience retrospectively. The reader may well ask, then, whether the following examination of Wordsworth's development is worthwhile. I believe that it is. First, this period in Wordsworth's life is too important to abandon because of methodological overscrupulousness, provided, of course, that one proceeds with caution. Second, *The Prelude,* although not autobiography, is a record of Wordsworth's spiritual growth and therefore does possess evidentiary value if it is read with care and tact.

Wordsworth went up to St. John's College at Cambridge in October, 1787. Entrance to Cambridge was Wordsworth's entrance to a great world, the world in which dreams of splendid social success could become true. Wordsworth writes of his arrival at Cambridge as the fulfillment of a dream. "I was the Dreamer, they the Dream" (*Prel.* III, 28). He wastes no time in dressing himself in a manner suitable for playing a role in this world. He is newly attired as by a "Fairy's power" (*Prel.* III, 34) in the clothing of a gentle class. He powders his hair for the first time. Wordsworth is quick in asserting how very special he was. He writes:

> I was a chosen Son.
> For hither I had come with holy powers. . . .
> (*Prel.* III, 82–83)

He goes on to tell of the extraordinary power of his mind. His mind is a "force" capable of working on the "visible universe" "changes" like those wrought by "time, and place, and seasons" (*Prel.* III, 85–88). He may have been a relatively poor and obscure fellow who did not otherwise distinguish himself in competitions or exert himself to take the Tripos (a final examination for honors instituted at Cambridge in the first half of the eighteenth century), but the hidden undervalued prince, the Odysseus disguised to the suitors by his rags, is clearly visible in this grand self-description. He writes that "often among multitudes of men," he was

> Unknown, unthought of, yet I was most rich,
> I had a world about me; 'twas my own,
> I made it. . . .
>
> (*Prel.* III, 140–143)

Wordsworth portrays himself as a young man who, without relinquishing his own high conception of himself, withdraws from active society where he might receive recognition of his worth. The bookish scholarly dedication required for success in the Tripos, from which Wordsworth also withdrew himself, may seem far removed from success in the active world, but success in these examinations could give access to prominence, recognition and worldly success in the world outside of the library. Whether he withdraws because something in him inhibits any manifest social attempt to demonstrate egoistic mastery, as I believe, or whether he held back because Cambridge seemed too mean a place to warrant special endeavor—whether, that is, he sought a larger world—this I cannot say. But of "The thirst of living praise" stirring "A fervent hope of rigorous discipline," he says, "Alas! such high commotion touch'd not me" (*Prel.* III, 343–349).

Wordsworth offers hints of the reason for his fundamental alienation from Cambridge society. After he has adjusted somewhat to Cambridge life, he tentatively enters the social world. The results are unfavorable. Like a cancer he finds growing in him:

> a treasonable growth
> Of indecisive judgments that impar'd
> And shook the mind's simplicity.
>
> (*Prel.* III, 214–216)

The charge of treason suggests that the regnant power of his mind was to him its simplicity—its simple and direct relation to the living universe. Society, Wordsworth seems to have believed, interfered with this direct relationship, and therefore interfered with what made Wordsworth unique and imperial. Only when he could see the possibility of society becoming simple, or of society coming into direct contact with the processes of the living universe, could he actively enter the social world. In the same vein he later tells us that on entering the social world on his return to Hawkshead during his first summer vacation, his "authentic sight of reason" became "perplex'd" (*Prel.* IV, 295–296). He writes of his clothes, now of latest fashion, that they seemed

> To prey upon my strength, and stopp'd the course,
> And quiet stream of self-forgetfulness.
>   (*Prel.* IV, 293–294)

Clothing is an article that symbolizes singularly well man's acceptance of and integration with society. This passage describing Wordsworth's summer vacation would seem, then, to ratify his judgment that involvement in an active social world impaired him because it preyed upon his mind's simplicity.

But a more sustained reading of this passage reveals suggestions of sexuality and aggression latent in the pursuit of an active social life that seems to weaken the theory about himself that Wordsworth somewhat self-servingly advances. This is the theory that participation in social life corrupted the integrity of his most significant identity, that of poet, much as the city impairs and corrupts Michael's Luke. Wordsworth says that social pleasure seduced him from his habitual simple pleasures found in nature and books. The choice of the verb "seduce" seems to imply that active participation involves some sexual need, even if only a symbolic one. Here is the passage in question

>   . . . a swarm
> Of heady thoughts jostling each other, gawds,
> And feast, and dance, and public revelry,
> And sports and games (less pleasing in themselves,
> Than as they were a badge glossy and fresh
> Of manliness and freedom) these did now

Seduce me from the firm habitual quest
Of feeding pleasures, from that eager zeal,
Those yearnings which had every day been mine,
A wild unworldly-minded Youth, given up
To Nature and to Books. . . .

(Prel. iv, 272–282)

This passage strongly suggests that participation in society afforded
a symbolic gratification of some constituent part of his sexuality.
Social life seduces him; it is a badge of manliness. Tentatively it
would seem that the social world afforded satisfaction of his egoistic desire to exercise mastery, to wield power, to be, that is, the
prince capable of possessing everything, including women and all
that this implies. At the very least the passage seems to suggest that
society confronted Wordsworth with the possibility of sexuality and
sexual fulfillment which, to the degree that it was forbidden him,
may have created anxiety. And it is possible that Wordsworth was
accurate in noting that society weakened him, because society
might cause emotional energy that might otherwise be used by the
ego to be diverted away from the ego. This diverted energy might
be channeled into the creation of anxiety.

Wordsworth does much to confirm the notion that social action brings into play the impulse toward mastery when in the
conclusion of the same passage he declares that active social life
impaired "Th' authentic sight of reason." Wordsworth then describes the being who emerges when social life has perplexed authentic reason. The description is of a predatory being "with vile
claws" *(Prel.* iv, 302).

Society is not the only area that afforded opportunities for forbidden egoistic assertion. Self-assertion also manifested itself in
choice of vocation. The forces of family authority demanded that
he become either a lawyer or a curate. But Wordsworth wished to
pursue a literary career of some kind and such a vocational wish
was "proud rebellion."

                    I was detached
Internally from academic cares,
From every hope of prowess and reward,
And wish'd to be a lodger in that house
Of Letters, and no more; and should have been

Even such, but for some personal concerns
That hung about me in my own despite
Perpetually, no heavy weight, but still
A baffling and a hinderance, a controul
Which made the thought of planning for myself
A course of independent study seem
An act of disobedience towards them
Who lov'd me, proud rebellion and unkind.
(*Prel.* vi, 29–41)

Wordsworth, looking back at his college years, calls his failure to rebel a "bastard virtue . . . cowardice" (*Prel.* vi, 42–43). The personal concerns and family obligations hang about Wordsworth like clothing. They are external to him and, indeed, conceal him. It is his refusal or inability to divest himself of these lendings that he retrospectively sees as cowardice and a bastard virtue.

The picture of Wordsworth that emerges at the end of his Cambridge years is that of a young man filled with egoistic desires that are restrained at every turn, either by some internalized restricting force, his family, or both. The shock of "loving-liking" is forbidden him; the opportunity to engage and dominate society is forbidden him; the freedom to choose his own career is likewise forbidden him. Thus thwarted, many of his impulses, both conscious and unconscious, blocked, Wordsworth might have remained unfulfilled, "A Poet only to myself" (*Prel.* x, 200), "vegetating on a paltry curacy" (*E.L.* 59). But this was not to be. At this important, possibly decisive, moment in Wordsworth's life, his emotional conflicts became deeply involved with the social conflict of the French Revolution. In an historically more stable period, his own emotional conflicts might have resolved themselves independently of larger social conflicts, but from the moment Wordsworth became actively involved with the politics of the French Revolution, his emotional life was no longer an independent one. His inner life, to borrow one of Wordsworth's favorite metaphors for emotional development, was caught up in the river of the French Revolution and was twisted in its currents.

Unlike some of his generation, Wordsworth did not immediately enthusiastically support the French Revolution. He explains this by writing that to one born in a free country, England, raised in a district almost free of deference to hereditary aristocracy, Cumberland, and educated in a university in which member fellows treated each other as citizens in a republic, Cambridge, the events in France at first seemed in no way out of the ordinary,

> If at the first great outbreak I rejoiced
> Less than might well befit my youth, the cause
> In part lay here, that unto me the events
> Seem'd nothing out of nature's certain course,
> A gift that rather was come late than soon.
>   (*Prel.* ix, 249–253)

Wordsworth first saw revolutionary France on July 13, 1790 when he crossed from Dover with his fellow Cantabrigian, Robert Jones, in order to begin a walking tour of France, Switzerland and Italy. They entered France "and found themselves plunged into the festivities of the great 'Federation Day' of the French Revolution."[4] Though Wordsworth did not yet become a partisan, he did participate in the joyous celebration of the newly free French Third Estate. He describes participating in a festive banquet filled largely with delegates returned from Paris.

> The Supper done,
> With Flowing cups elate, and happy thoughts,
> We rose at signal giv'n, and form'd a ring
> And, hand in hand, danced round and round the Board;
> All hearts were open, every tongue was loud
> With amity and glee. . . .
>   (*Prel.* vi, 404–409)

During Wordsworth's first trip to France, his checked impulses did not yet find release through active participation in revolutionary politics. Such participation and the consequent release of those pent-up impulses would come some two years later. It is possible, however, to find indirect signs of this stored-up aggressiveness in the metaphors and similes Wordsworth uses to describe his physical progress during his walking tour of 1790. He and Jones pursue a "march . . . of military speed." They are "Keen Hunters" who are as "Eager as birds of prey" (*Prel.* vi, 428–436). These journey metaphors seem to betray a dammed-up and violent charge of egoistic energy, as well as a certain degree of discharge of energy as well. Whether Wordsworth used this imagery because he was retrospectively aware of the aggressive impulses during his tour with Jones, or whether, on the other hand, he retrospectively read back into his account of the tour feelings of aggression present only when he wrote *The Prelude* cannot be determined.

But Wordsworth was not ready in 1790 to become a political activist. Though a social being, he was as yet too immature to realize fully the social aspects of his being. Wordsworth conveys this in a brilliant simile. After describing "the Swiss exulting in the fate/Of their near Neighbors" and "the Brabant Armies on the fret/For battle in the cause of Liberty," he writes:

> A Stripling, scarcely of the household then
> Of social life, I look'd upon these things
> As from a distance, heard, and saw, and felt,
> Was touch'd, but with no intimate concern;
> I seem'd to move among them as a bird
> Moves through the air, or as a fish pursues
> Its business, in its proper element. . . .
> (*Prel.* vi, 688–699)

The image of likening himself to a fish moving through water has a deceptive appearance of simplicity. On the one hand, a fish pays no special attention to water. But on the other hand, this inattention is not due to the insignificance of water for the fish. Quite the contrary. The fish is not especially aware of the water precisely because water is so important for the fish, precisely because it is the very necessity without which piscine existence would be impossible. If existence and water are almost interchangeable terms for the fish, the fish could not conceive of existence without water. So the fish takes water as a given and is unaware of it. Wordsworth is truly like the unconscious fish. In his immaturity, Wordsworth takes society for granted. He is not yet aware that it is vital for his sustained existence. He is not conscious that he is a social being. He cannot be aware, therefore, of how important the unfolding French Revolution is to him.

Immediately after likening himself to the heedless bird or fish, Wordsworth concludes Book vi of *The Prelude* with the following declaration that he was not dependent upon society for his pleasures:

> I needed not that joy, I did not need
> Such help; the ever-living Universe,
> And independent spirit of pure youth
> Were with me at that season, and delight
> Was in all places spread around my steps
> As constant as the grass upon the fields.
>   (*Prel.* VI, 700–705)

This passage is significant in that by telling under what conditions Wordsworth may be independent of society as a source of joy it also tells, by implication, what conditions will be necessary to make him seek out joy in the political and social world. Wordsworth is independent of the political and social world, not because he does not need joy but because he has his own personal sources of joy. Implicitly when he turns to active social life in order to find happiness it will be out of need. Either youth and the living universe will no longer be able to fulfill his needs or he will have turned away from the gratification afforded by youth and nature, seeking joy in society instead. Perhaps after having graduated from Cambridge, the lack of any settled plan for a future career triggered terror of future impoverishment, "Cold, pain, and labour, and all fleshly ills" (*P.W.* 2:239). Fear of impoverishment was, as I have noted, the form in which anxieties of contraction typically manifested themselves for Wordsworth. If Wordsworth were burdened by an especially intense charge of anxiety he would have less emotional energy free to produce joy. Although during his walking trip he had had joy enough, now he would have to turn to other sources to find it. He would then have turned, out of need, to the political activity then available to a proponent of the French Revolution, because "the ever-living Universe," and the "independent spirit of pure youth" could not supply enough joy for one wracked by anxiety.

Whatever suppositions may be made as to why Wordsworth became a proponent of the French Revolution, and more will be made, the bare history of his involvement is known. Wordsworth

shrank from the idea of "vegetating on a paltry curacy." With his
uncle pressing him to return to Cambridge temporarily in order
"to study the Oriental languages" (E.L. 61), the better to suit himself for the clergy, he hit upon the scheme of becoming "a travell-
ing tutor to some wealthy youth."[5] But before he felt himself qual-
ified to undertake this, he deemed it necessary to return to France
in order "to perfect his knowledge of French."[6] Was this plan but
a rationalization behind which lurked the desire to go to France in
order to break with his past and the limitations that his family,
both the quick and the dead, placed upon him? France offered
him a chance to become involved in the teeming world of revolutionary politics. It would be a fine place to make such a break with
his past. Perhaps he unconsciously remembered what he had seen
the previous summer:

> How bright a face is worn when joy of one
> Is joy of tens of millions.
> (Prel. vi, 359-360)

Such a recollection could easily give rise to the idea that the forces
repressing his impulses for self-fulfillment might be more effectively fought if he joined himself to a collectivity "of tens of mil-
lions" all of whom seemed, like him, to be struggling against traditional restraints and limitations.

Whether or not he went to France unconsciously determined
to become a revolutionary, he crossed from Brighton to Dieppe on
November 27, 1791. From Dieppe he traveled to Paris and from
Paris he traveled to Orleans in order to improve his knowledge of
the French language. It was in Orleans that he first met and began
his love affair with Annette Vallon, whose family were Royalists,
some time early in 1792. When Annette returned to her home in
Blois early in the spring of that year Wordsworth followed her. It
was in Blois that Wordsworth met Michel Beaupuy, a captain in
the revolutionary armies. Beaupuy played a role in converting
Wordsworth to the ideals of the French Revolution, to a conviction of the rights of man and to a disdain for the aristocracy's
demand for special honor and privilege. In Wordsworth, Beaupuy
found a willing pupil. Wordsworth was soon a convinced adherent
of the French Revolution.

This is not the place to give a detailed biographical account of Wordsworth's doings. Rather it is my wish to attempt to understand what motivated William Wordsworth to become an advocate of the French Revolution. Many another English youth of Wordsworth's generation joined him in such advocacy. It is likely that many of them came to support the revolution for reasons similar to Wordsworth's. Though this study may incidentally shed light on the motives of Wordsworth's corevolutionists, it will do so only by the way. What, then, in Wordsworth's unique character motivated him to support the French Revolution?

I have suggested that Wordsworth found himself at an impasse by the age of twenty-two. His impulses towards sexual fulfillment, social domination and free choice of a career seemed to be restrained not only by his living uncles but also by the monitions of the dead father whom he bore within himself. If Wordsworth found himself thwarted, "bewildered and forlorn," the French Revolution was a suitable struggle that he could join in order to break through his personal impasse. As did the blind boy in the poem "The Blind Highland Boy" (*P.W.* 3:88–96), written in 1806, Wordsworth wished to fulfill his heroic dreams of self-assertion. Both Wordsworth and the blind boy wish to fulfill themselves in defiance of familial authority. The blind Highland boy disobeys his mother's injunction that he never sail on Loch Leven. The boy's rebellion is crushed. He is saved, against his will, from being swept into the turbulent currents of the lake, and perhaps ultimately down to the sea. Writing of the rebellious period during which he sought fulfillment in and through the French Revolution, Wordsworth describes himself as having been on a "road/That leads direct to the devouring sea" (*Prel.* ix, 4). The comparison of the young rebellious Wordsworth to the blind Highland boy is not fanciful. Both rebelled against authority, both were almost destroyed, and both ended by accepting the authority they had flouted.

Wordsworth looked upon the politics of the Revolution as an avenue by which his imperial nature could become manifest. He could become a "Power" independent of and even opposed to his father. Speaking of France as it appeared to him at the time of his second visit, he writes:

> The land all swarm'd with passion, like a Plain
> Devour'd by locusts, Carra, Gorsas, add
> A hundred other names, forgotten now,
> Nor to be heard of more, yet were they Powers,
> Like earthquakes, shocks repeated day by day,
> And felt through every nook of town and field.
>   (*Prel*. IX, 177–188)

Wordsworth, whose growth had been fostered by tutelary powers, sought now in his own turn to become a "Power" as potentially destructive as an earthquake. The Revolution seemed to open the way for hundreds to become Powers. In the simile of the earthquake the aggressiveness of the restrained egoism is visible. He writes almost immediately afterward that

> . . . though untaught by thinking or by books
> To reason well of polity or law

he still valued the area of public affairs as a realm for possible greatness even though he realized that he might have to pay for his greatness with suffering. His heart, he says,

> Beat high and fill'd my fancy with fair forms,
> Old Heroes and their sufferings and their deeds. . . .
>   (*Prel*. IX, 200–210)

Earlier, writing of his experience in London perhaps prior to his second trip to France, he says

> . . . I sought not then
> Knowledge; but craved for power, and power I found
> In all things. . . .
>   (*Prel*. VIII, 754–756)

Finally, as evidence that the French Revolution offered Wordsworth an avenue of escape from the limitations that had been imposed upon his personal strivings, and therefore an avenue toward the fulfillment of the realization of his imperial idea of himself, it would be useful to consider Wordsworth's apparent identification in fantasy with Francis the First. Wordsworth describes himself walking with Beaupuy along the Loire discussing great public issues of the day. Wordsworth lapses from political discourse into daydream.

From earnest dialogues I slipp'd in thought
And let remembrance steal to other times. . . .
(*Prel.* IX, 445-446)

When Beaupuy shows his young English companion Romerentin and recalls how Francis the First wooed his beloved Lady, communing "By cresset and love beacons," Wordsworth reflects

. . . 'mid these frequent monuments
Of Kings, their vices and their better deeds,
Imagination, potent to enflame
At times with virtuous wrath and noble scorn,
Did also often mitigate the force
Of civic prejudice, the bigotry,
So call it, of a youthful Patriot's mind,
And on these spots with many gleams I look'd
Of chivalrous delight.
(*Prel.* IX, 494-502)

It seems probable that Wordsworth has identified the amorous Francis the First with the heroic ideal of himself as public and erotic hero. The French Revolution was the means by which Wordsworth sought to make this ideal a reality. It is precisely from discussions of the Revolution that Wordsworth slipped into heroic erotic fantasy.

And of course, for Wordsworth, mature erotic fulfillment and acceptance of politically revolutionary principles were biographically deeply connected. Wordsworth began his affair with Annette Vallon only shortly before his political transformation. It is possible that the two events were causally as well as temporally linked. Though Wordsworth says in the 1805 edition of *The Prelude* that man was subordinate to nature in his love until "three and twenty summers had been told" (*Prel.* VIII, 483), de Selincourt points out that in the D text of *The Prelude* the figure is "two and twenty." De Selincourt goes on to say: "If my interpretation is correct, this shifting of interest from Nature to Man would coincide with his plunge into humanitarian politics and the dawning of his love for Annette" (*Prel.:* 580).

Wordsworth's breakthrough from love of nature to love of man came with his sexual involvement with Annette. In this rela-

tionship, his sexual passion again turned to a human figure, Annette. His passions had previously been involved, however elabo-
rately, and with whatever sublimations, with nature, and nature
may, in turn, be said to have been a replacement for his forever
absent mother, Ann. The love affair with Annette represented
Wordsworth's break with the restraints that had been put upon
him. The causal connections between his relationship with Annette Valon and his adherence to the Revolutionary factions in
France seem to be clear. After he had shaken his inhibitions in
regard to Annette it was both more possible and more necessary for
him to overcome the limitations placed upon him by traditional
political attitudes. Having joined what Blake referred to as the
"Devils party" [7] by permitting himself sexual freedom, it was understandable for him to justify himself by becoming an active
member of the that party. He became an earnest supporter of new
claims for personal rights and liberties. He attacked traditional
social institutions that had limited personal freedom. In this way
he unconsciously supplied himself with ideological justification for
the liberties he and Annette had taken. He was no longer alone in
opposing familial and paternal restrictions. Now he knew

> How bright a face of joy is worn when joy of one
> Is joy of tens of millions.
> *(Prel.* VI, 359–360)

Wordsworth, himself, probably did not make a conscious connection between active participation in mature sexuality and active
participation in revolutionary politics, as Blake did, at least on the
level of ideas. He was not like William Blake. He would very
likely have recoiled at any suggestion that revolutionary politics
was or ought to be connected with sexual freedom. He did not en-
dorse free love. The connection between his new politics and his
new sexuality very likely remained hidden from him. This inferred
failure of connection would have been facilitated by Annette's
strong Royalist inclinations.

It seems almost certain that there was an enormous amount
of denial on his part as to how radically he had broken free of the
power of the introjected restaining authorities in him. He pretends
to see a continuity between social life as he had experienced it at

Cambridge and the social life his new political ideals would bring
into being. He writes:

> . . . nor was it least
> Of many debts which afterward I owed
> To Cambridge, and an academic life
> That something there was holden up to view
> Of a Republic, where all stood thus far
> Upon equal ground, that they were brothers all
> In honour, as in one community,
> Scholars and Gentlemen, where furthermore,
> Distinction lay open to all that came,
> And wealth and titles were in less esteem
> Than talents and successful industry.
>
> (*Prel.* IX, 225–235)

Our knowledge of the social life in late-eighteenth-century Cambridge suggests that Wordsworth's portrait is highly misleading at
best. But one must bear in mind how urgently Wordsworth strove
to deny and minimize his break with his past, how urgently he
sought to erase from consciousness any trace of his assault on the
memory of the father of his childhood and all the aristocratic connections that his father had represented and stood for. Only by
bearing this in mind is it possible to read seriously this unconscious parody of life at Cambridge. Where is the university to
which Halévy refers:

> During the seven months of the term the wealthiest could spend
> several thousands. It was difficult to live in a town where these rich
> spendthrifts set the fashion, under £100 to £150 a year. The poor
> student was condemned to a precarious and humiliating existence
> in an environment necessarily unfavorable to serious study.[8]

Where is the Cambridge in which tutors competed for wealthy and
influential aristocratic students, even helping these students with
their examinations in the hope of future preferment?

Wordsworth's denial of his rejection of the authorities that he
had internalized in early life took on a form other than an idealization of his recent past in order to bring it into conformity with
his revolutionary present, so that little discrepancy could be seen.
In fact, during this period Wordsworth experienced an intense

kind of filial love. This love represented an effort on Wordsworth's part to deny that his feelings for his father were ambivalent, that they contained hatred, as well as love and the desire to emulate his father. Wordsworth expressed his love and denied his antipathy in a way that is typical of adolescent or late adolescent men who are attempting to formulate an identity independent of that formed by identifications with their real father. He set up a new father figure, a transitional father figure, so to speak, representative of the sought-after new identity. By loving this transitional father and thereby experiencing filial piety, Wordsworth could more easily deny the repudiation of the real father.

Michel Beaupuy, eleven years Wordsworth's senior, was the transitional father figure Wordsworth found. Wordsworth's need had probably created earlier such figures, such as William Taylor, the Headmaster of Hawkshead Grammar School while Wordsworth was a student there, who was the first to interest Wordsworth in poetry and to encourage him to write it. But at this stage of Wordsworth's development, Beaupuy was an ideal choice. He possessed many characteristics that enabled Wordsworth to bind himself to him by ties of identification. Like Wordsworth, Beaupuy was a solitary. Beaupuy had been spurned by his fellow officers for his revolutionary sympathies and been left in relative isolation. He was "rejected by the rest/And with an oriental loathing spurn'd" (*Prel.* IX, 295–296). Like Wordsworth, at this point in Wordsworth's development, Beaupuy's character was free of demonstrable conscious egoistic self seeking.

> A meeker Man
> Than this liv'd never, or a more benign
> Meek, though enthusiastic to the height
> Of highest expectation. . . .
> (*Prel.* IX, 297–300)

Beaupuy's noble birth was significant because it made it possible for Wordsworth's grandiose ideal of himself to identify with Beaupuy; for of Beaupuy Wordsworth writes "By birth he rank'd/With the most noble" (*Prel.* IX, 308–309). Finally, though himself an aristocrat, Beaupuy speaks out against aristocratic privilege, against the "voluptuous life/Unfeeling" (*Prel.* IX, 352–353) of royal courts and for justice for the poor and the oppressed. In this last respect Beaupuy was, as a father figure, opposed to Wordsworth's real father, John, who spent his life as a professional legal retainer to a powerful aristocratic family, the Lowthers.

Wordsworth had denounced the "voluptuous life/Unfeeling" in the poem "Nutting" written in 1798 (*P.W.* 2:211–212). In this poem he describes himself as a young boy who had found an unspoiled hazel nook, dallied there in a "Voluptuous" mood, and then plundered the grove with "merciless ravage," a formulation that could easily be recast to read "unfeeling ravage." He then cautions a "dearest Maiden," presumably Dorothy, to "move . . . In gentleness of heart . . . ," to be, that is, unlike the unfeeling voluptuary who had desecrated the "virgin scene."

The Wordsworth family's troubled and bitter relationship to the House of Lowther is yet another determinant in Wordsworth's unconscious negative feelings for his father and his bitterness toward the aristocracy. These twin bitternesses would make it far less difficult for Beaupuy to convert the young Wordsworth to the cause of the French Revolution. The father of the Lowther family, for whom John Wordsworth worked as legal agent, was given the title of Lord Lonsdale. The family had enormous parliamentary power. John Wordsworth's employer had occasion to confer honorary freedom on 14,000 coal miners whom he employed in the family's enormous collieries, in order that they vote for the Lowther candidates for Parliament in the corporation of which Lowther was master. He performed this trick with success on three occasions.[9] In 1781 it was Lowther who first sent the younger Pitt to Parliament (*Lakes* 326). From 1768 to 1832 the Lowthers held unquestioned electoral sway in Cockermouth. They controlled no less than six of the ten local seats (*Lakes* 326). These are only some instances of the enormous power of the Lowther family. This power was to inflict great hardship upon the children of John Wordsworth.

At his death in 1783, John Wordsworth's financial affairs were in disorder. His employer, Sir James Lowther, owed him £4,700 spent out of pocket in his employer's behalf. But due to both John Wordsworth's carelessness and Sir James's brutal aristocratic high-handedness, it was difficult to establish the validity of the claim. The orphaned Wordsworth children were faced with the prospect of gentle destitution unlike anything that they had known. If this experience was not the original source of William's terror of future impoverishment, it almost certainly strongly reinforced any such as yet potential fears. Years of litigation failed to secure payment of the debts. The Wordsworth children were dispersed to different relatives and were often made only too aware that they were poor and dependent relations. Only years later, in 1802, was the validity of the debt acknowledged by Sir James's cousin and successor, Sir William, and a settlement reached, for £8,000.

Young William may well have perceived his father's death and failure to provide security for him as an abandonment and may have felt anger and bitterness towards his father as a result. When Wordsworth became an antiaristocratic republican, he rebelled against the social system which his father had served, against the Lowthers and perhaps through the Lowthers against his father as well. His father and some of the resentment he may have had against his father were both connected with the mighty Lowthers. Wordsworth's "Letter to Bishop Llandaff" written in 1792 makes bitter reference to the British law's ability to tear the fleece from a litigant's back (Prose 1:47). Possibly his bitterness over his contested patrimony was part of the rage that sparked his personal rebellion.

The tale of "Vaudracour and Julia," pathetic both in its content and in its execution, supplies evidence that Wordsworth's rebellion against the aristocratic principle was as well a rebellion against the father, here seen as callous and dictatorially restrictive. Since the rediscovery of Wordsworth's affair with Annette Vallon (I say rediscovery because Wordsworth himself never tried to conceal his relationship with Annette or their daughter Caroline), critics have been tempted to read the story of Vaudracour and Julia as a disguised account of his affair with Annette. Without attempting to assert that such conjectures are utterly false, I believe the central autobiographical impulse behind the tale (if indeed there is any such impulse) lies far closer to Wordsworth's home. The noble Vaudracour reflects Wordsworth's princely estimation of himself. That his father is also noble is implicit. A noble son must have a noble father. Further, it is typical of the child that his early years are governed by a grandiose overestimation of his father and his father's powers. [10] In the dream lives of both children and adults the father is commonly represented by a king. [11] Who then is Julia, whom the father so unyieldingly forbids Vandracour to marry? In part, of course, she may indeed be Annette. But why then such paternal intransigence leading even to the son's arrest? The question is valid, of course, only if one seeks an autobiographical meaning beneath the manifest social one. If the tale may be read as hidden autobiography, then Wordsworth may give a possible clue as to Julia's identity, but only if it is conceded that the autobiographical material in the story is hidden from Wordsworth as well as from his readers. Wordsworth writes of the two lovers that

> From their cradles up . . .
> The pair had thriven together year by year. . . .
> (*Prel.* ix, 569–571)

From his cradle up Wordsworth had thriven with the love of two women, or more precisely, a woman and a girl, either one of whom or both, for that matter, could be Julia. Wordsworth grew up both with his mother and his sister Dorothy. The father would have ample reason for ruthlessly forbidding his son fulfillment in either match.

It is not to be expected that Wordsworth would simply passively accept the thwarting of such passionate wishes. He probably harbored rage, perhaps even murderous rage against the powerful father who stood in his way. In *The Interpretation of Dreams* Freud writes of the story of Oedipus:

His destiny moves us only because it might have been ours—because the oracle laid the same curse upon us before our birth as upon him. It is the fate of all of us, perhaps, to direct our first sexual impulse towards our mother and our first hatred and our first murderous wish against our father. [12]

And in *The Ego and the Id* Freud writes of the son that as a result of the Oedipus complex:

His identification with his father then takes on a hostile colouring and changes into a wish to get rid of his father in order to take his place with his mother. [13]

But one of the most striking aspects of Vaudracour's personality is the total absence of rage against his father. It seems positively queer that when Julia "coupled with his Father's name some words/Of vehement indignation," Vaudracour "Check'd her." Wordsworth writes

> . . . for thought
> Unfilial, or unkind, had never once
> Found harbour in his breast.
>   (*Prel.* IX, 712–716)

As a literary touch this detail is disastrous. It is all but impossible to regard the passive, helpless and ultimately literally idiotic Vaudracour with any sympathy. But if Vaudracour's passivity towards his father is seen not as an awkward bit of melodrama but as an integral part of a piece of fantasy then it is possible to make sense of this sorry tale.

A fantasy that gave expression to unconscious forbidden desires and hatreds would be a structure analogous to a dream. Even if the forbidden wishes found expression, they would only reach Wordsworth's consciousness after having been subjected to distortions and censorship. Affects would be transformed into their opposites and perhaps displaced as well. If this is so then it is possible to see Vaudracour's passive acceptance of his father's tyrannical behavior as murderous rage transformed into its opposite. But the rage is not only converted into its opposite; it is also displaced. Vaudracour's father uses his influence to have his son arrested by a *lettre de cachet*. In an uncharacteristic act of violence Vaudracour murders one of the three armed men sent to arrest him and severely wounds another. So guilt-stricken is Vaudracour at this act of self-defense that he tells Julia

> "Thou no longer now art mine,
> I thine; a Murderer, Julia, cannot love
> An innocent Woman. . . ."
>   (*Prel.* IX, 707–709)

Again, as literature this bit of ridiculous melodrama is out of place in a work of art as great as the 1805 version of *The Prelude*. But as a piece of psychopathology it is quite comprehensible. The rage at the father is displaced in this fantasy away from the father onto the insignificant instrument of ruffian power, the murdered arresting officer. This would explain the ridiculous disavowal of his right to Julia. Such a disavowal would be appropriate to the murderer of one's father. Even Vaudracour's wish that his father banish him to a distant country retreat may be read as a transformed version of Vaudracour's wish to banish his father.

The story of Vaudracour is of too slight a literary interest to merit such examination if it were not that the story contains evidentiary value for understanding the motives that brought Wordsworth to become a partisan of the French Revolution. Vaudracour, in exile, becomes a wasted "imbecile mind."

> Nor could the voice of Freedom, which through France
> Soon afterward resounded, public hope,
> Or personal memory of his own deep wrongs,
> Rouse him. . . .
>
> (*Prel.* IX, 930–934)

But not so for Wordsworth. The fantasy about Vaudracour turns into its opposite, Wordsworth's response to "the voice of Freedom." Wordsworth saw in the Revolution an opportunity to do what he had not been able to do, what Vaudracour was unable to do, that is, break free from the restraints imposed on him by the father within him. Wordsworth used what appeared to be the convulsive birth of French liberty to liberate his restrained desire to be the prince, to achieve, that is, control both over the real world and control over the world created by his projected emotions.

Wordsworth's identification with the Revolution and with those who fought to defend it was intense. Just how intense is made clear by a comparison between the description of French patriots marching out of Blois to defend the frontiers recorded in Book IX of *The Prelude*, on the one hand, and the sonnet "With ships the sea is sprinkled far and nigh," on the other. In the sonnet Wordsworth depicts himself staring out to sea at many ships, some "at anchor," some "veering up and down." Suddenly his attention is fixed upon one special ship of which he says "I pursued her with a Lover's look." In a letter to Lady Beaumont dated May 21, 1807, Wordsworth explains how he comes to fix on one particular ship.

All at once, while I am in this state, comes forth an object, an individual, and my mind sleepy and unfixed, is awakened and fastened in a moment. . . . this Ship in the Sonnet may, in a manner still more appropriate, be said to come upon a mission of the poetic Spirit, because in its own appearance and attributes it is barely suficiently distinguish[ed] to rouse the creative faculty of the human mind. . . . (M.L. 148–149)

In other words Wordsworth is drawn from lethargy by an arbitrary imaginative identification with one ship, which he follows with great interest. Here is the sonnet:

> With Ships the sea was sprinkled far and nigh,
> Like stars in heaven, and joyously it showed;
> Some lying fast at anchor in the road,
> Some veering up and down, one knew not why.
> A goodly Vessel did I then espy
> Come like a giant from a haven broad;
> And lustily along the bay she strode,
> Her tacking rich, and of apparel high.
> This ship was nought to me, nor I to her,
> Yet I pursued her with a Lover's look;
> This Ship to all the rest I did prefer:
> When will she turn, and whither? She will brook
> No tarrying; where She comes the winds must stir:
> On went She, and due north her journey took.
>
> (P.W. 3:18)

In Book IX of *The Prelude* Wordsworth describes how while he watches the patriot troops marching out of Blois to the frontiers, his eye would arbitrarily settle on one face and he would love that unknown patriot. Having read Wordsworth's comments to Lady Beaumont one has an idea of how intense an identification such seemingly arbitrary visual selection entailed. Wordsworth, then, strongly identified with the soldiers going forth to defend their Revolution. It has already been shown that Wordsworth had harbored a wish to become an army officer.

> Meanwhile, day by day, the roads . . .
> Were crowded with the bravest Youth of France,
> And all the promptest of her Spirits, link'd
> In gallant Soldiership, and posting on

To meet the War upon her Frontier Bounds. . . .
Even files of Strangers merely, seen but once,
And for a moment, men from far with sound
Of music, martial tunes, and banners spread
Entering the City, here and there a face
Or person singled out among the rest,
Yet still a Stranger and belov'd as such,
Even by these passing spectacles my heart
Was oftentimes uplifted. . . .

(Prel. IX, 266–287)

Not only did Wordsworth identify with the revolutionary patriots, but he became an extravagant enthusiast in their cause as
well. The Revolution was good, a cause

. . . which no one could stand up against
Who was not lost, abandon'd, selfish, proud,
Mean, miserable, willfully deprav'd,
Hater perverse of equity and truth.

(Prel. IX, 289–292)

By clear implication those who stood up for the cause were not
lost, and not vicious, but charitable, humble, noble, good; they
would love both truth and equity. Obviously Wordsworth was no
tepid supporter of the French Revolution.

If a continuing examination of Wordsworth's relation to the
French Revolution has any hope of remaining useful, it will no
longer be possible to continue distinguishing only between those
who supported the Revolution and those who opposed it. Many
groups with different aims and beliefs supported the Revolution
and likewise many diverse groups joined in opposing it. Jacques
Roux or Gracchus Babeuf may be said to have supported the Revolution, but what did they have in common with Lafayette or even
Brissot, for that matter, both in some sense supporters of the Revolution?

Wordsworth gave his support to the faction called the Brisso-
tins, named after their foremost spokesman Jacques Pierre Brissot
de Warville. This group is remembered primarily by the name
Girondins, after the Gironde district from which many of the
members came. The division in the Bolshevik ranks, following

their ascension to state power in Russia, as to whether their primary task lay in consolidating the revolution at home or in spreading it abroad had an antecedent in the debates of 1791 in the French Legislative Assembly between those favoring a revolutionary war against all tyrants and those opposing such a war. Brissot and his followers were leading advocates of such a war. According to George Lefebvre they "consorted with the business bourgeoisie . . . who did not regard with disfavor a war that would bring lucrative contracts to suppliers." [14] Albert Soboul makes the same point.

> Nor was the idea of a war totally without its attractions to the world of commerce, since those supplying the armies were always sure of substantial profit margins. But they preferred a continental war against Austria to a naval war against England, since that would place in jeopardy the West Indian trade and the continued prosperity of the ports. Hence the Girondins unleashed a land war as early as April 1792 but did not declare war on Great Britain until the following February. [15]

Almost alone Robespierre led the losing debate against the war.

The internationalist enthusiasm of the Girondins had enormous emotional appeal for Wordsworth. Their internationalism seemed to offer him the possibility of a universal community of brotherhood and liberty, a universal world of natural affections. Moreover, the Girondins, however radical they might appear to an Englishman, were representatives of the business bourgeoisie. They were not so radical or plebian as the Mountain, their soon-to-be victorious rivals in the Jacobin Club and the Legislative Assembly. The Mountain derived much of its support from the Parisian *menu peuple*. Even Thomas Paine, who had been denounced as a Jacobin and forced to flee England, was too moderate for the Committee of Public Safety dominated by Robespierre. Paine almost lost his life during the Terror. The Girondins, however, offered a revolutionary style that could be socially compatible with that of an English gentleman and former Cantabrigian.

But Wordsworth could not, or at least did not, know that there was a fatal contradiction between the Girondins' means and their ends. The Girondins were like a man trying to reach an object reflected in a mirror. The closer he approaches the mirror the farther away he moves from the desired object that he sees reflected on the surface of the glass. [16] The Girondin ideal was that of a decentralized federal public. But the war they helped to bring into being drew France away from decentralization and towards a highly centralized government controlled by the Committees of Public Safety and of General Security. Wordsworth could view such developments only with horror. Furthermore, Wordsworth's political ideal of an affective community of independent producers conflicted with the social composition of the Girondins and their heirs, the Thermidorians. The Girondins represented the forces of capitalist development that had struggled to achieve economic freedom from the restrictions of the *ancien régime* and later from Robespierre's Maximum. Soboul analyzes the class character of the Girondins:

> The Girondins were the representatives of the propertied middle classes, the commercial and industrial bourgeoisie, whose interest it was to defend property rights and economic liberty against the restrictions demanded by the sans-culottes. [17]

The forces of capitalist development that the Girondins sought to unleash would have accelerated the processes of the concentration of capital and the separation of the individual worker from his means of production. Of this Wordsworth understood little.

The future society that Wordsworth saw in the ideals proclaimed by the Girondins answered one of Wordsworth's most pressing emotional needs. Wordsworth saw himself as being suspended between a Golden Age lying irretrievably in the past and a terrifying annihilated future waiting inevitably before him. The Revolution seemed to destroy this opposition by replacing the dark night of the annihilated future with the new day of a future Golden Age.

"Descriptive Sketches" offers a picture of Wordsworth living through the dawn of the Golden Age in 1792. The sketches are of the Italian, Grison, Swiss, and Savoyard Alps. In "Descriptive Sketches," there is no past Golden Age lost beyond the power of repossession, as hinted at in "An Evening Walk." The present in the dawn of 1792 is mixed. There is both great suffering and the possibility of utter annihilation, on the one hand, and domestic fulfillment on the other. The future, however, is clearly bright.

The present in "Descriptive Sketches" is not free from the terror of destruction. Being may be extinguished in a moment, but significantly for the young Girondin looking to the future for a perfected society, in this poem such extinction occurs only outside society, only in isolation. The poem contains two examples of such solitary extinction. In the first, a "Grison gypsy," having barely escaped being swept to her death when a wooden bridge that she is crossing is destroyed by a flood-swollen river, is left waiting in darkness for a hungry wolf who is being drawn near by the cries of the gypsy's infant.

> Vex'd by the darkness, from the piny gulf
> Ascending, nearer howls the famish'd wolf,
> While thro' the stillness scatters wild dismay,
> Her babe's small cry, that leads him to his prey.
>
> (P.W. 1:56)

The second example of solitary extinction is that of the lone chamois hunter who is buried in an avalanche while his wife and child wait in fear for his return.

Wordsworth is not content to use the example of these two unfortunates to make his point. If he wants the reader to understand that true social community affords a buffer against personal suffering, then the reader had better be told so explicitly.

> Hope, strength, and courage, social suffering brings,
> Freshening the waste of sand with shades and springs.
>
> (P.W. 1:54)

What is the nature of the social oasis as Wordsworth portrays it in "Descriptive Sketches"? It is a traditional community such as one might have thought had disappeared with the passing of simpler times. It is a community of independent producers each of whom owns the means of production adequate for the support of his own family:

> Once Man entirely free, alone and wild,
> Was bless'd as free—for he was Nature's child.
> He, all superior but his God disdain'd,

Walk'd none restraining, and by none restrain'd,
Confess'd no law but his reason taught,
Did all he wish'd, and wish'd but what he ought.
As Man in his primaeval dower array'd
The image of his glorious sire display'd,
Ev'n so, by vestal Nature guarded, here
The traces of primaeval Man appear.
The native dignity no forms debase,
The eye sublime, and surely lion-grace.
The slave of none, of beasts alone the lord,
He marches with his flute, his book, and sword,
Well taught by that to feel his rights, prepar'd,
With this "the blessings he enjoys to guard."
(P.W. 1:172–74)

This ideal community is given an Alpine setting. Later with some significant modifications it will be set in Westmorland and Cumberland. It is important to recognize that Wordsworth is not merely describing the character of an individual who by means of synecdoche represents the whole community. This passage does not constitute praise of the noble solitary. That this is so is made clear in a later, but parallel passage in *The Prelude* that records Wordsworth's response, not to this or that Swiss shepherd, but, rather, to a simple and dignified communal way of being:

Sweet coverts did we cross of pastoral life,
Enticing Vallies, greeted them, and left
Too soon, while yet the very flash and gleam
Of salutation were not pass'd away.
Oh! sorrow for the Youth who could have seen
Unchasten'd, unsubdu'd, unaw'd, unrais'd
To patriarchal dignity of mind,
And pure simplicity of wish and will,
Those sanctified abodes of peaceful Man.
My heart leap'd up when first I did look down
On that which was first seen of those deep haunts,
A green recess, an aboriginal vale
Quiet, and lorded over and possess'd
By naked huts, wood-built, and sown like tents
Or Indian cabins over the fresh lawns,
And by the river side.
(*Prel*. VI, 437–452)

But Wordsworth does not believe that this ideal community need be limited to the Alps or that it ought to be so limited. If tyrannical courts and artificial aristocratic hierarchy can be eliminated, this ideal community predicated upon freedom and equality can spread and perhaps become the norm.

> In the wide range of many a weary round,
> Still have my pilgrim feet unfailing found,
> As despot courts their blaze of gems display,
> Ev'n by the secret cottage far away
> The lily of domestic joy decay;
> While Freedom's farthest hamlets blessings share,
> Found still beneath her smile, and only there.
>
> (P.W. 1:84)

Not only do households and villages benefit from freedom, but

> —Yet, hast they found that Freedom spreads her pow'r
> Beyond the cottage hearth, the cottage door:
> All nature smiles; and owns beneath her eyes
> Her fields peculiar, and peculiar skies.
>
> (P.W. 1:86)

If not only the community but the natural world thrives and is filled with joy when men are released from tyranny, why should mankind wait upon the time? Men should, therefore, unite to end the reign of tyranny and bring on a new universal Golden Age. This moment is at hand. A page is about to be turned in universal history.

> —Tho' Liberty shall soon, indignant, raise
> Red on the hills his beacon's comet blaze;
> Bid from on high his lonely cannon sound,
> And on ten thousand hearths his shout rebound. . . .
>
> (P.W. 1:88)

The result of liberty's triumph should by now be predictable:

> Lo! From th' innocuous flames, a lovely birth!
> With it's own Virtues springs another earth. . . .
>
> (P.W. 1:88)

Finally, with the victory of the forces of liberty, the tyrants are to be annihilated, to be hurled into the abyss of nonbeing:

And grant that every sceptered child of clay,
Who cries, presumptuous, "here their tides shall stay,"
Swept in their anger from th' affrighted shore,
With all his creatures sink—to rise no more.

(P.W. 1:88–90)

Perhaps George III and his retainers might be among those swept "from th' affrighted shore."

If Wordsworth has extricated himself from the fate of being suspended between a golden past and an annihilated future he has done so at a price. He has relinquished his vision of himself as the unique and powerful prince of the family romance for a less exalted position. In the coming age of glorious freedom he will not be uniquely princely. He will be of many, one. All of mankind is to be elevated in glory. In relinquishing his private princedom in favor of universal liberty, Wordsworth was striving to create a social world to act as a sufficient anodyne for his pain. By merging himself with a body larger than himself—here a social body, a body politic—Wordsworth was recapitulating consciously what he had earlier done unconsciously in the grandiose moments of the sentiment of being, when he also merged with a larger body, in that case Nature. There is a further and perhaps more significant recapitulation at work as well. Wordsworth would relinquish his personal myth of the unique hidden prince only for a compensatory social myth, that of the Golden Age, of Paradise.

> . . . the whole earth
> The beauty wore of promise, that which sets,
> To take an image which was felt, no doubt,
> Among the bowers of paradise itself,
> The budding rose above the rose full blown.

(Prel. x, 702–706)

But Paradise itself is but a return to an earlier state. Freud remarks that "Paradise itself is no more than a group phantasy of the childhood of the individual."[18]

Wordsworth by embracing the Girondin cause was, unbeknownst to himself, becoming entangled in a web of contradiction. Wordsworth's most powerful and most valued experiences were of intense, pleasurable, but rare psychic states. The Alpine community idealized in "Descriptive Sketches" was for him an emotionally bound community. But Girondin ideology, despite some genuflection to the sentimental aspects of Rousseau's thought, was a hard-headed ideology of a newly released bourgeoisie that saw infinite horizons before it. The political economy of the Girondins made no allowances for Wordsworth's idealized cotters. Within that political economy Wordsworth's free independent producers would, it is true, be allowed, but their freedom would be the freedom of free trade, the freedom to sell their produce as commodities at market prices or to refuse to sell at market prices and withhold their goods from the market. Such freedom does not seem to be what Wordsworth had in mind.

It appears that Wordsworth's acceptance of the Revolution was based upon a failure to perceive the contradictions between Girondin political philosophy and his own ideal of a community of natural affections. Just such natural affections, called prejudices by Edmund Burke, were central to Burke's attack on the rationalist doctrines of the French Revolution. Further, Wordsworth's community of Swiss yeomen and later of the world of Grasmere corresponded in size and intensity with "the little platoon" [19] that Burke had opposed to what he had seen as the unnatural universals offered by the political philosophy that defended the principles of the French Revolution. Girondin rationalism clashed as well with Wordsworth's intensely felt experiences with nature. Wordsworth had unsuccessfully attempted to combine mechanical materialist philosophy and the social world of natural affections. This false unity was to receive a severe blow when England entered the war against France in February 1793. It is possible that for a while Wordsworth was to resolve these contradictions by endorsing, at least partially, the materialism of Godwin, thereby retreating from the organic and affective aspects of human experience.

As late as May 19, 1792, writing to William Mathews from Blois, Wordsworth praises England in high terms. Wordsworth admonishes Mathews not to despair of his future maintenance. "You have the happiness," he writes, "of being born in a free country, where every road is open, where talents and industry are more liberally rewarded than amongst any other nation in the Universe" (E.L. 77).

Whether or not Pitt wished for war with revolutionary France is not clear. On February 17, 1792 while defending his budget Pitt predicted fifteen years of peace. But the Decree of December 15, by which the French Convention in effect guaranteed to support a dictatorship of Belgian Revolutionaries by force of French arms, and the opening of the Scheldt, forced Pitt's hand. On December 20 Pitt asked for 20,000 sailors. In January he halted shipments of grain and raw material to France, and on January 24 the French ambassador was given his passport. On February 1, the French Convention responded by declaring war on England.

Wherever the blame really lay, Wordsworth blamed England. The conflict shook his moral life as it had never been shaken before.

> And now the strength of Britain was put forth
> In league with the confederated Host,
> Not in my single self alone I found,
> But in the minds of all ingenuous Youth,
> Change and subversion from this hour. No shock
> Given to my moral nature had I known
> Down to that very moment; neither lapse
> Nor turn of sentiment that might be nam'd
> A revolution, save at this one time,
> All else was progress on the self-same path
> On which with a diversity of pace
> I had been travelling; this a stride at once
> Into another region.
>
> (*Prel.* x, 230–242)

History had penetrated Wordsworth's unconscious mind. Wordsworth had unconsciously rebelled against his father, the English social structure in which his father had actively participated and, through that social structure, against England itself. But until there was open conflict between England and France, Wordsworth had been able to deny his intense ambivalence about England, "conflict of sensations without name" (*Prel.* x, 266). Wordsworth's relationship with Annette probably exacerbated the intensity of his self-conflict. To the extent that his affair with her represented a re-pudiation of the limitations that his father and family had placed upon him, England's war effort against France may have been

seen as a retaliation against him for transgressing the paternal restrictions. England, his fatherland, had taken an action that made
the continuation of the "rebellious" liaison difficult, if not impossible. Wordsworth's confusion as to how to fulfill his role as lover
and father now that war had broken out between France and
England probably contributed to Wordsworth's troubled state. He
could no longer deny the ambivalence, the conflict of emotions,
because history had created an open conflict from which he could
not hide. Events had thrown his conflicted feelings into consciousness.

Part of the shock felt when England went to war against
France stemmed from the unconscious ambivalence Wordsworth
felt towards his father. True, he had rebelled against the father
who was the internalized "Thou shalt not" within himself. But if
he rebelled in order to become a more assertive individual whose
desires could be fulfilled, he was also, by rebelling against his father, rebelling against the very figure who had been a model of
manly authority to him, a model that Wordsworth had internalized through the mechanism of identification. Wordsworth
had loved his father and had keenly felt his loss. In a letter that
Dorothy wrote in late July 1787 she told Jane Pollard, "Many a
time have Wm [William], J [John], C [Christopher], and myself
shed tears together, tears of the bitterest sorrow, we all of us, each
day, feel more sensibly the loss we sustained when we were deprived of our parents, and each day do we receive fresh insults
. . ." (E.L. 3). The insults and disrepect Dorothy goes on to enu-
merate are the insults the Wordsworth children received as a result
of being dependent poor relations. In a letter to Jane Pollard in
November of the same year, Dorothy is more precise about the
loss that she and her brothers so lament. "Never, till I came to
Penrith, did I feel the loss I sustained when I was deprived of a Father" (E.L. 9). To the Wordsworth children their father had been
a source of strength. To William, he had been a model of authority and power.

The moral shock Wordsworth received when England joined
the confederated host was due not only to his identification of England with his father but to his identification of England with his
mother as well. He had experienced what he thought of as organic

interchanges between himself and the English landscape. Among other things, English nature had been for him a surrogate mother. English landscape had fed him pure organic pleasure. He was but an extension of this maternal landscape, a leaf off her tree. He was one

> . . . who with the breeze
> Had play'd, a green leaf on the blessed tree
> Of my beloved country. . . .
>
> (*Prel*. x, 254–256)

Now he was faced not only with conflicted feelings towards his father, but also with the question of whether or not loyalty to France and the liberated power it seemed to promise him, meant a separation from, and repudiation of, the very mother his new power was to bring him. As a result the green leaf on England's tree "was cut off,/And toss'd about in whirlwinds" (*Prel*. x, 258–259).

Wordsworth, cut off and tempest tossed, was whirled in a complete circle. Previously his conscious politics had been based on love of all of humankind. He felt betrayed. His rage against his father, no longer submerged, manifested itself now as hatred of England and of the First Coalition, his unconscious anger now as conscious anger against England, his fatherland. If counterrevolutionaries denied the validity of the universal love proclaimed by the defenders of the French Revolution, and saw, instead of love, the principle of diabolic destructiveness, Wordsworth was willing to comply. Instead of love he would show bitterness and rage.

> An active partisan, I thus convoked
> From every object pleasant circumstance
> To suit my ends; I moved among mankind
> With genial feelings still predominant. . . .
>
> In the main outline, such, it might be said,
> Was my condition, till with open war
> Britain opposed the Liberties of France;
> This threw me first out of the pale of love;
> Sour'd and corrupted upwards to the source
> My sentiments, was not, as hitherto,
> A swallowing up of lesser things in great;
> But change of them into their opposites. . . .
>
> (*Prel*. x, 737–765)

For Wordsworth there emerged what was to become a fateful association of rage and abstract intellect. The passage just quoted continues:

> And thus a way was opened for mistakes
> And false conclusions of the intellect. . . .
> (*Prel.* x, 766–767)

And still later:

> This was the time when all things tending fast
> To deprivation, the Philosophy
> That promised to abstract the hopes of man
> Out of his feelings, to be fix'd thenceforth
> For ever in a purer element
> Found ready welcome. Tempting region that
> For Zeal to enter and refresh herself,
> Where passions had the privilege to work,
> And never hear the sound of their own names. . . .
> (*Prel.* x, 806–814)

Now that Wordsworth had been "Sour'd and corrupted" he came to identify with "the ancient Prophets" (*Prel.* x, 402), with the voice of destructive fate. Watching the tumult of counter-revolutionary war he felt ready to utter jeremiads. He felt himself to be connected somehow with God in his manifestation as dispenser of wrath. Here is another aspect of the egotistical sublime. It rescues Wordsworth from being the helpless passive and contracted watcher of calamity and turns him into an active power. Psychologically it is more painful to feel oneself to be a helpless object than it is to feel oneself to be an active subject.

> And in their rage and dog-day heat I found
> Something to glory in, as just and fit,
> And in the order of sublimest laws;
> And even if that were not, amid the awe
> Of unintelligible chastisement,
> I felt a kind of sympathy with power,
> Motions rais'd up with me, nevertheless,
> Which had relationship to highest things.
> (*Prel.* x, 412–419)

Now Wordsworth is embittered. He feels himself to be something of a wrathful prophet. Further, he is under the spell of what he will later see as a degenerate and false philosophy. What, then, are the results for Wordsworth in the realm of political philosophy? The answers are to be found in the antiaristocratic, antimonarchical and thoroughly republican "Letter to Bishop Llandaff" written in February or March 1793, though never published.

In January 1793 Richard Watson, Bishop of Llandaff, a onetime supporter of the French Revolution, turned apostate. In an appendix to a volume of sermons he had already prepared for publication, he denounced the Revolution. The twenty-three year old Wordsworth was stung by this apparent breach of political faith and replied in the unpublished letter. The letter begins with a striking image borrowed from Addison. As a result of his apostasy Llandaff, crossing the immense bridge of moral life, has fallen.

> . . . you have at last fallen, through one of the numerous trap-doors, into a tide of contempt to be swept down to the ocean of oblivion. (*Prose* 1:31)

Opposition to the French Revolution, that is to say, is a course that leads to ultimate contraction, to destruction. Wordsworth then goes on to take a position that is especially worthy of note since, like so much in the "Letter," it is directly opposed to the position Wordsworth will take in his next political tract, the essay on the Convention of Cintra, published in 1809. It is worth stopping to note passages in the "Letter" which will be directly contravened in the later Cintra tract. Such discrepancies supply some measure of the degree of change in Wordsworth's political thought over an interval of sixteen years. Wordsworth suggests that moral judgment should be governed by reason, for "under the influence of reason, it is regulated by the disproportion of the pain suffered to the guilt incurred" (*Prose* 1:32–33). Nothing could be further from the Wordsworth of 1809 than this use of analytic reason to reach moral conclusions. Wordsworth is commenting here on what he believes is the proper use of pity as a corrective to what he sees as the pity Llandaff wastes on the decapitated Louis XVI.

Wordsworth goes on to castigate Llandaff for not realizing

"that a time of revolution is not the season of true Liberty" (*Prose* 1:33). Wordsworth laments that in overthrowing a despotism it is often necessary to use despotic means. But he goes further; he sees revolution as war. He almost advances to the more specific identification of revolution and class warfare. He writes of "a state of war between the oppressors and the oppressed" (*Prose* 1:34). Such warfare is a precondition for setting aside traditional morality in favor of the interests of expedience. The question of ends subsumes the question of means. Wordsworth writes epigrammatically, "Political virtues are developed at the expense of moral ones" (*Prose* 1:34). Nothing will mark Wordsworth's mature political theory more than his violent repudiation of any political action that is not based on moral ground.

Wordsworth defends the revolutionary government's appropriation of the clergy's wealth. He rejects Llandaff's claim that the French should have used the British Constitution as a model. Wordsworth then defends republicanism. He declares "that much of human misery, that the great evils which desolate states, proceed from the governors' having an interest distinct from that of the governed" (*Prose* 1:36–37). This idea, that social evils stem from a disjunction of the interest of the governed and the governors, will continue to play a significant role in Wordsworth's political philosophy. But Wordsworth will draw different conclusions from it in 1809 than he does in 1793. In 1793 Wordsworth says that the problem should be solved by eliminating the distinction between governed and governors. He wishes to distribute effective power to the people through a "system of universal representation" (*Prose* 1:37).

Wordsworth boldly declares himself to be republican, a daring assertion to make at this time in a manuscript even being considered for publication. But Wordsworth follows this assertion with a statement that marks him as a Girondin, one who may support the interests of the common people but who clearly sets himself off from them and perhaps sets himself above them as well. Because of the abuses "of the executive power" it has come about that "if at this moment the original authority of the people should be restored, all that could be expected from such restoration would in the beginning be but a change of tyranny" (*Prose* 1:38). Such tyranny, however, would be both temporary and self-correcting. From behind one of the similes Wordsworth uses to illustrate this point his condescension to the "people" clearly shows itself. Wordsworth believed that the "people" needed educating before they would be fully fit to rule. Here Wordsworth anticipates, somewhat, the antirevolutionary position that he will articulate in June 1794:

> The animal just released from its stall will exhaust the overflow of its spirit in a round of wanton vagaries, but it will soon return to itself and enjoy its freedom in moderate and regular delight. (*Prose* 1:38)

Whatever Wordsworth's conscious opposition to Edmund Burke, this analogy between the common people and a wanton stable beast that will eventually learn moderation is uncomfortably close to Burke's epithet "a swinish multitude."[20] There is a latent paradox here that will have to be explored later. While Wordsworth is an avowed republican it is possible to detect in his language an aversion to the common people. After Wordsworth gives up moral questions in despair and turns away from the French Revolution, no longer regarding it as the first step in the regeneration of mankind, he grounds his creed in the celebration of hard-working shepherds, farmers, peddlers, waggoners and the like.

There is something else about his analogy between the newly liberated common people and a beast released from its stall that is worthy of attention, something that links Wordsworth with William Blake. The analogy suggests that the *ancien régime* had been repressing the energy of its subjects and the release of repressed energy is necessary before the people can "enjoy its freedom in moderate and regular delight." We are close here to Blake's "Damn. braces: Bless relaxes"[21] and "He who desires but acts not, breeds pestilence."[22] Here also is the connection between Wordsworth's politics and his personal psychology. The tyrannic government that represses energy is the father who represses his son's desires to fulfill himself. To destroy the repressing regime is to destroy the repressing father. This connection is, of course, not unique to Wordsworth's psyche, but may be common to most, if not all, men.

There is something else implicit in this analogy, something which will remain, in a slightly different form, a fixed idea on Wordsworth's political thought. The people newly released from tyranny, the "animal just released from its stall," constitute the governing class. The governing class is ignorant. The result of their initial ignorance is that society will resubmerge into tyranny. The problem is how will the governing class gain wisdom and moderation. This problem is real and important, and for the young Wordsworth very easily solved. He believes that the new governing class will learn automatically through experience. He will later draw different conclusions. But what is of significance is the reversal, perhaps reversal unawares, of Plato's solution to a central problem of political theory: How does one make sure that the governing class is both wise and just? Plato's solution expressed in *The Republic* is to create a group of wise men who know the True and Beautiful. The problem as Plato poses it is the opposite of the problem as Wordsworth sees and will continue to see it. For Plato the problem is, how can men who have risen to a vision of the True, the Beautiful, and the Good be induced to participate in something so base and inconsequential as the governance of the polis. For Wordsworth the problem is different. For him the problems is how to inculcate wisdom into those who have already chosen to rule.

Wordsworth goes on to expound for Llandaff the workings of a republic as he, Wordsworth, conceives it. "As laws, being but the expression of the general will, would be enacted only from an almost universal conviction of their utility, any resistance to these laws, any desire of eluding them, must proceed from a few refractory individuals" (*Prose* 1:39). It becomes apparent here that Wordsworth has as yet no conception of political interest in an economic and social sense. He assumes that once the repressing few have been removed, the remaining population will be harmonious and united in its voting and response to enacted legislation because the ability to see the truth, that is, reason, is universal. He does not yet see what Burke had already seen in his *Reflections*,[23] that the Revolutionary government was a class government installed in the interest of the triumphant bourgeoisie. Wordsworth accepts political forms and arguments as historical absolutes, with no notion of the social and class interests that lie behind them.

An example of this political innocence is Wordsworth's implicit acceptance of laissez faire. If primogeniture, corporate bodies, "all that monopolizing system of legislation whose baleful influence is shewn by the depopulation of the country," and the "innumerable statutes whose constant and professed object is to lower the price of labour," in short all forms of government intervention in the economy are done away with, then beggary will be eliminated as will bastardy (*Prose* 1:43)! Wordsworth has no idea that the economic doctrine that he espouses is historically a specifically bourgeois one, that it is not a doctrine that can be validated by an appeal to abstract reason, and that it is destructive of the rural community of independent producers that is so dear to him.

Wordsworth attributes the collapse of the rural natural economy, that he so values, to the power that the English aristocracy has brought to bear on Parliament in support of its selfish interest. Wordsworth sees rural depopulation; he sees "sad relicks" who "owe their very existence to the ostentatious bounty of their oppressors"; he sees prostitution, and attributes its existence to "aristocratical prejudices." Wordsworth's belief that the sad relics owe their existence to the "bounty of their oppressors" is as close as Wordsworth will ever come to Blake's sardonic observation that

> Pity would be no more,
> If we did not make somebody Poor. . . .[24]

By 1797 Wordsworth would already be writing "The Old Cumberland Beggar" (*P.W.* 4:234–240), a poem that defends the beggar's right to beg rather than be placed in a work-house. The beggar, as Wordsworth has come to see him by 1797, performs a moral function in society. He affords even the humble the opportunity to give charitably to someone in even greater need than he. People should not be deprived of the right to feel pity and give charity.

What is striking, upon reflection, is that Wordsworth accuses the landed aristocracy of destroying the traditional "natural" economy at the very same time that he lends his support to free trade, the program of the financial and industrial bourgeoisie. For reasons which I shall explain in greater detail in a later chapter, it was precisely the political economy of the mercantile, financial and industrial bourgeoisie that was the most corrosive force with which the traditional or in Marx's usage "Natural"[25] economic structure had to deal. Was Wordsworth blind to the opposition between business capital and natural political economy? Did he not realize that he was supporting the very economic forces that he would do better to oppose?

The answers to these questions are not at all as simple as they seem. True, Wordsworth would eventually come to see that industrial and financial capital set in motion forces to which he was opposed. For this reason he came more and more to support the traditional large land-owners as a counterweight to the forces of manufacture and commerce. It was in order to preserve this counterweight that he opposed the Reform Bill of 1832. But, on the other hand, he was correct early in 1793 in opposing the landed aristocracy as a force that was destructive to the natural economy of the independent individual worker of the land. The aristocracy was creating mendicant "sad relicks" by driving freeholders and copyholders from their land. The aristocracy was creating at least the illusion of "depopulation of the country" (*Prose* 1:43) by consolidating many small land holdings into large unified holdings. Wordsworth lived at a time of political revolution, when this very aristocracy was being attacked as a parasitic and oppressive class. Seeing the depredations the ariostocracy was working on the land, Wordsworth joined the revolutionary attack upon the aristocracy. Further, and perhaps above all, it is necessary to recognize that in initially supporting mercantile, financial, and industrial capital, as opposed to land-owning capital, Wordsworth was not simply making a choice that he later came to see as wrong. The intellectual assumptions about political economy that led Wordsworth to oppose landed capital were the dominant and most progressive assumptions available to him. Wordsworth took Adam Smith and the climate of opinion Smith created as given. There were no alternate fully developed political economic systems for Wordsworth to choose from.

What can be made of this seeming confusion? Wordsworth

was correct in attacking the aristocracy for destroying the traditional, natural economy. At the same time, Wordsworth erred when he sided with the business bourgeoisie. What then could he have sensibly done? There was, in fact, no rational political course open to Wordsworth, for in a fundamental sense, though he did not and could not know it, the English landed aristocracy was not really at odds with the interests of manufacture and commerce, in that all three were components of a capitalist class, enriching itself not from feudal dues and tribute, but from ownership of the means of production. They were three different manifestations of a complex and long-evolving system of organizing the means of production and reproduction while at the same time extracting profit from them. They were, that is, three different manifestations of that complex social and historical entity known as capitalism—in Marx's words, "a definite social production relation, belonging to a definite historical formation of society. . . ."

> It [Capital] is a means of production monopolized by a certain section of society, confronting living labour-power as products and working conditions rendered independent of this very labour-power, which are personified through this antithesis in capital.[26]

Because Wordsworth came to political consciousness at a time before even the most radical reformers could conceptualize an economic and social system for ordering the means of production and reproduction other than capitalism, it was impossible for Wordsworth to avoid contradicting himself, as he did both when he opposed the aristocracy and when he supported it. My point is an extension of a central observation in Carl Woodring's definitive study, *Politics in English Romantic Poetry*. Woodring writes, "it is my argument that none of the philosophical bases and justifications of liberalism available to the English poets of 1789–1832 could be harmonized with the convictions that motivated their poetic practice."[27]

The identification of the traditional English aristocracy as a capitalistic class would have been difficult for Wordsworth or any contemporary observer to make. The aristocracy hid its capitalist nature, or base, by means of mystification in the realm of ideology, or superstructure. It attempted to maintain its traditional paternalistic attitude toward the poor by spending large sums on poor relief. It attempted to disavow its capitalist nature by maintaining feudal titles and to some extent feudal honors. It maintained its Fieldingesque attitudes of the jolly squire loving his hunt and his ale. Marx, writing in 1852, discussed the bourgeois nature of the traditional landed families:

> We speak of two interests of the bourgeoisie, for large landed property, despite its feudal coquetry and pride of race, has been rendered thoroughly bourgeois by the development of modern society. Thus the Tories in England long imagined that they were enthusiastic about monarchy, the church, and the beauties of the old English Constitution, until the day of danger wrung from them the confession that they were enthusiastic only about *ground rent*. [28]

And indeed, the aristocracy functioned as a capitalist class. It rationalized agricultural productions; it concentrated capital in agriculture in order to lower the composition of agricultural capital by raising the proportion of capital spent on the materials of production. It paid for increased drainage, increased use of fertilizer, the implementation of more productive seed and superior breeds of live stock, and the use of expensive and improved agricultural machinery. In doing so it decreased the proportion of capital spent as wages, both relatively and in some cases absolutely. It converted some surplus value in the form of rent into surplus value in the form of profit. Raymond Williams in his superb study *The Country and the City* lays bare the aristocracy's ability to exploit the countryside in a capitalist manner while maintaining the posture and image of a traditional beneficent squirearchy.

However inadequate it may have been for his needs, Wordsworth's political thought was the vehicle that expressed the method by which he hoped to satisfy his need for community. His political thought evolved rapidly. In early 1792 he has not yet committed to supporting the French Revolution. By 1793 he had written a republican tract defending the execution of Louis XVI and the general violence that attended the revolutionary process. By June 8, 1794 he had changed again. He was still one to "disapprove of monarchical and aristocratical governments, however modified." But he no longer defended the revolution. He wrote, "I recoil from the bare idea of a Revolution," and "I am a determined enemy to every species of violence" (*E.L.* 119).

The Girondins' fall from power on June 2, 1793 when twenty-nine Girondin deputies were expelled from the Convention by force and arrested, their leaders destined for the guillotine, must have done much to dispell the romance with which the idea of revolution had been invested for Wordsworth. If this is so, then the establishment of revolutionary government led by the Montagnards and their leader Robespierre, did even more to disillusion Wordsworth. The Terror, a consequence of the Montagnard revolutionary dictatorship, may have been the deciding factor in turning Wordsworth against the idea of revolution.

By June of 1794 Wordsworth, perhaps after studying William Godwin's *Political Justice*, which eschewed violent political revolution, came to believe that there was a valid alternative to revolution. The enlightened elite must educate the mass of men. It is a "duty incumbent upon every enlightened friend of mankind," that "he should diffuse by every method these rules of political justice." If men are left free to seek the truth, republican social change must follow. "Freedom of inquiry is all that I wish for . . ." (*E.L.* 124–125).

Yet the rate of social change promised by a campaign of nonviolent education might well appear to be slower than the speed with which revolution might bring about change. If this were so, then the longed-for international community lay further away in the future than Wordsworth might wish. The intensity of Wordsworth's longing for such community is demonstrated by his response to the events of 9 Thermidor. On 9 Thermidor (July 27) 1794, less than two months after Wordsworth wrote that he recoiled from the idea of revolution, Robespierre fell from power. The next day, July 28, Robespierre and his two closest associates on the Committee of Public Safety, Saint-Just and Couthon, were guillotined. Wordsworth was walking along the sands of the Leven estuary, after having visited the grave of William Taylor, his beloved Hawkshead master, when a passing horseman shouted to him that "*Robespierre was dead*" (*Prel.* x, 536). Even after having lived through one disillusioning year of the Montagnard dictatorship and the Terror, even after having repudiated the very idea of revolution, the need was so great for the large community that the Revolution seemed to promise, that Wordsworth's faith in the Revolution was immediately rekindled by the news.

> Great was my glee of spirit, great my joy
> In vengeance, and eternal justice, thus
> Made manifest. 'Come now ye golden times,'
> Said I, forth-breathing on those open Sands
> A Hymn of triumph, 'as the morning comes
> Out of the bosom of the night, come Ye:
> Thus far our trust is verified; . . .'
> Then schemes I framed more calmly, when and how
> The madding Factions might be tranquillised,
> And, though through hardships manifold and long,
> The mighty renovation would proceed. . . .
>
> (*Prel*. x, 540–557)

Within an instant Wordsworth is again intensely involved in the workings of the Revolution. His psychological need for what the Revolution seemed to offer must have been very great, indeed.

By November of the same year, it is possible to detect yet another change in Wordsworth's political development. I have already indicated that Wordsworth had been simultaneously influenced by two contradictory, almost mutually exclusive, political ideals: Girondin ideology, on the one hand, and the belief in an affectively bound community of natural producers, on the other. It is a fair assumption that Wordsworth was reading at least some of the contemporary republican literature, but there is no indication that he accepted all of the political and social assumptions of Girondin ideology. However, it would be somehow odd if he admired Girondin leaders and spokesmen while failing to respect the ideals and principles that these leading Girondins upheld. At about this time he came under the influence of William Godwin's necessitarian essay *Political Justice*. Wordsworth became so heavily influenced by Godwin as to become, for a brief while, a convert to Godwin's anarchistic necessitarianism. Godwin and the republican pamphleteers were influenced by a school of thought that was decidedly abstract and rationalistic in its tendency. Abstract reason was elevated to decisive importance. The affective powers were ignored or, as with Godwin, spurned. Condillac and La Mettrie both contributed to this highly rationalistic world view. This view denied the significance of the intense spiritual experiences and relationships that Wordsworth knew and valued highly. This rationalism stressed the significance of effective as opposed to affective power. Under the influence of this powerfully seductive philosophy which, with its reductionist rationalism, offered the possibility of explaining and understanding everything, Wordsworth temporarily rejected the strong and significant passionate aspect of his character. He subscribed instead to a rationalistic materialism that seemed to promise unlimited power over the real world. Perhaps at some level of consciousness, Wordsworth realized the existence of a contradiction between his idea of a community of individual producers bound by ties of love and duty and the Girondin idea of an economically free community that was to be brought into being by real, rather than by emotional power. For a while at least, Wordsworth turned his back on the powerful part of himself that craved intense organic experience and chose abstract rationalistic experience instead.

Wordsworth gave a clear indication of this moral and political development when on November 7, 1794 he wrote in a letter to William Matthews, "I begin to wish to be much in Town [London]; Cataracts and mountains are good occasional society, but they will not do for constant companions" (E.L. 136). It need scarcely be said that this is not Wordsworth writing in his most Wordsworthian voice.

Wordsworth was now committed to using abstract reason as a tool with which to gain mastery, to posses effective power. Wordsworth writes caustically in *The Prelude* of this period when the individual intellect seemed all powerful and autonomous:

> How glorious! in self-knowledge and self-rule,
> To look through all the frailties of the world,
> And, with a resolute mastery shaking off
> The accidents of nature, time and place,
> That make up the weak being of the past,
> Build social freedom on its only basis,
> The freedom of the individual mind,
> Which, to the blind restraint of general laws
> Superior, magisterially adopts

> One guide, the light of circumstances, flash'd
> Upon an independent intellect.
>
> *(Prel.* x, 820–830)

In discussing Wordsworth's response to England's entry into the war against France, the association in Wordsworth's mind of abstract reason and aggressiveness has already been indicated. Now Wordsworth has fully committed himself to the use of abstract reason. Later he would come to realize the high degree of aggressiveness that was associated with that commitment. He describes his speculative examination of "ancient institutions," "custom and written law," "moral sentiments as props/And emanations of these institutes," and "old opinions" in terms of a brutal vivisection.

> I took the knife in hand
> And stopping not at parts less sensitive,
> Endeavoured with my best skill to probe
> The living body of society
> Even to the heart; I push'd without remorse
> My speculations forward; yea set foot
> On Nature's holiest places.
>
> *(Prel.* x, 851–879)

There is a hint here of something other than an analytic exploratory vivisection, a hint of brutal aggressive assault. He did not withhold his knife. He pushed, without remorse, the knife blade of his speculation. Wordsworth then changes his metaphor. He was not a probing anatomist, but a relentless prosecuting attorney arraigning all traditional institutions and modes of thought. Wordsworth writes

> Thus I fared,
> Dragging all passions, notions, shapes of faith,
> Like culprits to the bar, suspiciously
> Calling the mind to establish in plain day
> Her titles and her honors. . . .
>
> *(Prel.* x, 889–893)

This image of Wordsworth as the vigorous, powerful advocate of uncompromising rationalism bringing tradition and dogma to be arraigned is the reversal of an image he had given of himself earlier in a description of a nightmare that he had had recurrently. In the dream he is a doomed unheard pleader of a doomed cause. The later powerful image is to the helpless nightmare image what the latent dream thought is to the distorted manifestation of that thought. Wordsworth writes that he was haunted for years by dreams in which he vainly pleaded before the unjust tribunals of the Terror.

> I scarcely had one night of quiet sleep
> Such ghastly visions had I of despair
> And tyranny, and implements of death,
> And long orations which in dreams I pleaded
> Before unjust Tribunals, with a voice
> Labouring, a brain confounded, and a sense
> Of treachery and desertion in the place
> The holiest that I knew of, my own soul.
> (*Prel*. x, 374–381)

To say that the latent content of this recurrent dream is that of being a relentlessly effective revolutionary prosecutor is to suggest that the nightmare is an anxiety dream in which the pleasurable sensations brought about by the fulfillment of the wish in the manifest dream thoughts are converted into their opposite, terror and dread, by the vigilant dream censorship. The content of the dream thoughts has undergone reversal as well. The hidden wish is the wish to become the powerful saving orator and leader of the Revolution, a prince, rather than be the contracted Wordsworth who was "Mean" and "little graced with power/Of eloquence even in my native speech" (*Prel*. x, 132–133). The dreamwork in this recurrent nightmare converts the princely Wordsworth of the latent wish into the helpless contracted Wordsworth of the manifest dream.

The dream that Wordsworth records here is rich and complex, and one would do well to remember Freud's observation that no dream can be completely interpreted. When Wordsworth writes of feeling "treachery and desertion" in his soul he echoes his state of mind after he had been frightened into returning the borrowed boat.

> . . . in my thoughts
> There was a darkness, call it solitude,
> Or blank desertion. . . .
>
> (*Prel.* I, 420–422).

In echoing the stolen boat episode Wordsworth linked the dream of the Terror with a moment in which he had been punished for exercising the impulses to mastery that I believe are hidden in his later recurrent nightmare.

Unless the last lines of the above passage are read in relation to the stolen boat passage the last line of the poetic recollection of the anxiety dreams seems to ring false. Wordsworth might well have felt deserted as he pleaded hopelessly before the unjust tribunals but he may not have felt, in these dreams, a desertion in the holiest place he knew of, his own soul. This, perhaps, is not an autobiographical reminiscence, but rather a moral judgment. Wordsworth believed that he had had to suffer these dreams as a penance. He had betrayed England. He had betrayed something within himself. He had failed to check his desires for power. And for betraying his homeland and his family he felt guilt. The guilt is evident in the line I have just referred to written after Wordsworth had ceased his apostasy. It is visible, however, even in one of the major poems he wrote while still a Girondin, a poem later to become "Guilt and Sorrow" (*P.W.* 1:14–127).

"Guilt and Sorrow" is perhaps as polemical a poem as Wordsworth ever wrote. Written over a period of years and under the different titles "The Female Vagrant" and "Salisbury Plain," it was started perhaps as early as 1790 or 1791 [29] and completed in 1797. It attacks a range of social evils—engrossing, enclosing landlords; the horrors of war; kidnapping by press gang; a society so callous that it leaves a homeless woman to starve; and capital punishment. It illustrates Godwin's theory that criminals are created by social circumstance rather than by radical evil. In this case the discharged soldier and murderer is portrayed as being kind to the female vagrant and to a child abused by its father. He is clearly not radically evil even though he is a murderer. On November 20, 1795 Wordsworth wrote to Francis Wrangham that his purpose in the poem is partly "to expose the vices of the penal law and the calamities of war as they affect individuals" (*E.L.* 159).

Wordsworth's guilt at betraying England and the personal relationships symbolized by England is expressed in "Guilt and Sorrow" by a probably unconscious identification with the murderer, the vagrant former sailor. To the degree that this identification exists, Wordsworth had indicted himself of, or excused himself for, action correlative to theft and murder, as I shall attempt to demonstrate. To begin with, during the summer of 1793 Wordsworth himself walked alone across Salisbury Plain. When the former sailor first appears he is a solitary "Traveller on the skirt of Sarum's Plain" (*P.W.* 1:95). Like Wordsworth who had left Annette, the sailor had left, or to be more precise failed to return to his wife. Wordsworth had failed to return to Annette. It is probable that in some sense Wordsworth and Annette had, for a time, thought of themselves as married. Annette referred to William as her husband in her early letters to him, and throughout her life she referred to herself either as Madame William or Veuve Williams.[30] Another link between Wordsworth and the sailor is the terrifying encounter with a gibbet. The sailor, while pursuing his way across the plain, sees a man hanging in chains.

> Now, as he plodded on, with sullen clang
> A sound of chains along the desert rang;
> He looked, and saw upon a gibbet high
> A human body that in irons swang,
> Uplifted by the tempest whirling by. . . .
> (*P.W.* 1:98)

This apparition has a violent effect upon the ex-sailor because "It was a spectacle which none might view . . . but with shuddering pain." The sailor faints. "He fell, and without sense or motion lay . . ." (*P.W.* 1:99). The student of Wordsworth should be aware of a resonance between this bit of narrative from "Guilt and Sorrow" and one of the significant moments in *The Prelude* already discussed, when the young Wordsworth retreated from a moldering gibbet and mounted Penrith Beacon. In both Wordsworth's experience with the gibbet at Penrith Beacon and the sailor's experience on Salisbury Plain a strong wind plays a part. If the vision of a gibbet has a powerful effect upon the sailor-vagrant, the vision of the mouldered gibbet powerfully affects Wordsworth in a different way, and becomes one of the "spots of time" that possess for him a "vivifying Virtue" (*Prel.* xi, 258–260).

Wordsworth's biographer, Mary Moorman, writes that the sailor's vision of the gibbet and his reaction to it "takes us far back into a Cumberland childhood, when a little boy, riding alone and astray among the fells, came face to face with a gibbet, and after a moment of panic, saw the world under a strange new aspect of 'visionary dreariness' of indescribable mental intensity and power."[31]

Perhaps more significant than the sailor's having experienced, as did Wordsworth, an extraordinary moment relating to a gibbet, is the emotional state the after-shock creates for him.

> As doth befall to those whom frenzy fires
> His soul which in such anguish hath been tossed
> Sinks into deepest calm, for now retires
> Fear a terrific dream in darkness lost
> The dire phantasma which his sense had crossed
> The mind was still as a deep evening stream.
>
> (P.W. 1:99)

Here in the comparison of the mind to a stream, in the sudden unexpected calm that follows a moment of great psychological intensity, it is possible to discern Wordsworth's description of his own mind. In the words of Mary Moorman, "In this last wonderful line Wordsworth the poet seems suddenly to look out at us. . . ."[32]

Another link between the sailor and Wordsworth is that both have the experience of being told the life story of the female vagrant. The sailor is told the story by the female vagrant as they find shelter from the stormy night. Wordsworth says of the story of the woman's misfortunes "All that relates to her sufferings as a sailor's wife in America, and her condition of mind during her voyage home, were faithfully taken from the report made to me of her own case by a friend who had been subjected to the same trials and affected in the same way" (P.W. 1:330).

These links suggest that Wordsworth unconsciously identified with the sailor-vagrant, who was guilty of murder. In this identification is located guilt that Wordsworth felt at betraying England

and his father by rebelling against them. He betrayed the principles of the French Revolution as well, and guilt for this secondary betrayal may also be expressed by his identification with the murderer. Finally as this identification between Wordsworth and the sailor seems to function as a pharmakos for Wordsworth's burden of guilt, remorse about having abandoned Annette may well find expression in the same identification. The sailor who bears the weight of guilt is shown to be kind and gentle. He listens to the female and offers her encouragement. He comes to the defense of a young boy threatened by his own father. At an inn children gather about his knees to receive his tenderness. Finally he meekly submits himself to justice and stoically accepts the sentence of death by hanging. By having such a gentle, good man represent the guilty aspect of himself, Wordsworth makes it possible for the reader to see the efforts of his unconscious mind to justify himself and minimize his guilt. From this perspective, the character of the sailor is a compromise formation in which Wordsworth's opposing impulses find expression. On the one hand, the part of Wordsworth that wants to be punished for its transgressions seems to identify with a murderer and a thief who is hanged for his crimes. On the other hand, part of Wordsworth seems to repudiate any guilt. This part of him finds expression in the sympathetic sailor who, despite a momentary lapse, is loving and pure.

It is possible to see in Wordsworth's revolutionary development the seeds of his own repudiation of republican politics. Wordsworth found himself driven to take an extreme mechanistic and rational intellectual position. "Guilt and Sorrow" bears witness to an enormous amount of unconscious guilt, and Wordsworth may have felt conscious guilt as well. Not only would it be a strain to endure such guilt, but the very presence of guilt was an indication that his father's values which he had struggled to defeat still had power over him. Just how much power remained to be seen. Finally, the Revolution was accompanied by continuous violence in the form of incessant warfare and periodic French domestic turbulence. The constant presence of such manifest violence made it almost impossible for Wordsworth to deny the violence of the impulses that drove him to take up his revolutionary position. The violence necessitated the expenditure of enormous quantities of emotional energy in the effort to deny his aggressiveness.

External and historical events in France enabled Wordsworth to detach his sympathies from the French Revolution, thereby releasing himself from the strains that were accumulating and making continued adherence to the cause of the Revolution painful and untenable, although the price he paid for relinquishing this revolutionary position was very high. He would have to endure a terrible siege of depression, during which his conscience punished his ego with denunciations and reproaches. Wordsworth was able to turn against the French Revolution when the French armies became so successful and occupied so much territory outside of France that they came to be seen not as defenders of an ideal but as aggressors themselves, conquerors who only sought selfish gain.

> And now, become Oppressors in their turn,
> Frenchmen had changed a war of self-defence
> For one of conquest, losing sight of all
> Which they had struggled for. . . .
> (*Prel.* x, 792–795)

After the fall of Robespierre, the Thermidorians found that their treasury was empty. If they chose to economize by disbanding their already ill-equipped army they faced not only the threat of foreign invasion and reinstitution of the monarchy, but also the threat that the army would refuse to disband, and, under the leadership of its officers, take power in a coup d'état. The Thermidorians chose to send the armies beyond the French borders, both to support themselves by living off the land, and to send needed treasure back to Paris. The French armies had success both in Italy and Spain in September and October 1794. They occupied Holland and demanded exorbitant payments as well as hostages. By January 1795, the French occupied all the territory west of the Rhine. Belgium was annexed in 1795. In the words of Ernest de Selincourt, "to Wordsworth, to whom the Revolution was an ideal of universal freedom and brotherhood, this [the conquest] was the renunciation of their faith" (*Prel.*, p. 604). Though the French invasion and conquest of Switzerland came some three years after Wordsworth's position had already begun to change, it was a conquest that would make it impossible ever to reverse his turn away from France. For in attacking Switzerland, the Revolution came in direct conflict with the Swiss communities that he had idealized in "Descriptive Sketches."

Wordsworth had turned to the French Revolution because it seemed to offer him community. That community seemed to offer him a dwelling place for his princely self. He had sought not only community but release from constraints placed upon him. He sought, that is to say, a community in which his princely self could achieve security and recognition. He sought access to both affective and effective power. When he adopted the highly rationalist analytic outlook of some of the most advanced republican thinkers, he surrendered possible access to affective power.

In rejecting the French Revolution Wordsworth, who had already rejected access to emotional power, denied himself access to physical power as well. He was now in the painful state of contraction that approached nonbeing. Having joined himself to the Revolution in order to destroy the dictates of the father and thereby achieve complete power, he was now devoid of both forms of power and seemingly at the mercy of the paternal force that could punish him with utter annihilation. He was made to suffer by this internal power. His depression was a manifestation of the reproaches that he heaped upon himself. The impairment in Wordsworth's ability to function was a measure of the disorganization the remorseless negative conscience wreaked upon Wordsworth's ego.

It is appropriate and perhaps somewhat ironic, therefore, that Wordsworth presents his collapse into moral confusion as a peripeteia. Wordsworth is, in the beginning of the passage that ends in this collapse, exercising decisive actual power in arraigning traditional beliefs such as might be associated with his father, whom Wordsworth associated with traditional aristocratic, monarchical power. Then, at what seems to be a moment of power, Wordsworth is hurled into a state of despair. The passage is extraordinary in the force of its ironic peripeteia when read in the above light.

> Thus I fared,
> Dragging all passions, notions, shapes of faith,
> Like culprits to the bar, suspiciously
> Calling the mind to establish in plain day
> Her titles and her honours, now believing,

Now disbelieving, endlessly perplex'd
With impulse, motive, right and wrong, the ground
Of moral obligation, what the rule
And what the sanction, till demanding *proof*,
And seeking it in everything, I lost
All feeling of conviction, and, in fine,
Sick, wearied out with contrarieties,
Yielded up moral questions in despair. . . .

                              (*Prel*. x, 889–901)

Wordsworth's attempt to overcome the authority whom he had internalized in his psyche resulted in his loss of both affective and effective power. It is likely that on some level Wordsworth felt this loss as a kind of retributive vengeance. In one sense, at least, the attempt to eliminate the restrictive power of the father might have been self-defeating for Wordsworth because it was precisely his father who may have supplied, for Wordsworth, a model of masculinity. Wordsworth had taken up this model by identifying with his father. To eradicate utterly this masculine image in the quest for unrestricted masculinity might have proved something of a contradiction. But from another perspective it was this very failure to eliminate the power of the father and the consequent obedience to paternal limitations that differentiates Wordsworth from William Blake. Blake insisted upon becoming a pure creative subject and would accept no limitation that would render him a relatively passive object. Blake, at least within the framework of his myth, insisted that Nobodaddy be overthrown. Of course, the absolute difference of class perspective between Blake, the laboring artisan, and Wordsworth, the Cambridge gentleman, should on no account be underestimated when comparing the two men.

For a life as well documented as Wordsworth's, remarkably little is known about his crisis of the spirit except that it overcame him and that through the ministrations of his sister, Dorothy, the redemptive power of nature, and later the adulatory support given him by Coleridge, he recovered from this crisis. He tells us that the recovery enabled him to return to his true relation to nature, that nature "Revived the feelings of my earlier life" (*Prel*. x, 925).

But as I shall attempt to show, much had changed. We do know something about his spiritual crisis, and several things can be inferred about the process of his recovery. It was Wordsworth's conviction that joy was a reward for worth. He writes of himself at one point as being "unworthy of the deeper joy" (*Prel.* IV, 382). If Wordsworth was found unworthy after the collapse of his failed egotism, then he was unworthy of and devoid of joy. Wordsworth must have felt himself helpless, buffeted by immense destructive forces. He writes that the French Revolution was a path that led him to "the devouring sea" (*Prel.* IX, 4).

It was Wordsworth's fate to be caught up and almost destroyed by historical forces that he could not fully understand. Yet without understanding those forces, Wordsworth nonetheless attempted to help to make history. Marx wrote perhaps the most powerful comment on man's attempt to make history:

> Men make their own history, but they do not make it just as they please; they do not make it under circumstances chosen by themselves, but under circumstances directly encountered, given and transmitted from the past. The tradition of all the dead generations weighs like a nightmare on the brain of the living. [33]

Wordsworth tells us that memories of his role, however minor, in the French Revolution weighed on his brain like a recurrent nightmare.

Wordsworth, emotionally weakened and battered, would have had reason to fear annihilation, but the now dominant paternal forces offered a compromise instead. For a price, suffering, he could have affective power, provided that he relinquish his claims to effective power. Wordsworth would compromise his original and more grandiose desire for both forms of power, while, on the other side, the still-living psychic father within him would compromise by taking an intermediate position between the reproachful, stern, ever-limiting tyrant, on the one hand, and the internalized model for the attainment of absolute masculine self-assertion, on the other. But the acceptance of suffering as an ineluctable aspect of being was the price that Wordsworth had to pay in order to negotiate this compromise that released him from the realm of contradiction. Suffering is the mark of the covenant Wordsworth entered with one godlike father that was within him. The annihilating power, like Bercilac's third blow, had stopped short. Wordsworth had been saved from the abyss of nonbeing and this gift of life was marked by the acceptance of pain.

I hope that a close reading of *The Borderers*, especially its preface, never published during Wordsworth's lifetime, and of Wordsworth's early drafts of "The Ruined Cottage," will demonstrate that Wordsworth emerged from his spiritual crisis having repudiated effective power, which he had come to see as prideful, egoistic and aggressive, and having accepted affective power as the greatest power to which he could attain. Further, I hope to demonstrate that he emerged from the crisis having come to believe or rather to perceive that suffering was an inevitable part of human existence and that personal suffering was the price he would have to pay for having been allowed to escape from his spiritual crisis.

Wordsworth's first attempt at establishing an adequate community for himself failed. He had hoped, in the community that the French Revolution had held before him, to find a place in which he could fully realize all of his potential energies. This hope remained unfulfilled, but his need for community remained. In the next chapter I shall examine how Wordsworth's ideal of being shifted from one who possessed both effective and affective power to one who possessed affective but not effective power. And I shall examine as well the nature of the community that was congruent with this new ideal.

THREE

COMMUNITY FOUND: PART I

WORDSWORTH did succeed in finding a form of social community to which he could ally himself: the social community of the dalesmen in the Lake counties of England. At first glance this choice seems to be so natural and inevitable as to be self-evident. After all, so it might seem, after having attempted to join the social world of brotherhood held out by the French Revolution, Wordsworth simply returned to the form of social community in which he had grown up. In his end was his beginning. So the idealization of Grasmere Vale was a simple and inevitable result of his disappointed hopes in France. Nothing remarkable here; everything quite natural and inevitable. But the matter is far more complex.

It was suggested in the previous chapter that it would be necessary to read carefully *The Borderers*, its preface, and the earliest version of "The Ruined Cottage" in order to understand how Wordsworth came to accept a community that satisfied the need for affective power while denying access to effective power. This form of community was a compromise between the community of affective and effective power that he had sought and the punished condition devoid of either form of power with which the retributive forces within had threatened him. As a result of this compromise

> . . . sanguine schemes,
> Ambitious virtues pleased me less, I sought

119

For good in the familiar face of life
And built thereon my hopes of good to come.
(*Prel.* XII, 65–68)

After I have discussed *The Borderers*, I shall examine, from several perspectives, the compromise emotional and social formation that is marked by affective power without effective power, reading Wordsworth's poetry in order to illuminate the different aspects of this emotional and social formation. Further, I shall attempt to describe the nature of the community that was to become Wordsworth's social ideal. I hope to show that this community is bound together by imaginative force, rather than by utilitarian calculation. In it, land is partrilineally inherited, and the family is governed by paternal authority.

In the character Oswald and in the preface to *The Borderers* written with the play between 1796 and 1797, Wordsworth paints a portrait. The key to understanding this portrait is the realization that Wordsworth's capacity for profound introspection antedates the autobiographical blank verse that was to make up *The Prelude.* Oswald and the individual described in the play's preface comprise an introspective portrait of the artist as a young revolutionary. The correspondence between Oswald and Wordsworth is less remarkable when one notes that Oswald was shaped by "reflections I had been led to make during the time I was a witness of the changes through which the French Revolution passed" (*P.W.* 1:343). Writing at Racedown in 1796 and 1797, Wordsworth had become repelled by the fugitive glimpses he had caught of the thwarted egoistic desires within him that sought fulfillment. He became aware of aggressiveness so intense that it would destroy what it could not obtain, although it is not clear how much of what he glimpsed he recognized to be himself (or, to be more precise, his potential self) and how much he attributed to creative insight. But he certainly had come to understand that egoistic passions can, upon reaching consciousness, dress themselves in the seemingly selfless guise of analytic reason. Much of the message of *The Borderers* and its preface is contained in the wry observation in *The Prelude* that while he was a revolutionary enthusiast, "passions had the privilege to work,/And never hear the sound of their own names . . ." (*Prel.* X, 813–814).

The preface to *The Borderers*, never published in Wordsworth's lifetime, is an attempt to analyze the workings of a particular type of criminal mind. It is clear that the man he is trying to describe is not Oswald, the Iago-like villain of the play, but that person or that class of persons whom Oswald is made to represent. The man he is attempting to describe is the man driven to commit crimes by his involvement in the French Revolution; someone who had continued along the path Wordsworth himself had traveled before he had been brought to a jarring halt when he gave up moral questions in despair.

Wordsworth asks us to conceive of a brilliant but excessively proud young man who "has deeply imbibed a spirit of enterprize in a tumultuous age" (*Prose* 1:76). That is to say, we are asked to conceive of someone living in a revolutionary period in which careers are open to talent, or of a zealous patriot aspiring to public power. Wordsworth, who fantasized at playing a redeeming role in France, had imbibed this spirit of enterprise as had the rising class of bourgeois entrepreneurs. "He goes into the world and is betrayed into a great crime." As a result "That influence on which all his happiness is built immediately deserts him" (*Prose* 1:76). He is mired in guilt. Wordsworth had inadvertently written an abstract and summary of the tale of Oedipus. It is not my intention to suggest a literary allusion or source. It is only that Wordsworth, in writing this play (which is, by the way, the story of a man who kills a father in order to obtain a wife), is in the grip of what Freud would later call the Oedipus complex. Wordsworth had been driven by an intense unconscious wish to overcome restraints his father had placed upon him. Wordsworth did not have the power to carry through his rebellion, and therefore he halted, overcome with remorse and despair. Oswald represents someone who was able to carry the rebellion further, someone who like Oedipus was betrayed into a terrible crime and consequently hurled from innocence, influence and power. He acts out, and in this way discharges homeopathically, some of Wordsworth's fantasies of what would happen to him if, despite guilt and punishment, his egoistic desires had continued unrestrained.

For the criminal whose psychological portrait Wordsworth is painting, guilt is so closely linked with the loss of power consequent upon his guilt that by extrapolation it would seem that a reaccession to power would result in elimination of guilt and that guilt is merely the psychic representative of loss of power. "The recovery of his original importance & the exhibition of his own powers are therefore in his mind almost identified with the extinction of those painful feelings which attend the recollection of his guilt" (*Prose* 1:76). Wordsworth presents here the morality, if such a word be allowable, of the infant who in his egoistic desires is governed only by what Wordsworth would come to call in another context "the grand elementary principle of pleasure," someone whose ego development had reached but not grown beyond the pleasure ego.[1] What satisfies the infant's desire for pleasure is good; what thwarts it, bad. This primitive and utterly egoistic morality persists in the adult mind, though it is not always visible or even accessible to conscious scrutiny. In his preface to his only play, Wordsworth delineated the ruthless egoism he had been prevented from pursuing. In a reaction deferential to the restraining power within him, he had turned from such egoism in disgust. Again, the human infant may provide a model for such a reversal, for in the process of its development the contents of its bowel, for example, once regarded as a fascinating and pleasurable object, comes to be regarded with revulsion. Such a reversal is called a reaction-formation.[2]

What is important for any understanding of Wordsworth is that the egoism and aggressiveness that he came to repudiate were consciously linked in his mind with the French Revolution; the economic and social groups that had supported Girondism; the industrial, mercantile and financial bourgeoisie; and significantly, the mechanistic rationalism, which, descending from Condillac and LaMettrie, had been an ideology of the antifeudal bourgeoisie.

For Wordsworth, emerging from the depression caused by a loss of faith in radical politics, revolution, the bourgeoisie, limited rationalism, and lying behind them egoism and aggressiveness, were the stuff that evil was made out of. That which attempted to destroy or erode the traditional aristocratic social order against which Wordsworth had fought would now or soon come to be seen as being evil. Wordsworth was undergoing a process of change the first effects of which would soon become visible. He did not experience an instantaneous conversion.

If Wordsworth was undergoing such a process of change, then a passage in "The Communist Manifesto," written in 1848, is particularly relevant to Wordsworth's developing disgust for the bourgeoisie and all that was associated with it:

> The bourgeoisie, wherever it has got the upper hand, has put an end to all feudal, patriarchial, idyllic relations. It has pitilessly torn assunder the motley feudal ties that bound man to his "natural superiors," and has left remaining no other nexus between man and man than naked self-interest, than callous "cash payment." It has drowned the most heavenly ecstacies of religious fervor, of chivalrous enthusiasm, of Philistine sentimentalism in the icy water of egotistical calculation. It has resolved personal worth into exchange value and, in place of the numberless indefeasible chartered freedoms, has set up that single, unconscionable freedom—free trade. In one word, for exploitation, veiled by religious and political illusions, it has substituted naked, shameless, direct, brutal exploitation.[3]

Marx and Engels consciously describe the aggressive, calculating and ruthless egoism of the same bourgeoisie that Wordsworth had responded to with equal disgust but without the same kind of political consciousness. Marx and Engels created the historical materialist critique of bourgeois society. Wordsworth had helped to create the Romantic critique of the same society.

The character whom Wordsworth describes "cannot exist without occupation" and is continually committing new crimes. Accordingly, "his reason is almost exclusively employed in justifying his past enormities & in enabling him to commit new ones," and "he has a sophism for every crime" (*Prose* 1:77). Thus pride and sophistic reason come to be seen as joint producers of crime and evil. It is, then, the desire to restore power to oneself by any means, but always with sophistic argument, that Wordsworth hates as he had intuited it in himself and was later to see it in Bonaparte. Rationalistic calculating egoism is the voice that justifies the rage of someone who is criminally opposed to the traditional moral order. When Wordsworth writes "We murder to dissect" (*P.W.* 4:57), the line is heavily overcharged because analytical reason was linked associatively with murderous retaliatory rage. The criminal described in the preface "Presses truth and falsehood into the same service." He is a fallen man who "dallying with moral calculations

. . . becomes an empiric. . . ." He "disguises from himself his own malignity by assuming the character of a speculator in morals . . ." (*Prose* 1:77–78).

The rage behind the sophistic reason is Wordsworth's rage when the paternal forces checked his hope of fulfilling his imperial nature and pushed him to the verge of nonbeing, devoid of power of any kind. Someone pushed to the brink of nonbeing is in only attenuated contact with reality. His reasoning will be erring, false and specious as a result. He is not likely to understand reality clearly. Only people who have a secure hold on being can see life in its organic wholeness.

If rage and murder are associated with destructive analytic reason, then by implication peace and intimations of immortality are associated with an imaginative vision in harmony with the natural order. Wordsworth was coming to understand how inadequate analytic reason was in any attempt to comprehend the complexity of the moral life. He discovered that man did not do good because it was in his enlightened self-interest to do so. Good was not the result of any felicific calculus. Rather Wordsworth came to understand, perhaps to discover, the link between the moral life, the "principle of pleasure" (*Prose* 1:140) and the unconscious. Unremembered, and therefore unconscious pleasures, could influence "the best portion of a good man's life" (*P.W.* 2:260). His discovery of the intimate relationshhip between the unconscious and the moral life contributed to Wordsworth's rejection of narrow rationalism.

If the preface to *The Borderers* shows that Wordsworth had come to reject egoism as being ineluctably linked to pride, rationalism, and evil, it is important to appreciate the larger context in which this emotional development took place. The larger context is the play itself. For *The Borderers* is very much a play about fatherhood. The play demonstrates in its own way that the moral order of the world is contingent upon the security of the father's power. The father, here Herbert, is a centripetal force in the moral world. Without him the center cannot hold. Chaos is come again. When the protagonist, Marmaduke, is told that Herbert, the father of Idonea, intends to prostitute his daughter's virtue by giving her over to the unscrupulous Clifford, Marmaduke exclaims

"Father!—to God himself we cannot give a holier name . . ."
(P.W. 1:148–149).

Marmaduke is, of course, deceived in what he has been told about Herbert. Marmaduke is the leader of a band of men along the troubled Scotch-English border during the thirteenth century. The altruistic Marmaduke loves and is loved by Idonea, daughter of Herbert, who, old and blind, depends upon his daughter and opposes the match between his daughter and Marmaduke. Oswald, an evil and duplicitous member of Marmaduke's band, is driven to do evil because like the figure described in the prologue, he had been betrayed into a great crime. He has become a moral "empiric" (Prose 1:78). While convincing Herbert to have Idonea marry Lord Clifford, he also contrives to convince Marmaduke that Herbert is not Idonea's father but that he has duped her into believing he is. Further, Oswald convinces the credulous Marmaduke that Herbert intends to give Idonea over to the degenerate Clifford. Idonea can be saved, and justice done, Oswald insists, only if Marmaduke slays the blind, helpless Herbert. Marmaduke cannot nerve himself for the fell deed, but instead turns Herbert to wander upon a stormy moor. Herbert ultimately dies of exposure. When Marmaduke learns that he has been deceived into killing Herbert, he adjures his right to Idonea and condemns himself to a life of solitary wandering and penitence.

As I have said, The Borderers is a play about a man who murders a father in order to obtain a wife. It is not coincidental that this theme is, as is the history of the criminal described in the preface, linked to the Oedipus legend. Like Oedipus, Marmaduke is self-condemned to a life of wretched homeless wandering. He will be, that is, a solitary. For Wordsworth the state of being solitary, in one of its aspects, was one that could border on the feared state of nonbeing. It is worth noting that Wordsworth, in creating Marmaduke as the hero of The Borderers, fulfilled in Marmaduke Freud's precondition for being a hero. "A hero," says Freud, "is someone who has had the courage to rebel against the father and has in the end victoriously overcome him." [4] Herbert is not only Idonea's father; he is, in the world of the play, the principle of fatherhood itself.

And it is precisely to the degree that Herbert embodies the

principle of the sacredness of fatherhood that the play is revelatory of Wordsworth's emotional condition between 1796 and 1797 when he wrote it. Moreover, not only is Herbert an emblem of paternity, but he is an emblem of the traditional moral and social order as well. It is to the point here to note that his claim to be a baron, challenged throughout the play, is vindicated at the play's end. The values of love of father for child, and of child for father, of respect for age, of respect for social rank, of the martial valor of a nobleman, and of the responsibility of the community to care for the helpless all cluster about him. He is a veritable sun in a solar system of affective values.

Opposed to him in the moral economy of the play is Oswald, the moral empiric. To him all the traditional uses of this world are humbug. Having suffered intense remorse after having been duped into stranding the captain of his ship on a waterless rock, he underwent a moral revolution.

> When from these forms I turned to contemplate
> The World's opinions and her usages,
> I seemed a Being who had passed alone
> Into a region of futurity. . . .
>
> (P.W. 1:200)

There is only one law that he will obey:

> . . . the immediate law
> From the clear light of circumstances, flashed
> Upon an independent Intellect.
>
> (P.W. 1, 187)

From the preface it is clear that Oswald represents, for Wordsworth, the partisan of the French Revolution, the revolutionary bourgeois and bourgeoisie. Of the bourgeoisie Wordsworth had already intuited what Marx and Engels later expressed, that it would "wherever it has got the upper hand . . . put an end to all feudal, patriarchial, idyllic relations."

The action of the play works out for Wordsworth, as in a fantasy or dream, the conflict between his desire for egoistic self-assertion and the imperative to respect the father and the moral and social worlds the father represents, Oswald representing the former and Herbert the latter. The father or that part of Wordsworth's psyche that respects his father must be destroyed if Wordsworth's egoism is to be released from bondage. Oswald's survival is predicated on the destruction of Herbert and all that respects Herbert. The result of the conflict is for Wordsworth devastatingly clear. If respect for the father is removed the result is moral chaos. The father is a gravitationally powerful star that holds in order the affective and moral system that revolves about him, while illuminating it with significance.

Further, like John Wordsworth's, Herbert's power is not diminished by death. It is after his death that his claim to the title of baron is acknowledged. Those who thwarted him in life do not remain unpunished. Oswald is killed. Marmaduke is not allowed to achieve sexual fulfillment as a man. He gives up his claim to Idonea, and must wander alone until death, with little food or rest—a solitary thrust out to the very margin of being. The consequences of expressing murderous rage at the father and resentment at the limitations he has imposed are dire. So Wordsworth gives up his attempt to break through the restraints his internalized father had placed upon him. He gives up his attempt to destroy this father. He relinquishes his attempt to attain effective power. Instead, he accepts the moral and social world that the image of the father represents. This does not, of course, mean that Wordsworth's rage against his father is eliminated. Though buried deep within him, it still remains an active agent. Marmaduke commits himself to a life of despair. Depression often is the manifestation of rage turned inward against the self. Wordsworth himself comes to accept suffering as part of his lot, as well as part of the lot of humanity itself. A year after *The Borderers* was completed Wordsworth was to write on revisiting the banks of the Wye, after an absence of five years, that he was able to hear now a sound that had eluded him before, "The still, sad music of humanity" (*P.W.* 2:261). Wordsworth's newly won tragic sense of the human condition may well be in part a result of the rage at the father who denied him princely status. Now this rage was turned inward against himself and Wordsworth came to understand better the pain and the sense of lost promise that constitute some of the harmonies of the still, sad music.

For Wordsworth, rage was destructive and anarchic. It was not for him creative. Savage indignation could not lacerate him and thereby provoke bitter works of literary genius. Wordsworth became aware that this was true of himself. He gave up an attempt at social satire that he was writing jointly with his college friend, Francis Wrangham, admitting that he had no touch for satire (M.L. 89). Moreover, the intense pleasure of communion with nature led to the sentiment of being which was in turn an experience that Wordsworth turned into the subject of great poetry. This pleasurable communion was not accessible to Wordsworth when he was filled with rage. Rather, a peculiar kind of passiveness, of receptivity, was required before this joyful interaction with nature was possible. To create great poetry, then, it was necessary for him to create a buffer between himself and his rage. A stabilizing surrounding community might well help him sustain such a buffer.

Looked at from a slightly different perspective, the moral crisis that caused Wordsworth to abandon his attempt to obtain the fulfillment of all of his egoistic desires, and consequently to accept paternal authority, may be seen as what has popularly come to be called a crisis of identity of late or delayed adolescence. From this perspective the question of his identity revolved around the nature of his relationship to his mother. Up until the emotional crisis, following his disillusionment with republican politics, he had never been able fully to accept the reality of his mother's death. She had continued to live, for him, a sublimated but intense existence in or as Nature. So long as she continued to be a potentially accessible figure for him, he could continue to harbor hopes of princely fulfillment in possessing her. He could sustain this hope only if he accepted the condition of perpetual adolescence. But when he actively broke with restraining tradition and attempted to realize his imperial nature, to win his mother to himself, his attempt met with failure.

Faced with the bitter reality that he could never reattain the Golden Age of unity with his mother, he relinquished his hopes and claims to the stern demands of the father. He would be guided no longer by the grand principle of pleasure but instead by the severe principle of reality associated with the stern and severe father. He would, that is, grow from adolescence to adulthood. Emerging from this crisis of identity, he was a changed person. The Golden Age now lay irrevocably in the past. The loss of his mother was admitted. He would no longer be the object, cared for and loved as a child. He would become a subject, a fully creative subject, a great poet. Wordsworth's new ability to hear the "still, sad music of humanity" on the banks of the Wye is thus overdetermined. The new sadness that has humanized his soul comes from the recognition that the loss of his mother is permanent.

The pain of this loss must have been a terrible ordeal for Wordsworth. It is my speculation that having worked through the pain of this loss over a period of several years, he gave unconscious expression to it in Goslar in the cold winter of 1799. I believe that the Lucy, whose death or possible death is the subject of the great elegiac Lucy poems, and Emma, whose death is mourned by Matthew in "Two April Mornings" written during the same winter, are girls through whose deaths Wordsworth symbolically and unconsciously mourns his mother. Only after he had completed the until-then uncompleted task of mourning his mother's death could he free himself to examine his past and write *The Prelude*. Some lines from "Two April Mornings" express the unbearable pain of his now-acknowledged bereavement. He cannot allow himself such suffering again. Matthew, turning from his daughter Emma's grave, sees a beautiful young girl. He says of that moment:

> "There came from me a sign of pain
> Which I could ill confine;
> I looked at her, and looked again:
> And did not wish her mine!"
> (P.W. 4, 71)

Wordsworth's hypothesized crisis of identity could explain the decline in intensity of Wordsworth's interactions with nature, a decline that Wordsworth first describes in "Tintern Abbey." Unlike his experience on the banks of the Wye in 1793, the sounding cataract no longer haunts him, in 1798, like a passion. The woods, "Their colors and their forms" are no longer "An appetite; a feeling and a love." He no longer experiences "aching joys" and "dizzy raptures" (P.W. 2:261). It is not, I think, insignificant that the terms used to describe his feelings five years earlier are terms appropriate to erotic passion. But now five years later, following his crisis of identity, he must acknowledge the actuality, the finality of his mother's death. She can no longer be sought for in and through nature. Nature can no longer offer him such intense pleasure. As he was to write in the first part of the great "Intimations Ode" written in 1802, "there hath past away a glory from the earth" (P.W. 4:279). What has replaced this glory? The answer in both "Tintern Abbey" and the "Intimations Ode" is the same. Having grown through and out of his identity crisis Wordsworth came to accede to the harsh reality principle. He has become a man. His wish for his mother could not be satisfied. Clearly the human condition was one that necessitated great frustration and sustained pain. He developed "the faith that looks through death," "the philosophic mind" (P.W. 4:284). This maturation was consequent upon his completing the incompleted process of mourning for his mother.

It would be incorrect to assume that, having relinquished his claim to wield effective power, Wordsworth relinquished all his bitterness towards his father. This bitterness was still capable of appearing in disguised form as late as 1807 and 1808 when he first wrote "The White Doe of Rylstone" (P.W. 3:281–340). In this poem Wordsworth's resentment of the limitations that his father had placed upon him takes a curiously childish form. It is typical of a child that when reprimanded for doing something inappropriate he or she will reply, "But you do it, too!"[5] In "The White Doe of Rylstone" Wordsworth says of his father, in effect, "But you do it, too." For in "The White Doe" the father, Norton, is the rebel against the Crown and Church of England. The father is even excuted for his rebellion.

Wordsworth's crisis following his disillusionment with the French Revolution was but the first stage in resolving the bitterness against his father, a bitterness that was part of his family romance.[6] A second series of developments helped to bank the intensity of

Wordsworth's bitterness by forcing Wordsworth to come to identify more completely with his father. One of a child's greatest wishes is the wish to be grown-up like its parents. Much of childish play is playing at being grown-up, and thereby in fantasy anticipating the desired growth.[7] In the family romance, so common among children, the desire to be grown-up manifests itself as the desire to replace the parent of the same sex as the child. John Wordsworth was both a husband and a father. Young William, if he was much like other children, envied his father's ability to fulfill these two roles, that he, William, was incapable of fulfilling. So that when Wordsworth married Mary Hutchinson on October 4, 1802, he fulfilled his childhood wish to be a husband, like his father, and to the degree that he had succeeded in becoming like his father, he came to identify with him that much more than he already had. This identification was further intensified when on June 18, 1803, Wordsworth became the father of his first legitimate child, his son John. The intensification of Wordsworth's unconscious identification with his father reinforced the tendencies that were already at work binding the poet to the traditional moral and social values that his father had held. Wordsworth thus moved that much further from his earlier republican views. But the nuclear, and in Wordsworth's case extended, family that reinforced Wordsworth's commitment to the traditional social order, could not exist in isolation. A Wordsworth household committed to traditional values would be rendered more stable by being surrounded and supported by a larger social community committed to those same traditional values.

After there had disappeared a glory from the earth, because nature had ceased to be invested with his mother's presence, nature could no longer function as successfully as it had in the past as the stabilizing gate or wall that prevented Wordsworth from contracting into the "abyss of idealism" (*P.W.* 4:463). His dependence on society to act as a stabilizing agent would be that much greater. In London when the face of everyone he met was a mystery to him, he had contracted toward nonbeing. A mutual community, one in which he could perceive recognition and reciprocal confirmation of self in every face he met, would be a stay against the confusion of impending dissolution. Recognition in the faces of those about him would fall far short of being acknowledged as a prince, but it was preferable to an anomic social world in which no recognition was possible. Wordsworth had accepted a compromise between princely realization on the one hand and annihilation on the other.

I have chosen to call this compromise Wordsworth's covenant with his father. In the emotional crisis consequent upon the abandonment of youthful radicalism Wordsworth had found himself without either effective or affective power. He must have felt himself vulnerable to annihilation. He survived, but his emergence from the emotional crisis, which I have also viewed as a crisis of identity, was predicated upon compromise with traditional authority. Rather than possessing effective and affective power, he would possess only affective power, and even this compromise was purchased at the price of the acceptance of suffering. I have attempted to show in relation to *The Borderers* how Wordsworth came to turn away from assertive power with revulsion, associating it with egoistic and destructive impulses. I have also shown the suffering Wordsworth experienced when he came to recognize the irrevocable loss of his mother. In the following pages I shall examine the power that Wordsworth was granted in the convenant, further examine the significance of suffering as a sign of that covenant, and briefly examine some poems that bear upon the compromise formation that I call the covenant.

The potency that Wordsworth is granted is the power to work freely in the realm of creating poetry. To be sure, the ability to create poetry may be a form of assertive power, but that this was not so for Wordsworth is, I believe, demonstrable. The gift of the ability to create poetry is for Wordsworth a compensatory one.

Wordsworth himself demonstrated an uncommonly acute understanding of his own intrapsychic processes. In "Home at Grasmere," begun in 1800 and mostly completed in 1806, he indicates that he is aware of processes whereby his aggressive impulses were transformed into their opposites and also diffused into other more acceptable psychic aims. That is to say, he is aware both of the process of reaction-formation and of sublimation. Nature, he tells us, has transformed his aggressive impulses into the ability to write poetry, but only about gentle subjects. The ability to create poetry is a reward or dower for relinquishing his aggressiveness. He has, that is, exchanged effective power for affective power.

> While yet an innocent Little-one, with a heart
> That doubtless wanted not its tender moods,
> I breathed (for this I better recollect)
> Among wild appetites and blind desires,
> Motions of savage instinct my delight
> and exaltation.
>
> (P.W. 5:336)

At this point in his life he loved the "daring feat" (P.W. 5:336) however disobedient. Even now as an adult his spirit is set in motion by a martial tale.

> Yea to this hour I cannot read a tale
> Of two brave Vessels matched in deadly fight,
> And fighting to the death, but I am pleased
> More than a wise man ought to be. I wish,
> Fret, burn, and struggle and in soul am there. . . .
>
> (P.W. 5:337)

But nature has checked the fretful and burning impulses in him—"But me hath Nature famed . . ."—she has treated him like a "turbulent Stream/Some nursling of the mountains" (P.W. 5:337). She has quieted him by leading him "Through quiet meadows."

> Her deliberate Voice
> Hath said, "Be mild and cleave to gentle things,
> Thy glory and thy happiness be there.
> Nor fear, though thou confide in me, a want
> Of aspiration, that *have* been, of foes
> To wrestle with, and victory to complete,
> Bounds to be leapt, darkness to be explored,
> All that inflamed thy infant heart, the love,
> The longing, the contempt, the undaunted quest,
> All shall survive—though changed their office, all
> Shall live,—it is not in their power to die."
>
> (P.W. 5:337)

Evidently Wordsworth also intuited that time did not exist in the unconscious, that no strong drive "that inflamed the infant heart" could ever die.

Wordsworth will be a poet. There is in him "an internal brightness . . . that must not pass away" (*P.W.* 5:335). But Wordsworth must not express his "wild appetites and blind desires" in his poetry. The "longing, the contempt, the undaunted quest" that had inflamed his infant heart must not find expression in his verse. This aggressiveness must be tamed like the turbulent mountain stream that is calmed in "quiet meadows." It is here that I suspect that Wordsworth demonstrates an awareness, however oblique, of the processes of sublimation and of reaction-formation. In his poetry "Of ill-advised Ambition and of Pride" he must "stand clear" (*P.W.* 5:335). Moreover, he must not write "Of scorn and condemnation personal/That would profane the sanctity of Verse" (*Prel.* x, 644–645). In the avoidance of aggressiveness and egoistic assertation in Wordsworth's poetry, it is, perhaps, possible to find one reason for the subjective nature of his verse. If Wordsworth is to be so hedged around with limitations as to what can be fit objects of verse for him, he will transform subject into object. He, the subject, will be the object of his verse. He will write *The Prelude.*

The injunction that he not write of "wild appetites and blind desire" may help to explain the relative sexlessness of Wordsworth's poetry, a sexlessness parodied by Shelley in "Peter Bell the Third," written in 1819:

> But from the first t'was Peter's drift
> To be a kind of moral eunuch,
> He touched the hem of Nature's shift,
> Felt faint—and never dared uplift
> Her closest, all—concealing tunic.[8]

So Wordsworth, having relinquished all power in his emotional crisis, not only survived, but was able to regain affective power. The price he had to pay the paternal forces in order to survive was the acceptance of suffering. The suffering may well have been due to his final acknowledgment of his mother's loss, of the inaccessibility of the princely Golden Age. But suffering also had symbolic significance. It was the mark of the covenant. It was the bow placed in the sky as a mark that the father in him had relented, that Wordsworth would continue to exist.

Egoistic impulses have been thwarted by the father. The result is rage, but the rage has been turned inward and is felt as depression, that is, as suffering. But suffering is significant. If one suffers, one must exist; one must be. Not "I think, therefore I am" but rather "I suffer, therefore I am." The annihilating power has stopped short. Man has been saved from the abyss of nonbeing, yet the reprieve is marked by pain. Even more, as the Pedlar in the 1797 text of "The Ruined Cottage" says, suffering seems to indicate a reality more profound than the phenomenal world, a reality beyond "The passing shews of being."[9] We receive intimations of this infinite world not only through moments of joyous transcendence and cosmic unity, but also in moments in which we experience and contemplate suffering. For Wordsworth, for whatever reason, suffering seems not to lead to the perception of existential, weightless absurdity, but rather to a vision of the infinite. Pain tells him, as it were, "This cannot be all. There must be more." But the more is "beyond the passing shews of being"; it is not accessible. Rather than intensifying the belief in the limitations of the phenomenal world, suffering denies the limitations of this world. In *The Borderers* Oswald says

> Suffering is permanent, obscure and dark
> And shares the nature of infinity.
> (P.W. 1:188)

Wordsworth thought enough of these lines to use them as part of an inscription to "The White Doe of Rylstone," published in 1815.

What is important for Wordsworth is that the spectacle of suffering, in that it may reinforce the meditative sympathetic imagination, can serve to strengthen the bonds of community. In "The Old Cumberland Beggar," written in 1797, Wordsworth shows that the spectacle of suffering serves to bind man to his fellow man. Speaking of good people who see the decrepit Cumberland beggar in his wanderings, Wordsworth writes that "Some there are" who

. . . from this solitary Being,
Or some like wanderer, haply have received
(A thing more precious far than all that books
Or the solicitudes of love can do!)
That first mild touch of sympathy and thought,
In which they found their kindred with a world
Where want and sorrow were. . . .

(P.W. 4:237–238)

Those already poor have their sense of community strengthened by
the beggar.

. . . the poorest poor
Long for some moments in a weary life
When they can know and feel that they have been,
Themselves, the fathers and the dealers-out
Of some small blessings; have been kind to such
As needed kindness, for this single cause,
That we have all of us one human heart.

(P.W. 4:239)

Raymond Williams, writing from a different perspective, states,
"The spirit of community . . . has been dispossessed and isolated
to a wandering, challenging if passive, embodiment in the
beggar."[10]

In the terminology of Blake's mythic world, Wordsworth's
covenant is an acceptance of the realm of Beulah, a gentle moon-
drenched realm. It is at the same time an act of bad faith, a refusal
to force his way into the fiery, creative realm of Eden, in which,
alone, Wordsworth could become pure subject.

The sun is a sign of Wordsworth's covenant. It is "a
pledge/And surety of our earthly life . . ." (Prel. II, 185–186).
The rainbow, likewise, is such a sign. Wordsworth's heart leaps up
when he beholds "A rainbow in the sky" (P.W. 1:226). It is, like
its biblical counterpart, a symbol of continuity. Because of "natural piety," a state in which it may be presumed that egoism and
aggressiveness have been subdued, our days are bound together
and given continuity. Upon first seeing the Swiss valley communities that display "patriarchal dignity of mind" and "a pure simplicity of wish and will" (Prel. VI, 443–444), Wordsworth exclaimed

"My heart leap'd up . . . ." (*Prel.* VI, 446). It would seem that recognition of "patriarchal dignity" is a manifestation of the natural piety that allows days to be "Bound each to each . . ." (*P.W.* 1:226).

Having lost faith in the French Revolution and the community of brotherhood it had seemed to hold out, Wordsworth found his way into a new community. This community would have to be congruent with the dictates of the covenant. It would have to damp egoistic effective power and stress mutually reflexive affective bonds. It would be a community like those found in the Swiss valleys. Patriarchal "dignity of mind" and "pure simplicity of wish and will" would exist in this community. Wordsworth had committed himself to a social world of natural affections, smaller than the universal world of brotherhood that had seemed open to him but a few years before, a world corresponding in size and intensity to Burke's "little platoon." [11] In the second poem to the small celandine, "To the Same Flower," composed in 1802, Wordsworth writes

> Praise it is enough for me,
> If there be but three or four
> Who will love my little Flower.
> (*P.W.* 2:146)

The necessary size of his social world has dramatically shrunk from the period of revolutionary ardor when the whole world seemed to lie before him to be shaped and reformed.

The social world that Wordsworth committed himself to recapitulated his reshaped character structure. It was to be a community of people poor in effective power but rich in affective power. In his portrait of the community enjoying its rural fair under the shadow of Helvellyn, in the opening of Book VIII of *The Prelude*, Wordsworth delineates such a community.

In terms of worldly force the Lake Country dalesmen are no more than infants.

> How little They, they and all their doings seem,
> Their herds and flocks about them, they themselves,
> And all that they can further or obstruct!

Through utter weakness pitiably dear
As tender Infants are. . . .

                              (*Prel.* VIII, 50–54)

This seems, and perhaps is, a bit condescending, yet it must be admitted to be true. In terms of the affairs of the great world of state, of states in conflict, of history as an impressive tapestry of deeds and happenings, none of these rural folk is at all significant. They are powerless to influence nations or to shape human destiny. There may be some mute inglorious Miltons among them, but they will continue to remain mute and inglorious.

In this observation in the 1805 *Prelude* are the seeds from which Wordsworth's later Tory humanism would inevitably grow. The rural laborers, and perhaps the working class as a whole, is infantile in matters of power. The social order should treat them as children, care for them, protect them. The poor are to be cared for but seldom, if ever, given access to political power.

But Wordsworth's description of the rural shepherds and farmers as "tender infants" should be examined literally. An infant may be and in fact is physically helpless. But affectively he is a powerful creature. Precisely because his body is weak and vulnerable his needs are cared for. His cries of helplessness are heard and bring attention. The infant is privileged to enjoy an intense and powerful affective relationship with its mother. This experience is for most people the most intense love relationship that they will ever experience.[12] Further, infants are loved and doted on not only by mothers. And still further, the infant is autoerotic. If psychoanalytic theory is correct, the infant can satisfy itself sexually by pleasure sucking and other modes of self-gratification. The growing child has almost unlimited power in the realm of fantasy, and never again will its fantasies have such power to approximate the satisfactions of reality, unless the child's development is severely abnormal. Moreover, the older child is free to play. It might be free to make "one long bathing of a summer's day" (*Prel.* I, 294) or "Over the sandy fields" leap "through groves/Of yellow grunsel" (*Prel.* I, 297–298). It is as if the child's weaknesses were balanced by corresponding strengths. Although limited in effective power it has enormous affective power.

If the rural fairgoers are without influence in the great world they are affectively rich.

> Immense
> Is the Recess, the circumambient world
> Magnificent, by which they are embranced.
> (*Prel*. VIII, 46–48)

They are embraced, cared for. They are infants,

> and yet how great!
> For all things serve them; them the Morning light
> Loves as it glistens on the silent rocks,
> And them the silent Rocks, which now from high
> Look down upon them; the reposing Clouds,
> The lurking Brooks from their invisible haunts,
> And Old Helvellyn, conscious of the stir,
> And the blue Sky that roofs their calm abode.
> (*Prel*. VIII, 54–61)

Their childish position, as Wordsworth sees the fairgoers, reflects his own condition. He has retreated unconsciously from an attempt to usurp his father's power to the position of a child, as I have described the potencies available to the child. This is not to say that he became like a child again. The matter is far too complex for such assertions. There is clearly a difference between a great poet and a child, or between the same poet and himself as a child. However, it is possible to say that the character formation of the adult great poet was congruent with the character formation dominant in his childhood personality. When Wordsworth repudiated his own attempts to dominate the world, he entered into and idealized the emotional posture that he had maintained as a child. He idealized as well a social form that mirrored his new ideal of being. This congruence between social and emotional being was to be threatened by economic development and change, by capitalist development.

It would be appropriate at this juncture to examine the permutations of affective and effective power in order to see why affective power devoid of effective power had become his ideal. To have neither effective nor affective power is the state that Wordsworth most dreaded. It bordered on nonbeing. To be in such a state one would be an outcast, bewildered and depressed. People crushed by the burdens of excessive poverty or those city dwellers most degraded by their situation belong in this class.

To have effective power but no affective power was to be in the state that was most repulsive to Wordsworth. Bonaparte is emblematic of this class. He rules Europe, is an absolute tyrant, but is devoid of the capacity to feel

> The tenderest mood
> Of that man's mind—what can it be? what food
> Fed his first hopes?
>
> (P.W. 3:110–111)

Also in this contemptible class are the "monied worldlings." They "taint the air/With words of apprehension and despair." Their "riches are akin/To fear, to change, to cowardice, and death" (P.W. 3:119).

The next possible state was the state in which princely being was fulfilled, the state of possessing both affective and effective power. But the authority that he had internalized interdicted this state. Pursuit of it led to emotional collapse. Only one permutation remained, affective power and effective weakness. Wordsworth attained this after the compromise with the authority that had become part of his character. To have such power was to become an idealized member of the traditional natural economy. To be in such a state was to be in accord with nature, to avoid waging "foolish strife" (P.W. 4:72).

In the poem "Power of Music," composed in 1806, Wordsworth demonstrates how a man almost devoid of effective power is capable of generating an enormous affective field of force, the power of music. The man is blind. His debility limits his physical capacities. There may be many occasions when he is helpless and, like a child, dependent on help. But he is the source of emotional power so immense that it brings rushing passersby to a halt. The power is the power of the music he plays on his fiddle. Wordsworth could have entitled the poem "The Power of the Blind Fiddler" and thereby given power to the blind man himself. Wordsworth chose, rather, to displace the emphasis and make the music itself the powerful force. In this way, Wordsworth was able to create a character who embodied spiritual power combined with physical debility. Here is a stanza that demonstrates the degree of affective power that the fiddler generated. The field of force he creates is like a net capturing those who enter it.

> The errand-bound 'Prentice was passing in haste—
> What matter! he's caught—and his time runs to waste;
> The Newsman is stopped, though he stops on the fret;
> And the half-breathless Lamplighter—he's in the net!
> (P.W. 2:218)

If members of Wordsworth's idealized Cumberland or Swiss rural communities were without significant influence on the world, then, to the degree that the community was idealized, affective power must be idealized as well, in order to compensate for the powers that the communities lack. In "Power of Music" the strength of emotional power is emphasized. What about the quality of such power? Wordsworth affirms the quality of a life that affective power grants in a passage of Book VI of *The Prelude* describing life in the Vale of Chamouny. Life lived in such a place is more truly life than life lived in cities. The life of simple feeling is more real.

> Whate'er in this wide circuit we beheld,
> Or heard, was fitted to our unripe state
> Of intellect and heart. By simple strains
> Of feeling, the pure breath of real life,
> We were not left untouch'd.
> (*Prel.* VI, 469–473)

Wordsworth and his companion Jones are touched because in this account of the experience the life with its simple feeling is "real life" in its purity. Here man most completely realizes, in actuality as opposed to art, his spiritual essence, his species being.

Still observing the same community Wordsworth writes:

> With such a book
> Before our eyes, we could not chuse but read
> A frequent lesson of sound tenderness,
> The universal reason of mankind,
> The truth of Young or Old.
> (*Prel.* VI, 473–477)

Here Wordsworth equates "sound tenderness" with the "universal reason of mankind." This is highly significant. True reason, universal reason, is determined not by rigorous analytic logic, but by affectivity. By extrapolation, if tenderness is equal to reason, then callous brutality would be equivalent to irrationality. The affective, mutual rural community is the most rational form of social community. The city was at this point in history the social and demographic form most closely associated with capitalism. It was the social form that capitalism was bringing to rapid development in Manchester, for example. At the locus of the capitalist spirit "all feudal, patriarchal, idyllic relations" are being replaced by "callous cash payment," by "egotistical calculation." Because callousness and egotism are both concentrated and unrestrained in the city, the city, in which even neighbors may be unknown to each other, is an irrational social form that both symbolizes and renders more prevalent the failure of human connection. Human life as lived in cities is therefore not real, but a brutal lie, a falsification of the human spirit. Of what he had been told about London in his childhood, Wordsworth writes:

> . . . one thought
> Baffled my understanding, how men lived
> Even next-door neighbours, as we say, yet still
> Strangers, and knowing not each other's names
> (*Prel.* vii, 117–120)

This clearly is not a mutually reflexive, affectively bound community.

If the city was the demographic form that distorted and prevented significant human relationships, the rural community encouraged the development of such relationships. In *The World We Have Lost*, Peter Laslett notes the demographic factors that would help to create meaningful ties:

> . . . living together in one township, isolated, spatially, from others of comparable size, of very much the same structure, inevitably means a communal sense and communal activity, even if that activity is trivial and symbolic. . . .[13]

Elsewhere Laslett argues that in the small rural village, factors other than geographical isolation work to create strong mutual relationships.

> To the facts of geography, being together in one place, were added all the bonds which are forged between human beings when they are permanently alongside each other; bonds of intermarriage and of kinship, of common ancestry and common experience and of friendship and co-operation in matters of common concern.[14]

Wordsworth had many reasons for giving his allegiance to an affectively bound traditional community. For one thing, he associated such a community with his mother. He attributed his mother's sound and natural pedagogy in part to "faculties" instilled in her not only by the times but also by the "spot in which she liv'd" (*Prel.* v, 285–287), traditional Cumberland. The fact that her Cumberland environment helped ensure that she was "not falsely taught" and was without "presumption" (*Prel.* v, 266–269) or "jealousy" may have helped to make the traditional values of the Lake counties more significant.

An additional reason for Wordsworth's being drawn to the apparently stable traditional affective community was his desire to avoid being made to feel impotent. He could be made to feel helpless by being a member of an historical movement whose immense forces were beyond his control. Such loss of control would leave him an historical object rather than an historical subject. Wordsworth had allied himself with the Girondin faction of the Revolution and had watched helplessly as it was defeated by the Montagnards. After Robespierre was overthrown on 9 Thermidor, Wordsworth rejoiced, hoping for what he could view as revolutionary regeneration. Again he watched without possible recourse to action as the French became oppressors in their turn. That these events injured Wordsworth's self-esteem is suggested in a passage of the preface to *The Borderers*, in which he is delineating the character of the criminal mind he wishes to portray. I have already indicated the strong identification between Wordsworth and the character whose motives he attempts to disclose. Of this character Wordsworth writes:

The period in which he lives teems with great events, which he feels he cannot controul. That influence which his pride makes him unwilling to allow to his fellow-men he has no reluctance to ascribe to invisible agents. . . . (*Prose* 1:78)

Like Wordsworth, the criminal's pride is wounded by the fact that he cannot control the events of his time. Unlike Wordsworth, the criminal ascribes to invisible agents the power that his pride will not allow him to ascribe to his fellow-men. In order to avoid another such mortifying wound to his ego, Wordsworth commits himself to a quiet community that does not teem with great uncontrollable events.

The traditional social form to which Wordsworth gave his allegiance in yielding to an acceptance of the covenant was a quite specific one. The limitation of effective power is not the only significant characteristic of Wordsworth's ideal social community. Wordsworth's ideal community would be based on two additional and interrelated principles: paternal authority and patrilineally inherited private landed property. In writing to his friend, Thomas Poole, about the poem "Michael" on April 9, 1801, Wordsworth noted that in the poem it had been his intention "to give a picture of a man, of strong mind and lively sensibility, agitated by two of the most powerful affections of the human heart; the parental affection, and the love of property, *landed* property, including the feelings of inheritance, home, and personal and family independence" (*E.L.* 332). Society in the vale of Grasmere, as described in "Home at Grasmere," is ideal because it is "A true community, a genuine frame/Of many into one incorporate" (*P.W.* 5:334). All this is possible because this "true community" is ruled by "paternal sway" (*P.W.* 5:334). Further, here "Man! is Master of the field,/And treads the mountains which his Fathers trod" (*P.W.* 5:326). It would seem that there is one aspect of life in Wordsworth's ideal community in which effective power is not forbidden. A man may exercise effective power in the form of paternal authority within the limits of his own household.

Moreover, the tradition of obedience to the father reinforced the habit of deference to those who were hierarchically superior to oneself. Such a tradition worked to lessen the real power of those among the common people who might be seen as possessing some authority, including, paradoxically, fathers themselves. As Peter Laslett observes:

> Submission to the powers that be went very well with the habit of obedience to the head of the patriarchal family, and it had the extremely effective sanction of the universal fear of damnation to the defiant. [15]

The family- and father-dominated community that was Wordsworth's ideal was not the imaginative creation of a poet. It corresponded to the social reality of rural England, particularly of the Lake District of Wordsworth's time. The traditional community made the nuclear family the unit for nearly all activity. [16] The home was still the typical site of most labor. [17] A married laborer with two children might, by his family's labor, secure the equivalent of his own income without having to send his children to work in the mill (*Lakes* 265–266).

Textile operations were widely diffused in Lake Country homes. At the turn of the century there were still relatively few mills. Kendall was the most important wool center (*Lakes* 263). As late as 1800 most Cumbrians were manufacturers in miniature (*Lakes* 236). Knitted stocking manufacture was engaged in as a main or secondary occupation by many families in wool-producing areas (*Lakes* 264). Work took place in the home under parental supervision. [18] The wife of the head of the household spun flax. At night the husband carded and spun wool. The wife would, perhaps, sell the yarn at the Hawkshead Fair. In addition to spinning flax many Cumbrian women were involved in spinning lint for the family (*Lakes* 242).

Child labor was deeply rooted in the domestic textile industry. [19] Despite the work, most children were able to participate in games, dances and sports, unlike their unfortunate counterparts who were forced to enter a mill. [20] In Dorothy Wordsworth's journal entry for what seems to be October 4, 1802, she writes that outside of Thirsk she saw "a large Bonfire with Lads dancing round it, which is a sight I dearly love" (*D.W.J.* 157).

Wordsworth does not present Grasmere as an ideal community without a purpose in view. His hope is that by presenting such a community governed by the principles of paternal authority and patrilineally inherited landed property, he can help to preserve and propagate it. He hopes to

> Express the image of a better time,
> More wise desires, and simpler manners. . . .
>
> (P.W. 5:6)

Wordsworth's portrait of patrilineally transmitted land in which man "treads the mountains which his father trod" is, however, not an entirely accurate portrait of the social structure of the Lake counties. The location of the same family in the same holding generation after generation was not universal. In some parts of the Lake District, particularly among wealthy families, it was not even normal between 1730 and 1830 (*Lakes* 332). As old families died out or moved elsewhere, they were replaced by new families. Many large country estates came to be inhabited by new families enriched by coal mining and trade (*Lakes* 329).

I have been engaged in establishing the four fundamental characteristics of Wordsworth's ideal community: the inhabitants have no effective power; they have access to affective power; they are governed by paternal authority; and land is transmitted patrilineally through succeeding generations. I now propose to examine the nature of the force that bound each member of the community to each in natural piety. The most simple and direct statement that I can make is that the social glue of the ideal community was imaginative power. For Wordsworth the ability to love was a direct function of imaginative power.

In the first of his three "Essays Upon Epitaphs," all published in Coleridge's journal *The Friend* in 1810, Wordsworth suggests that social feeling, the ability to love beings other than ourselves, is rooted in an instinctive knowledge that we are immortal. If we did not believe in immortality we would not risk the unbearable pain of loss entailed in loving another mortal being. Therefore, social feeling, the very foundation of community, is based upon a belief in immortality. If we were to be brought up without a belief in immortality we would be unable to love:

> Were we to grow up unfostered by this genial
> warmth, a frost would chill the spirit, so

penetrating and powerful, that there could be
no motions of the life of love. . . .

(*Prose* 2:52)

What Wordsworth is saying is that feeling for others is predicated
upon an ability to break out of the self-containing boundaries of
self. The force that breaks through the shell of self and connects
the self with others is the imagination. Imagination is the centripetal force of community.

Wordsworth specifically identifies the imagination as a social
power in Book II of *The Prelude*. He writes of "the great social
principle of life/Coercing all things into sympathy" (*Prel*. II,
409–410). This power is even able to work in unlikely places such
as the heart of London. He writes of a rare moment when London
is breathed upon by the integrating coalescing power of the imagination.

> . . . among the multitudes
> Of that great City, often times was seen
> Affectingly set forth, more than elsewhere
> Is possible, the unity of man,
> One spirit over ignorance and vice
> Predominant, in good and evil hearts
> One sense for moral judgements, as one eye
> For the sun's light. When strongly breath'd upon
> By this sensation, whencesoe'er it comes
> Of union or communion doth the soul
> Rejoice as in her highest joy: for there,
> There chiefly, hath she feeling whence she is,
> And, passing through all Nature rests with God.
>
> (*Prel*. VIII, 824–836)

The most direct way of understanding this social power and of
seeing how closely Wordsworth held it to be related to what he
called the poetic faculty or creative imagination is to trace this
power back to what Wordsworth believed were its origins in every
individual. Wordsworth believed that the imaginative faculty originated in the relationship between the infant and its mother. First
the child takes from his mother. He "Doth gather passion from his
Mother's eye" (*Prel*. II, 243). His mother is the source not only of

passion but of the ability to integrate disparate objects, and it is this latter aspect of the imagination that Wordsworth calls the social power.

> Such feelings pass into his torpid life
> Like an awakening breeze, and hence his mind
> Even [in the first trial of its powers]
> Is prompt and watchful, eager to combine
> In one appearance, all the elements
> And parts of the same object, else detach'd
> And loath to coalesce.
>
> (*Prel.* ii, 244–251)

Likewise, the mother is the source of the individuating aspect of imaginative power. Describing the mother as a presence Wordsworth wrote:

> In one beloved Presence, nay and more,
> In that most apprehensive habitude
> And those sensations which have been deriv'd
> From this beloved Presence, there exists
> A virtue which irradiates and exalts
> All objects through all intercourse of sense.
>
> (*Prel.* ii, 255–260)

And in a natural fashion the child, that Being, learns to work creatively upon objects of his senses.

> Emphatically such a Being lives,
> An inmate of this *active* universe;
> From nature largely he receives; nor so
> Is satisfied, but largely gives again,
> For feeling has to him imparted strength,
> And powerful in all sentiments of grief,
> Of exultation, fear, and joy, his mind,
> Even as an agent of the one great mind,
> Creates, creator and receiver both,
> Working but in alliance with the works
> Which it beholds. —Such, verily, is the first
> Poetic spirit of our human life;
> By uniform controul of after years
> In most abated or suppress'd, in some,

Through every change of growth or of decay,
Pre-eminent till death.

(Prel. ΙΙ, 265–280)

I suspect that Wordsworth's high sense of what man can truly be if he fulfills his human nature derives, as well, from the infant's, or perhaps the child's, relationship to its mother. A fully human man, one in whom the poetic spirit remains preeminent until death, would be a man who had retained a sense of the profound intimacy that according to Wordsworth describes the relationship between mother and infant. This fully developed man might well be one who strove to live up to an ideal of perfection that he believed, on some level, to be a prerequisite for being an object worthy of the love of a highly idealized mother. He would strive to become the ideal heroic self loved by a perfect mother.

Wordsworth's faith in what man "may become" was a profound conviction that was not to be easily dispelled by evidence of human depravity:

Neither guilt nor vice,
Debasement of the body or the mind,
Nor all the misery forced upon my sight,
Which was not lightly passed, but often scann'd
Most feelingly, could overthrow my trust
In what we may become, induce belief
That I was ignorant, had been falsely taught,
A Solitary, who with vain conceits
Had been inspired, and walk'd about in dreams.

(Prel. VIII, 802–810)

Wordsworth's fully developed man is one who has enough imaginative social power to enable him to break through restricting barriers of egoism and demonstrate "the unity of man." He is a communal being. The human soul's "highest joy" is to attain "union or communion" with other men. The passage about London that I have already cited testifies to the high moral value that Wordsworth, the poet whose most typical subject is the solitary, placed upon community. In London one could occasionally see:

Affectingly set forth, more than elsewhere
Is possible, the unity of man,

> One spirit over ignorance and vice
> Predominant, in good and evil hearts
> One sense for moral judgements, as one eye
> For the sun's light. When strongly breath'd upon
> By this sensation, whencesoe'er it comes
> Of union or communion doth the soul
> Rejoice as in her highest joy. . . .
> (*Prel.* VIII, 826–834)

The conviction that man in his fully realized state was not to be limited by the narrow confines of the self led to a truly epic conception of man's possibilities. Beyond community, Wordsworth believed that man's true home is with the infinite.

> Our destiny, our nature, and our home
> Is with infinitude, and only there;
> With hope it is, hope that can never die,
> Effort, and expectation, and desire,
> And something evermore about to be.
> (*Prel.* VI, 538–542)

Wordsworth's theme, then, is truly epic. He is, as the Prospectus to *The Excursion* suggests, truly Milton's rival. His task is not Milton's; his task is not to "justify the ways of God to men." [21] Rather his vatic labor is to justify the ways of men to men. Wordsworth will sing of "the glory that redounds . . . to humankind and what we are."

> Be mine to follow with no timid step
> Where knowledge leads me; it shall be my pride
> That I have dared to tread this holy ground,
> Speaking no dream but things oracular. . . .
> (*Prel.* XII, 247–252)

So, social power is one form that the faculty of mind known as poetic spirit or imagination can take. When it takes the form of social power it brings objects outside the mind into relationship with one another; it agglutinates. In other forms, this faculty can act on objects outside the mind and alter the way that the mind perceives them. Working at its highest pitch, when it creates the sentiment of being, this faculty abolishes the distinction between subject and object by transforming the object world into subject.

If the "social power" can create union in a community as large and diverse as London already was, it would seem to be the key to social integration. It resolves latent contradictions between people by subjecting them to its power to create a social aggregate. Individual differences would therefore be changed, transformed into what they had not been before, in order to create harmony. This power to create unity is but the obverse of the power of the imagination to create uniqueness. In both cases the imagination transforms an object into something other than what it had been. An excellent example of the power of the imagination to render objects more singular rather than more typical is to be found in Book II of *The Prelude* just before Wordsworth describes the imagination as a social power:

> A plastic power
> Abode with me, a forming hand, at times
> Rebellious, acting in a devious mood,
> A local spirit of its own, at war
> With general tendency, but for the most
> Subservient strictly to the external things
> With which it commun'd. An auxiliar light
> Came from my mind which on the setting sun
> Bestow'd new splendor. . . .
>
> (*Prel.* II, 381–389)

Wordsworth described how, while at Cambridge:

> To every natural form, rock, fruit or flower,
> Even the loose stones that cover the high-way,
> I gave a moral life, I saw them feel. . . .
>
> (*Prel.* III, 124–126)

By creating for himself a unique and moral world to live in, Wordsworth renders himself unique. Because of his imagination projected onto fruit, flowers and highway stones, he is more completely individualized than he could have been without the power of his imagination. He literally inhabits a special world of his own.

> I was most rich,
> I had a world about me; 'twas my own,
> I made it. . . .
>
> (*Prel.* III, 141–143)

Imagination, then, is a key to Wordsworth's political thought, at least from 1797 to 1809. Through the power of imagination man can become fully individualized. Through the power of the imagination man can become fully socialized. Imagination could resolve the age-old dilemma of individual freedom versus social obligation, at least for someone who had fully cultivated his imaginative capacity. Man could be born free, enter society and never become enchained. From this would follow Wordsworth's devotion to everything that could develop the imaginative capacity in man and his abhorrence of everything that would deaden it, that would induce a "savage torpor" (*Prose* 1:128).

In order to achieve freedom, gross sensuality must be sublimated into imaginative power. To come under the sway of base sensuality is to become enslaved. Wordsworth asserts:

> I never, in the quest of right and wrong,
> Did tamper with myself from private aims;
> Nor was in any of my hopes the dupe
> Of selfish passions. . . .
> (*Prel*. xiii, 131–134)

Rather he

> . . . did with jealousy shrink back
> From every combination that might aid
> The tendency, too potent in itself,
> Of habit to enslave the mind. . . .
> (*Prel*. xiii, 136–139)

In the 1800 Preface to *Lyrical Ballads* Wordsworth states that it is the function of poetry to satisfy the human mind "without the application of gross and violent stimulants . . ." (*Prose* 1:128). The capability of rendering the mind susceptible to the effect of mild stimulants is "one of the best services in which, at any period, a Writer can be engaged. . . ." This service is especially "excellent . . . at the present day" (*Prose* 1:128).

> For a multitude of causes unknown to former times are now acting with a combined force to blunt the discriminating powers of the mind, and unfitting it for all voluntary exertion to reduce it to a state of almost savage torpor. The most effective of these causes are

the great national events which are daily taking place, and the encreasing accumulation of men in cities, where the uniformity of their occupations produces a craving for extraordinary incident which the rapid communication of intelligence hourly gratifies. (*Prose* 1:128)

Wordsworth finds that the quality of mind of his generation may best be described as being in a state of "savage torpor" because torpor implies that the mind can be stimulated only by progressively more and more violent stimuli. That is to say, the conditions in which men can be satisfied by means of moderate stimulation are being progressively destroyed. History itself is eroding the barrier between restraint and license. History's destructive forces are linked on the one hand with the French Revolution, "the national events which are daily taking place," and on the other with the Industrial Revolution which is "encreasing" the "accumulation of men in cities." Capitalist production, by means of the division of labor, impoverishes men's lives by causing a "uniformity of their occupations." The result of these destructive historical forces is a license devoid of true freedom.

By implication a free community would be devoid of that which would enslave the mind: selfish passions, vicious habits or gross sensuality. A free community is a community bound by the agglutinative social power of the imagination, as imaginative power would also allow each citizen to develop his individuality. In such a community members are not self-reflexively bound in upon themselves, not consumed by the savage torpor of egotism. Instead, the limits of the self are transcended and, by means of the social imagination and by empathy, the members of the community care for one another. But the socially binding imagination of a free community is connected with the absence of vice and sensuality. It is necessary that the community be spared torpor-inducing stimulation. Such vicious stimulation weakens, in every individual, the imaginative faculty that builds community. Freedom, virtue, and imagination all seem to be related to one another. True freedom is impossible without imagination which is, in turn, impossible without virtue.

There is one passage in *The Prelude* in which Wordsworth speaks at length of himself as a "Freeman." And it is significant, I think, that he should talk about his awareness of his great imaginative powers in the very passage that asserts his freedom. Even on this most subjective level freedom is directly related to imaginative power:

> I was a chosen Son.
> For hither I had come with holy powers
> And faculties, whether to work or feel:
> To apprehend all passions and all moods
> Which time, and place, and season do impress
> Upon the visible universe, and work
> Like changes there by force of my own mind.
> I was a Freeman. . . .
>
> (*Prel.* iii, 82–89)

Elsewhere in *The Prelude* Wordsworth describes a woman, either Dorothy or Mary, though the emphasis on passive acceptance would seem to signify Mary rather than the wild-eyed Dorothy. This maid "Was wholly free" (*Prel.* xi, 203). What accounts for such complete freedom? Her being is freed "from Appetites" (*Prel.* xi, 201).

> She welcom'd what was given, and craved no more.
> Whatever scene was present to her eyes,
> That was the best, to that she was attuned
> Through her humility and lowliness. . . .
>
> (*Prel.* xi, 207–210)

Freedom comes from acceptance of what is, from humility, and not from the arrogant sensibility that seeks gratification of every sensual impulse. Such arrogance and sensuality are slavery. There is only one form of true liberty. That is to be free from being dominated by sensuality. There are those who do not require extraordinary calls

> To rouse them, in a world of life they live,
> By sensible impressions not enthrall'd,
> But quicken'd, rous'd, and made thereby more fit
> To hold communion with the invisible world.
>
> (*Prel.* xiii, 101–105)

Of such capacities Wordsworth writes, "this alone is genuine Liberty" (*Prel.* XIII, 122). In the poem "To a Highland Girl" (*P.W.* 3:73–75), written in 1803, the speaker sees in the girl's face "The Freedom of a Mountaineer." It is possible to see freedom in her face,

> For never saw I mien, or face,
> In which more plainly I could trace
> Benignity and home-bred sense
> Ripening in perfect innocence.

Wordsworth's high sense of what man could be was intimately connected with his conception of a communal being. Further, I have tried to show that for Wordsworth the concepts of community, of moral probity, and of freedom were closely interrelated. Indeed, in the third of his "Essays on Epitaphs" he wrote, "local attachment . . . is the tap-root of the tree of Patriotism" (*Prose* 2:93). Wordsworth's definition of freedom in negative terms as freedom from license was representative of English thought in the late eighteenth and early nineteenth centuries. Wordsworth did not conceive of freedom in the positive terms of liberties that an individual might exercise. Rather for him the concept of liberty and that of duty were closely connected. In this he was representative of the England of his time. According to E. P. Thompson:

> The stance of the common Englishman was not so much democratic, in any positive sense, as anti-absolutist. He felt himself to be an individualist, with few affirmative rights, but protected by laws against the intrusion of arbitrary power. [22]

The Englishman "claimed few rights except that of being left alone." [23] In other words the Englishman made no claim for the right of effective power. Elie Halévy, addressing himself primarily to the first years of the nineteenth century, wrote of the English, "They now understood by liberty restraint self-imposed and freely accepted as opposed to restraint forcibly imposed by the Government." [24]

The man of letters, particularly the historian and the poet, could play an active role in strengthening the imaginative faculty that in one form helped to hold society together. The historian preserved for all future generations regenerative social spots of time that possess a "vivifying Virtue" (*Prel.* XI, 260) for society as a whole. Wordsworth and Beaupuis pick from among "bright spots" of "recorded time" salvational moments that told of past triumphs of truth.

> We summon'd up the honorable deeds
> Of ancient Story, thought of each *bright spot*
> That could be found in all recorded *time*
> Of truth preserv'd and error pass'd away,
> Of single Spirits that catch the flame from Heaven,
> And how the multitude of men will feed
> And fan each other, thought of Sects, how keen
> They are to put the appropriate nature on,
> Triumphant over every obstacle. . . .
>   (*Prel.* IX, 371–379; my emphasis)

The poet's role is both more difficult and more important than that of the historian. The poet's task is nothing less than to create community. The poet is to do this by creating imaginative realms that his readers may enter. His reader forgets "the heavy and the weary weight/Of all this unintelligible world" (*P.W.* 2:260). Such a destruction of narrow selfish concerns is a prerequisite for the development of community. After deprecating children's literature the intent of which is the development of the child's store of knowledge rather than of his imaginative faculty, Wordsworth wrote:

> Oh! give us once again the Wishing-Cap
> Of Fortunatus, and the invisible Coat
> Of Jack the Giant-killer, Robin Hood,
> And Sabra in the Forest with St. George!
> The Child, whose love is here, at least, doth reap
> One precious gain, that he forgets himself.
>   (*Prel.* V, 364–369)

And the child, needless to say, is father to the man. One of the proper functions of literature for the adult is to make him forget himself. Wordsworth is not, of course, arguing a case for literature

as mere diversion, for penny-dreadfuls. He is arguing for a literature that can make the reader look beyond the claustrophobic limitations of the self; make him transcend egoism and allow him to
engage in the world around him, aided by the power of sympathy.

There is even a suggestion in *The Prelude* that great poetry
recreates for its readers the relationship that is the emotional antecedent and model for all subsequent relationships between self and
other, the relationship between mother and child. At the beginning of Book v of *The Prelude* there is a meditation about the inevitable destruction of man's great cultural creations. In the subsequent episode of the dream about the Arab-Quixote,
Wordsworth more precisely defines man's highest cultural creations as "Poetry and geometric Truth" (*Prel.* v, 64). For man to
survive without these twin creations would be to survive while
remaining "Abject, depress'd, forlorn, disconsolate" (*Prel.* v, 27).
Such a state seems to resemble the condition of an infant without
its mother who is an "outcast . . . bewilder'd and depress'd" (*Prel.*
II, 261).

If one allows that there is sufficient emotional resonance between the state of a babe without its mother, and man without poetry, as Wordsworth has described them, then it would follow that
poetry and geometric truth satisfy the human spirit because they
present it with a symbolic reproduction of a precious and ever-to-
be-recreated relationship. They restore the lost infantine community between mother and infant. Perhaps poetry accomplishes this,
as Shelley suggested, by restoring to us the freshness and wonder
with which a child supposedly views the world, by purging "from
our inward sight the film of familiarity which obscures from us the
wonder of our being." [25] By serving to renew man's first experience
of community, in the form of intense communion, poetry might
facilitate man's participation in the larger world of social community.

Because imagination in the form of social power is the binding force that makes Wordsworth's favored form of community
possible, Wordsworth came to detest "naked self-interest" and
"egotistical calculation." He believed that they destroyed the sympathetic imagination that bound the community together. The intensity of Wordsworth's hatred of naked self-interest is revealed in

the significant but seldom discussed poem "Andrew Jones" (*P.W.* 2:463–464), written in 1798. Because the moral judgment rendered by the speaker in "Andrew Jones" coincides so closely with Wordsworth's own moral values, I believe that the speaker in the poem may be said to speak for Wordsworth. Wordsworth may have found his bitterness expressed too directly and too severely, because after 1815 he omitted the poem from his collected works. The poem is about a miserable wretch, Andrew Jones, who, because no one is looking, takes the two half-pennies that had been tossed to a poor cripple, before the hapless cripple could reach the two coins. Andrew Jones is clearly not governed by the power of sympathetic imagination. His ruthless egotism shows no respect for the community of natural affections. The poem begins with a veritable blast of rage:

> I hate that Andrew Jones: he'll breed
> His children up to waste and pillage.
> I wish the press-gang or the drum
> Would, with its rattling music, come,
> And sweep him from the village!

Andrew is refuse to be swept away. Moreover, his egotism will be punished by the father in the sublimated form of the authoritarian paternalistic state that will carry Andrew away in a press gang. Andrew will breed his children up "to waste and pillage." Andrew will foster rather than discourage destructive egotism in his children.

"Goody Blake and Harry Gill" (*P.W.* 4:173–176), also written in 1798, is another poem in which a rejection of the sympathetic imagination is punished, this time not with imprecation but with psychosomatic illness. In a bitter winter Goody Blake suffered from intense cold that "made her poor old bones to ache." She is too poor to afford fuel, so she raids the hedge of Harry Gill.

> Now Harry he had long suspected
> This trespass of old Goody Blake;
> And vowed that she should be detected—
> That he on her would vengeance take.
> And oft from his warm fire he'd go,
> And to the fields his road would take;

> And there, at night, in frost and snow,
> He watched to seize old Goody Blake.

He seizes her. Goody Blake falls to her knees and prays "O may he never more be warm." And he is never warm again.

For Wordsworth the egotism of Andrew Jones and Harry Gill is destructive of the traditional community regulated by a natural economy. But there is a social and demographic form in which such egotism is not the exception but rather the norm. This form is the city. Here Wordsworth is oppressed by

> . . . the weight of meanness, selfish cares,
> Coarse manners, vulgar passions, that beat in
> On all sides from the ordinary world
> In which we traffic. . . .
>
> (*Prel*. VIII, 454–457)

Wordsworth is thankful that he was brought up in nature:

> Happy in this, that I with nature walk'd,
> Not having a too early intercourse
> With the deformities of crowded life,
> And those ensuing laughters and contempts
> Self-pleasing, which if we would wish to think
> With admiration and respect of man
> Will not permit us. . . .
>
> (*Prel*. VIII, 463–469)

For a time, most likely when he was in London "mid the din/Of towns and cities" (*P.W.* 2:269), Wordsworth had had to endure "evil tongues . . . Rash judgments . . . the sneers of selfish men . . . greetings where no kindness is" and all "The dreary intercourse of daily life" (*P.W.* 2:162).

In cities, the egotistical calculation that capitalism, in all its forms, induced, deformed the human spirit. Shorn, for Wordsworth, of the power of imagination, which alone could lift man out of the narrow boundaries of self, the human spirit was reduced to a stunted egotistical caricature of what it was capable of becoming. Man could realize his species being in cities only with the utmost difficulty. What is most significant about the "contempts" bred by city life is that they are "self-pleasing."

Nature on the other hand is beneficent. In nature man reveals himself as an object worthy of imitation. He has a glory of his own, and the many shepherds who appear to the young Wordsworth, as they loom out of a luminescent mist, show that the word glory is appropriate both in its modern and its root acceptations. In nature man is literally "purified."

> But blessed be the God
> Of Nature and of Man that this was so,
> That Men did at the first present themselves
> Before my untaught eyes thus purified,
> Remov'd, and at a distance that was fit.
> <div align="right">(<i>Prel</i>. VIII, 436–440)</div>

In the poem "The Tables Turned" (*P.W.* 4:57), written in 1798 and supposedly at the expense of the young William Hazlitt, Wordsworth makes his point about nature's pedagogic power, although with a good measure of humorous exaggeration:

> And hark! how blithe the throstle sings!
> He, too, is no mean preacher:
> Come forth into the light of things,
> Let Nature be your Teacher.

And again in the same poem Wordsworth writes:

> One impulse from a vernal wood
> May teach you more of man,
> Of moral evil and of good,
> Than all the sages can.

These lines, unfortunately, will live forever for those who are intent on holding Wordsworth in contempt and are not above lifting lines out of their poetic context. Finally, nature, though gratifying, does not contribute to building a narrowly developed sense of self grounded on "fallacious hopes." Nature is a "Power":

> . . . the very quality and shape
> And image of right reason, that matures
> Her processes by steadfast laws, gives birth
> To no impatient or fallacious hopes,
> No heat of passion, or excessive zeal,
> No vain conceits, provokes to no quick turns

Of self-applauding intellect, but lifts
The Being into magnanimity. . . .
(*Prel.* XII, 25–32)

To be sure, the commonplace dichotomy between wholesome nature and the unwholesome city is not so absolute as to be
simple-minded, but it does exist. Rural England can produce an
Andrew Jones or a Harry Gill, and London, the artificer who at
the end of Book VIII of *The Prelude* tenderly brought his child to a
"spacious Grass-plot . . . For sunshine, and to breathe the fresher
air." The man held the child "in his brawny Arms" and "eyed it
with unutterable love" (*Prel.* VIII, 844–859). But however quali-
fied, the dichotomy between good nature and corrupting city does
exist in Wordsworth.

I have said that Wordsworth believed that the rural traditional
political economy was more salubrious to the full development of
human capacity than was the urban, capitalist political economy.
One aspect of Wordsworth's political thought, though not heavily
emphasized by him, transcends the limited categories of the
country and the city. I refer to the passage in the concluding book
of *The Prelude* that attributes to all men the ability and responsibility for developing their imaginative freedom. They can look to
no outside agency for help. Nothing can lessen or mitigate their
individual moral responsibility. They are all "Sufficient to have
stood, though free to fall," [26] or for that matter to rise.

Imagination having been our theme,
So also hath that intellectual love,
For they are each in each, and cannot stand
Dividually. Here must thou be, O Man!
Strength to thyself; no Helper hast thou here;
Here keepest thou thy individual state:
No other can divide with thee this work,
No secondary hand can intervene
To fashion this ability. . . .
(*Prel.* XIII, 185–193)

The implications of this passage for Wordsworth's political
thought seem clear, although I must stress again that this was not a
dominant element of his social philosophy. If "No secondary hand

can intervene" in helping man fulfill his imaginative potential, if man cannot benefit from any helper, then it would appear to be a matter of indifference whether he resided in the country or in the city. He would still be absolutely responsible for his imaginative development irrespective of secondary social help. No form of social community, no matter how ideal, can create a moral climate that will guarantee man's full development of his self, of his imaginative power. I must emphasize again that this position is only one aspect of a larger and sometimes contradictory body of ideas; but to the degree that Wordsworth asserts that the form of social community that a man inhabits is not decisive in determining that man's moral growth, Wordsworth rejects a tradition in Western social thought that reaches back to Plato. In *The Republic* Plato, through his protagonist Socrates, is unable to define the Good in relation to man without first defining the ideal republic in which man would be shaped. Since *The Republic*, ethical theory and political theory have been profoundly connected in Western thought. To assert that "No secondary hand can intervene" in elevating the human spirit is to turn away from the traditional connection between ethics and politics.

I have attempted in this chapter to formulate the moral, social, and political laws that govern the form of community that Wordsworth came to see as the ideal polity in the period following his emergence from a severe depression. He experienced this depression after he came to despair of the great promise that the French Revolution had, at first, seemed to hold out. This study has been, for the most part, a study of Wordsworth's poetry, so that the laws of polity that it attempts to describe are laws that govern the fictive social world portrayed in Wordsworth's verse. Often, indeed, the social formations that I refer to are latent and implicit rather than explicit. But the task of constructing a social world out of Wordsworth's poetry, a world governed by principles capable of being first identified, and then articulated, is a large one. If it can be accomplished at all, it cannot be done within the compass of a single chapter. I shall, then, extend my exploration of the social world latent in the poetry of Wordsworth's great decade to a second chapter.

FOUR

COMMUNITY FOUND: PART II

IN his book *The Country and the City*, Raymond Williams sees the idealization of the country at the expense of the city as a class-biased illusion. "It is, of course, a rentier's vision: the cool country that is sought is not that of the working farmer but of the fortunate resident." [1] Again he writes of the contrast between the idyllic country and the greedy city, "this contrast depends, often, on just the suppression of work in the countryside, and of the property relations through which this work is organized. . . ." [2] And once more he writes, relentlessly making his point: "What is idealised is not the rural economy, past or present, but a purchased freehold house in the country. . . . This is then not a rural but a suburban or dormitory dream." [3]

Williams insists that the exploitation of both man and nature that takes place in the countryside is realized and "concentrated" in the city and that, reciprocally, the profits from the exploitation of labor that goes on within the city penetrate the country as merchants and lawyers purchase country estates. [4]

The question that Williams raises bear heavily upon any sustained discussion of Wordsworth's political vision. Was Wordsworth's ideal rural community the product of a rentier's vision, a dormitory dream based upon the refusal to recognize the property relations around which rural work was organized? This chapter will attempt, at least provisionally, to answer this question. But while answering the question raised by Williams it is important to bear in mind an important distinction. Wordsworth was a writer, a poet, not a rentier. However closely his view of society might approximate the view of one whom Williams would call a rentier, Wordsworth came to his views out of a writer's needs. It would be an accurate generalization to say that Wordsworth looked upon himself as a wandering poetic recluse observing an Eden of work, himself happily rootless but admiring roots.[5] Although Wordsworth came to own property in both Cumberland and Westmorland, he never owned any house in which he lived. Even though these qualifications must be kept in mind in the following discussion, Wordsworth's idealization of Cumberland was similar enough to the idealization of a rentier to have social and political, as well as poetic, significance.

A reading of "Home at Grasmere" and parts of *The Prelude* seems to indicate that Wordsworth's social vision was indeed the idealized vision of a rentier. "Home at Grasmere" describes the Vale of Grasmere as containing a refuge of the hitherto lost Golden Age of the princely self:

> . . . surpassing grace
> To me hath been vouchsafed; among the bowers
> Of blissful Eden this was neither given,
> Nor could be given, possession of the good
> Which had been sighed for, ancient thought fulfilled
> And dear Imaginations realized
> Up to their highest measure, yea and more.
>
> (P.W. 5:317)

Wordsworth describes himself as having received one of what Freud describes in a letter as life's greatest pleasures, the fulfillment of the childhood wish.[6] This more than Edenic vale does not seem to be the locus of the toil, drudgery, and marginal economic existence of freeholder or day laborer working the land. Rather, it offers the "Perfect Contentment, Unity entire" (P.W. 5:318) that the blessed babe experiences in his communion with his mother, that prevents the infant from becoming an outcast, bewildered and depressed. Grasmere vale seems to offer Wordsworth a perceptual identity with the "Perfect Contentment, Unity entire" that the nursing infant experiences.

The notion that Wordsworth perceives Grasmere as a comforting maternal presence is reinforced when he cries to it to embrace him:

> Embrace me then, ye Hills, and close me in,
> Now in the clear and open day I feel
> Your guardianship. . . .
>
> (*P.W.* 5:317)

Not only does he ask to be embraced, a request that in itself could refer to a child calling to mother, or an adult to his or her lover, but he asks to be protected, more specifically guarded. The need to be guarded suggests that the desire to be embraced is the desire of a child for its mother. Nor is Wordsworth content with being embraced and guarded. He wishes to be closed in. He is asking the hills to enclose not only the vale, but also himself. In terms of Wordsworth's painful alternation between the expanded princely self and the contracted self, Wordsworth is asking for stability of self. He is asking for the unity of being in which his days would be bound by natural piety.

In the maternally comforting vale it is impossible to become an outcast, bewildered and depressed.

> For all things in this little world of ours
> Are in one bosom of close neighborhood.
>
> (*P.W.* 5:351)

Close neighborhood rules out the possibility of desolating solitude. This would seem to imply the converse of the principle that Wordsworth establishes in the first "Essay upon Epitaphs." There Wordsworth derives the possibility of community, "the social affections" (*Prose* 2:52) from man's certainty that he will never totally lose the objects of his love. This certainty results from the conviction of man's immortality. If, in the "Essay upon Epitaphs," the lessening of human anxiety of loss makes community possible, then the above two lines of verse from "The Tuft of Primroses," written in 1808, suggest the converse: that community lessens the anxiety of loss and separation.

Wordsworth expresses the dominant note in his social thought when he says that rural life, such as may be found at

Grasmere, plays a decisive role in helping man achieve imaginative fulfillment. Contact with the active universe lifts "the weight of meanness" and of "selfish cares." Wordsworth was fortunate because he first saw man in conditions of natural beauty:

> . . . first I look'd
> At Man through objects that were great and fair,
> First commun'd with him by their help. And thus
> Was founded a sure safeguard and defense
> Against the weight of meanness, selfish cares,
> Coarse manners, vulgar passions, that beat in
> On all sides from the ordinary world
> In which we traffic.
>
> (*Prel.* VIII, 450–457)

He was fortunate in

> Not having a too early intercourse
> With the deformities of crowded life. . . .
>
> (*Prel.* VIII, 464–465)

So in Wordsworth's social thought the nature of the community in which one learns to be human helps to determine the degree to which one becomes fully human.

That Wordsworth's vision of Grasmere is what Williams would call a suburban or dormitory vision is underscored by Wordsworth's repeated admission in "Home at Grasmere" that Grasmere is an idyll, an escape from the harrowing life beyond the vale. He calls Grasmere "A termination, and a last retreat" (*P.W.* 5:318). Further, Wordsworth writes a significant passage that ends with a wish to escape from "all remembrance of a jarring world" (*P.W.* 5:334). The Golden Age of the princely self is available to Wordsworth only at the price of turning his back on the world, of averting his eyes from all that might interfere with his "Perfect Contentment, Unity entire." This turning away from the outside world raises a question that will become significant for Wordsworth. What will happen when and if the outside world penetrates the enclosing mountains of the vale? For the moment it will be sufficient to deal with the intrusion into the vale of a band of itinerant gipsies.

In the *Biographia Literaria* Coleridge censures Wordsworth for being too severe in condemning the gipsies in Wordsworth's 1807 poem "Gipsies" (*P.W.* 2:226–227). Wordsworth finds it objectionable that a band of gipsies have remained "in the self-same spot" for "—Twelve hours, twelve bounteous hours." Coleridge suggests that Wordsworth is being insensitive. Perhaps the gipsies were badly in need of rest:

> . . . the poor tawny wanderers might probably have been tramping for weeks together through road and lane, over moor and mountain, and consequently must have been right glad to rest themselves, their children and their cattle for one whole day. . . .[7]

Although some of Coleridge's criticisms of Wordsworth are unfair, particularly some of his strictures on the "Intimations Ode," it would be unwise not to pause a moment over a poem that made so great a critic as Coleridge hesitate.

An examination of "Gipsies" reveals that Wordsworth was indeed oversensitive to the inactivity of a "Knot/ Of human Beings in the self-same spot" for twelve hours. But if Coleridge is at a loss to account for such oversensitivity and sees the poem as an example of "thoughts and images too great for the subject," the emphasis that this study has placed on Wordsworth's need for community should make Wordsworth's pique at the gipsies explicable. The gipsies seem in their torpor to be the types of anticommunity. The band of gipsies seems to be static and dead to Wordsworth. Their apparent lack of significant activity recreates, in its own way, the anomic quality of life in London in which every face that passed was a mystery, failing to reflect back to Wordsworth his own precarious being. It would seem that in order to support being reflexively a community must be vital and active, or perhaps interactive. Wordsworth describes the life the gipsies lead as being a "torpid life." Wordsworth may well be making a socially accurate observation about nineteenth-century English gipsies. The fact that tinkers were commonly regarded as pariahs and thieves makes it more clear that the vale's sanctity has been violated by an alien social group. But the word "torpid" suggests that their lives and their community itself are devoid of the power of affection. It is

precisely affection that opens up the "torpid life" of the blessed
babe. The babe

> Doth gather feelings from his Mother's eye!
> Such feelings pass into his torpid life
> Like an awakening breeze. . . .
>
> (*Prel.* ii, 243–245)

Wordsworth's response to the listless band of gipsies is an indication of how disturbed he will become when alien social forces press into his beloved vale. He calls upon the celestial bodies to bear witness to such unnatural inactivity.

> The weary Sun betook himself to rest;—
> Then issued Vesper from the fulgent West,
>   Outshining like a visible God
>   The glorious path in which he trod.
> And now, ascending, after one dark hour
> And one night's diminution of her power,
>   Behold the mighty Moon! this way
>   She looks as if at them—but they
> Regard not her:—oh, better wrong and strife
> (By nature transient) than this torpid life;
>   Life which the very stars reprove
>   As on their silent tasks they move!
>
> (P.W. 2:227)

It seems, then, that Wordsworth did see Grasmere and the surrounding country with something of a suburban or dormitory vision, but his vision did not deny the necessity of labor. Grasmere was, for him, a paradisiacal area, against whose outline the laggard and homeless gipsies stood out in ugly relief. Wordsworth's Grasmere had its own moral and political economy, based on what Marx called a natural economy as well as its own laws of social hierarchy. It is now my task to uncover and reconstruct the assumptions that underlay Wordsworth's ideal political economy and social hierarchy. Curiously enough this reconstruction will begin with the analysis of the political assumptions underlying a poem that is not set in the Lake District, but rather in London. It is not manifestly about social issues, as are such poems as "The Old Cumberland Beggar" and "The Last of the Flock," but rather about the pleasure afforded by music. Nor is the poem significant for its aesthetic merit. It is a very minor poem. The poem that I shall examine for its latent social assumptions is "Stray Pleasures" (P.W. 2:160–161), composed in 1806. I believe that the Tory humanist ideology of exchange based upon duty and reciprocity finds expression in this poem not because the poem is a conscious attempt to expound such an ideology, but because Wordsworth is so immersed in the ideology that he does not see it as such. Consequently, he is capable of expressing that ideology even when he is not aware that he is doing so. In short, he has absorbed it. Nevertheless, I suspect that some may find my reading to be forced. I wish those readers to be assured that the laws of polity that I derive from my reading of "Stray Pleasures" are amply supported by evidence from Wordsworth's letters and from Dorothy's *Journal*. For the reader who is disinclined to follow my reading of the poem, the evidence in the letters and Dorothy's *Journal* adequately proves the points I hope to make, and I shall draw on this evidence below.

In "Stray Pleasures" the speaker observes a "floating mill" on which he sees a "Miller with two Dames, on the breast of the Thames!" The three are "dancing merrily," but not to music that they have either created or occasioned.

> From the shore come the notes
> To their mill where it floats. . . .

The music is not theirs. It is a stray pleasure. It is "a prey which they seize/It plays not for them,—what matter? 'tis theirs. . . ." Yet by appropriating the pleasure of the music, they do not thereby lessen the quantity of pleasure to be enjoyed. Seemingly paradoxically, rather, they increase the quantity of pleasure, for the passing speaker is made gleeful by their appropriated merriment.

> They dance not for me,
> Yet mine is their glee!

It is the nature of pleasure, the reader is told, to extend ever farther from its initial source. And unappropriated pleasure legally becomes the property of whoever comes upon it.

> Thus pleasure is spread through the earth
> In stray gifts to be claimed by whoever shall find. . . .

The last stanza of the poem presents the reader with sources of this pleasure: spring showers and birds caroling. But showers and caroling as they are are not complete. There is, as yet, no system of distribution. Here Wordsworth introduces the wind necessary to spread the pleasure:

> If the wind do but stir for his proper delight,
> Each leaf, that and this, his neighbor will kiss;
> Each wave, one and t'other, speeds after his brother;
> They are happy, for that is their right!

Here the right to pleasure is made into a natural right; it is the right of the waves and the leaves to be happy. But even though wave and leaf are entitled to happiness, it does not follow that they will receive their birthright. Their birthright is conditional, as it depends on the workings of the distributive mechanism, the wind. They are happy if and only if "the wind do but stir. . . ." If the wind fails to stir, then happiness is not spread. Fortunately it is not a case of the wind blowing where and when it listeth. In this order of things the wind receives "proper delight" for stirring. In this moral order it is as blessed and as pleasurable to give as it is to receive.

I believe that the latent content of "Stray Pleasures" displays an order of property relations and of poor relief. Wordsworth's assumptions about this system of property relations are deeply rooted by 1806. They have become so integral to Wordsworth's consciousness that they can be taken for granted and projected, unawares, into a poem like "Stray Pleasures."

In this poem pleasure is like a use-value. It can be created, as in this poem, by the unknown musicians on shore. It can be found and used, as the three inhabitants of the windmill find it and use it in this poem. Presumably it is possible to be without pleasure as were the three before they appropriated the stray pleasure. It would even be possible to be not only without the use-value pleasure but also without the means of acquiring it. Conversely, it would be possible to be the source of large stores of pleasure. In the moral economy of the poem excess accumulated pleasure is not wasted but, rather, finds a way to satisfy others. Nonetheless, the theoretical possibility of hoarding excess pleasure exists.

The implications of this analysis should be obvious. Pleasure in the poem "Stray Pleasures" is a use-value that unconsciously and symbolically represents the use-values necessary to sustain life in a natural economy: food, shelter, implements of labor and so on. Here it is necessary to make an important distinction. Unlike the commodities necessary for survival, pleasure is indivisible. It cannot, then, be likened to food, or to clothing, or to tools, as each separate set of these commodities is divisible from the other. Rather, I think, it is necessary to see pleasure as representing an indivisible quantum of value, the quantum of value necessary for every member of society and for society itself to produce and reproduce its own being. A society possessing a smaller quantum of value would be an unstable disintegrating society, and a society possessing a larger quantum of value was not a possibility historically available to Wordsworth's imagination. Implicitly, the poem endorses a social system in which the few are morally justified in accumulating great wealth. For their great wealth does not deprive their fellow men of sustenance. Rather it is the necessary prerequisite for helping the unfortunate. Traditional economists would refer to this as the trickle-down theory of social distribution. It was the moral justification for the Whig and Tory English squirearchy's inequitable possession of wealth. The poor are not supposed to suffer from this system of distribution. Quite the contrary, they benefit from the overflow of the largess of their social superiors. In this poem Wordsworth expresses the distributive ideal of a Tory humanist.

The political economy that I find to be implicit in "Stray Pleasures" is an ideal political economy and differs in one very significant way from the traditional economists' trickle-down model. The political economy implicit in this poem is reciprocal. Value can trickle both up and down. As I shall attempt to demonstrate in my concluding chapter Wordsworth's conception of society was mythic, mythic not in the pejorative sense of fabulous and false, but in the sense that the anthropologist Claude Lévi-Strauss uses the term. For Lévi-Strauss mythic thought attempts to solve social problems: to replace social asymmetries with symmetries and to resolve through the method of mythic thought social contradictions that are ineluctably unresolvable on the level of social reality. In Wordsworth's mythic social world, for example, and these examples will be examined more closely in the last chapter, the gentle classes receive an inequitable proportion of the use-values distributed throughout the society. But, for their relative lack of use-values, the humble laborers receive a reciprocal spiritual prize, and not one that they must wait for the next world in order to enjoy. They are privileged to be the repositories of undistorted, undeflected pure humanity. Their direct and essential humanity is not pressed beneath layers of polite culture, false taste, and erudition. For this reason Wordsworth looks to them to find the human passions expressed in true and unmediated form. In his tract on Cintra Wordsworth suggests a further reciprocal exchange, which I shall examine later. If the wealthy possess more material goods than others they give up in return a degree of freedom. They are dependent upon the laboring classes, but the laboring classes are not dependent upon them.

It is clear that even with the reciprocity that this distributive system possesses, this system implies an antiegalitarian economic ethic. The accumulation of wealth is a social boon. In this political economy there is no exploitation, no forcible taking away of value from the producers of value. There is only possessing, on the one hand, and giving or distributing, on the other. Those that have have. Those that have not either receive directly from those that have or are given gleaning rights to appropriate the unused excess (precisely the social law that Harry Gill would not fulfill). Clearly Wordsworth is involved in a rentier's mystification of actual property relations. In the place of actual property relations a hierarchic social order is created in which none are exploited. Wordsworth's ideal community would be one in which everyone fit into the hierarchic structure of distribution.

Incidentally, to see pleasure as a use-value is to see pleasure as something that can be acquired. Pleasure can even be hoarded against feared future dearth. This insight offers another perspective from which to view Wordsworth's habitual tendency to store up the memories of beautiful landscapes for future enjoyment.

If pleasure, a use-value, became a value, that is a commodity value, how would Wordsworth respond? When confronted with a social order that converted all relations into commodity relations, all values into commodity values, Wordsworth would very likely be repelled. The consumption of pleasure in the form of a value would become totally egotistical. Sharing would no longer be an integral part of the moral order. The assumption that everyone had a right to a place in the social hierarchy would be discarded. A class would come into being that would appropriate pleasure and other values, leaving another social class from which value had been extracted. A world in which commodity ruled supreme would destroy the ordered, traditional, paternalistic, and natural economy. The development of wage labor would help to implement this process.

In the Lake counties surrounding Grasmere, production had not yet been totally subsumed by commodity production at the time of the opening of the nineteenth century. The production of use-values had not yet given way completely to production of commodity values. Producers did not primarily produce goods for the market. Even knitters and spinners produced, to some extent, for their own families (*Lakes* 246).

A concrete example of the distributive mechanism illustrated by "Stray Pleasures" can be found in a letter of Dorothy Wordsworth's. In a letter to Lady Beaumont dated November 5, 1805, Dorothy thanks the Beaumonts for having made a present of some game to the Wordsworth household.

> Again we all thank you for the game—it will almost make epi-
> cures of us—coming from you it will be such a feast, and we have
> had already another pleasure from it. Having a neighbor who is of
> Leicestershire we carried her a brace of the Partridges, and she es-
> teems them a great prize. (*E.L.* 636)

So Lord and Lady Beaumont give some of their bounty to the Wordsworths. The gift is more than sufficient, so the Wordsworths in their turn further distribute the bounty.

Indeed, one of Wordsworth's reasons for deploring poverty is that poverty deprives a man of the ability to participate actively in the distributive hierarchy. A poor man cannot be a subject in regard to distribution. He can only be an object. A poor man is deprived of what Wordsworth regards as a significant social potency. He does not have the power to inspire gratitude because he cannot give of himself, because he has nothing to give. In her biography of Wordsworth, Mary Moorman quotes a blank verse fragment that she assumes was to have been part of *The Recluse*. This fragment confirms that Wordsworth saw the poor man's inability to give as a deprivation, considering the social mechanism of distribution.

> What can we hope
> For one who is the worst of slaves, the slave
> Of his own home? The light that shines abroad,
> How can it lead him to an act of love?
> Whom can he comfort? Will the afflicted turn
> Their steps to him, or will the eye of grief
> And sorrow seek him? Is the name of friend
> Known to the poor man? Whence is he to hear
> The sweet creative voice of gratitude. . . .[8]

The old Cumberland beggar is valued precisely because he gives almost everyone and every being, except the little birds that eat the flour that falls from his palsied hand, the occasion to distribute part of their wealth. He leads them to "an act of love" and enables them to hear "The sweet creative voice of gratitude." He is not useless as the statesmen, who would pen him in a workhouse, believe him to be.

Dorothy, in her Journals, supplies evidence that even those far lower in social rank than Lord and Lady Beaumont participated in the nexus of distribution. Of May 22, 1802, she relates:

> We drank tea at a farm-house. The woman was very kind. There was a woman with 3 children travelling from Workington to Manchester. The woman served them liberally. Afterwards she said that she never suffered any to go away without a trifle 'sec as we have'. (*D.W.J* 127)

Pauperism was not unknown in the Lake counties (*Lakes* 290), and a society that saw the distribution of wealth to be an integral function of society would organize itself to deal with poverty. The Lake counties had such an organization. This would

tend to indicate that the system of distribution that underlay Wordsworth's poem "Stray Pleasures" existed in reality. This coincidence between social reality and Wordsworth's conception of social reality mitigates somewhat the negative image of Wordsworth
as a man with a dormitory vision.

A major part of poor relief in the Lake counties came out of
compulsory rates. The simplest kind of payment was payment in
cash or kind given directly to paupers living in their own homes
(*Lakes* 293). The disastrous Speenhamland system that drove down
wages by guaranteeing the relief recipient the difference between
his income and the money needed to purchase a given amount of
bread for his family was not much followed in the Lakes before
1832. In average parishes relief to the aged and infirm was £1.6d
per week (*Lakes* 306). Since bastards were a charge upon the
parish, officers bribed or forced expectant mothers to settle in other
parishes (*Lakes* 296). The majority of paupers lived outside of
workhouses (*Lakes* 306). Those poor regarded as being deserving
were not sent to workhouses; but the threat of the workhouse was
held over those poor who were regarded as being undeserving
(*Lakes* 301). The parish would in the end bury those for whom
private burial funds were unavailable. Dorothy records such a
burial in Grasmere in the September 3, 1800 entry in her *Journal*
(*D.W.J.* 38).

According to Peter Laslett begging was universal in traditional
society.[9] Dorothy's *Grasmere Journal* provides more than ample
evidence that this was so. On May 14, 1800 a woman "begged a
halfpenny" blaming her ill fortune to "hard times." Later that day
a woman "begged at the door" who had "buried her husband and
three children within a year and a half" (*D.W.J.* 16). On May 17
"a half crazy old man . . . begged a pin, afterwards a halfpenny"
(*D.W.J* 17). On May 19 a "little girl from Coniston came to beg
. . . her step-mother had turned her out of doors" (*D.W.J.* 17).
Come June 9 and a "poor Girl called to beg who had no work at
home and was going in search of it to Kendal" (*D.W.J.* 25). June
16 brought a seven-year-old boy who was begging for a meal.
"When I asked him if he got enough to eat he looked surprised
and said 'Nay' " (*D.W.J.* 28). Four days later "a poor man called,
a hatter." The "parish would not help him because he had imple-

ments of trade. . . . We gave him 6d" (D.W.J. 28). The hatter was in the same difficulty with his parish, it would seem, as was the shepherd in "The Last of the Flock." On December 22, 1801 Mary and William encountered a seventy-five-year-old man begging. He had "been 57 years at sea" but had no pension (D.W.J. 71). The next day a "broken soldier came to beg in the morning. Afterwards a tall woman, dressed somewhat in a tawdry style. . . ." (D.W.J. 73). On February 12, 1802 "a poor woman came, *she said* to beg some rags for her husband's leg which had been wounded by a slate from the Roof. . . . When the woman was gone, I could not help thinking that we are not half thankful enough that we are placed in that condition of life in which we are." (D.W.J. 89). This sudden recognition is but a prosaic version of Lear's belated fellow feeling for the poor naked wretches who routinely endure what it is Lear's misfortunes to bear on the storm-drenched heath.

Several things are remarkable about this sorry catalogue of beggars recorded in Dorothy's *Journal*. For one thing, it is difficult to comprehend the enormity of human suffering that is suggested here. For as an historical document, the *Journal* can do little more than hint at the true amount of forever unrecorded human suffering and social displacement. One is forced to ask whether anyone who did not have a rentier's vision could describe the Vale of Grasmere as being more blissful than Eden, as Wordsworth does in "Home at Grasmere," begun in 1800, at the same time that Dorothy is beginning her catalogue of mendicants, though mostly written as late as 1806. It is, of course, difficult to determine whether the moral sensitivity that a modern reader brings to Dorothy's account of what seems to be large-scale social displacement and suffering is not a sensitivity that has been created in the intervening century and a half, and therefore not to be expected in a journal written at the opening of the nineteenth century. Yet I am struck by how blandly many of these encounters are recorded. The entry for February 11, 1802 is troublingly typical. "Wm. still in his bed. 2 beggars today. I continued to read to him" (D.W.J. 88). Only twice does Dorothy seem to sense the full weight of the human actuality before her, first in her encounter with the pensionless old tar, and again in her encounter with the woman begging for rags. In Dorothy's defense, the fact that she took the trouble to record these encounters at all may be testimony to a sense of humanity that was troubled by the suffering that she saw almost daily. Finally, it is necessary to observe that the Wordsworth household obeyed the moral economy of distribution implicit in "Stray Pleasures." They gave of what they had to those who had less.

Grasmere could be an ideal community for Wordsworth, a retreat from "all remembrance of a jarring world" despite the presence of beggars. Of Grasmere he still found himself able to say in "Home at Grasmere,"

> That extreme penury is here unknown,
> And cold and hunger's abject wretchedness,
> Mortal to body, and the heaven-born mind. . . .
> (P.W. 5:325)

The result of this absence of extreme penury is

> That they who want, are not too great a weight
> For those who can relieve. Here may the heart
> Breathe in the air of fellow-suffering
> Dreadless, as in a kind of fresher breeze
> Of her own native element, the hand
> Be ready and unwearied without plea
> From tasks too frequent, or beyond its power
> For languor, or indifference, or despair.
> (P.W. 5:326)

In this Edenic community it is possible to confront and even to derive some pleasure from the suffering of economic hardship, because such hardship can be alleviated. It is possible to "Breathe in the air of fellow-suffering . . . in a kind of fresher breeze." Is it totally unfair to Wordsworth to find him, in this passage, to be morally self-satisfied and even morally insensitive? It might be justifiable to feel satisfied that all in need can be helped, but there is at least a suggestion here that it is pleasurable to live among needy who can be helped. And this is a refusal of human connection, a refusal that William Blake was incapable of making and one whose mechanism Blake understood with all the outraged irony of which he was a master:

Pity would be no more,
If we did not make somebody Poor;
And Mercy no more could be,
If all were as happy as we. . . .[10]

Wordsworth lived at a time in which few were able to envision a world in which there would be no poverty. Only a profound consciousness of some of the implications of the Industrial Revolution would make it possible for such a vision to be shared by many. This historical consideration suggests that it is anachronistic to bring Wordsworth to the moral dock, as I have done. But even when due attention has been given to the niceties of accurate scholarship, the moral vision of William Blake, Wordsworth's great contemporary, rises up to accuse Wordsworth of moral deficiency.

Wordsworth began "Home at Grasmere" in 1800, three years before the end of what E. P. Thompson calls the Golden Age of the cottage weaver,[11] and one year before Parliament passed the General Act of Enclosure, which greatly facilitated driving squatters from village common ground and marginal freeholders and copyholders from their holdings. How would Wordsworth respond to the increased social suffering and displacement brought about by increased enclosures and the stress caused by a slump among the cottage weavers? I have attempted to show that Wordsworth used the ravaged solitaries whom he encountered as psychic vehicles upon whom he projected his feared contracted self. Wordsworth, I have proposed, derived pleasure from the release the ravaged solitaries afforded him from his anxiety of contraction, but he paid for his pleasure by feeling guilt. When the speaker leaves the helpless and grateful Simon Lee, the speaker is mourning. It is possible that a marked increase in social suffering produced a quantity of guilt that overbalanced the forbidden pleasure afforded Wordsworth when he projected his ravaged self upon hapless "relicks." Whereas prior to the accelerating disintegration of the natural economy, he had been able to appease his guilt by finding lodgings for the discharged soldier or by giving alms to beggars, increased pauperism may have rendered such a solution unfeasible.

To put the matter another way, if when those who wanted were not too great a weight for those who could relieve, the heart could "Breathe in the air of fell-suffering . . . as in a kind of fresher breeze." Perhaps the breeze would become putrid if "extreme-penury" became more prevalent and those in want become too great a burden for those who could relieve. A quantitative social change could, after some critical point, produce a qualitative change in the way Wordsworth responded to the social world around him.

There were charities for the poor of the Lake counties other than public relief or the private dole. There were dispensaries to provide medicine and medical attention for the poor. These dispensaries were financed by public subscription. The earliest such dispensary was founded in Carlisle in 1782. Cockermouth followed in 1785 (Lakes 308). Charitable institutions such as these are indicative of a sense of a moral responsibility that the gentle classes had for the poor. In a letter to Jane Pollard dated December 7 and 8, 1788, Dorothy writes "We have, I think, visited most of the poor people in the parish . . ." (E.L. 23). Jane Austen portrays Emma making similar visits. In a letter to Lady Beaumont, dated July 23, 1806, Dorothy relays the news that one of the Wordsworth's former servants, Peggy Marsh, "overflows with gratitude" for the £5 that Lady Beaumont sent upon learning that Peggy's house had been damaged by fire (M.L. 56).

The single incident that best shows the gentry, Wordsworth included, banding together to help sustain the unfortunate is the tragedy of the Greens, first mentioned in Dorothy's March 28, 1808 letter to Catherine Clarkson (M.L. 203–204). George and Sarah Green, the poorest couple in Grasmere, had set out for Langsdale in order to attend a sale. They left their five youngest children in the care of their eleven-year-old daughter. George and Sarah fell to their deaths while returning home, leaving behind a brood of orphans and little property besides a heavily mortgaged bit of land. After describing this in much richer detail than I have given, Dorothy writes, "Since this melancholy event our thoughts have been chiefly employed in laying schemes to prevent the children from falling into the hands of persons, who may use them unkindly, and for giving them decent educations" (M.L. 206).

The Wordsworth household undertook to house, feed and clothe Sally Green, until she was old enough to care for herself. During the intervening period of about two years Sally was to be sent to school at Grasmere in order to learn to sew. Then the Wordsworths would try to find a place for her as a hired servant. In addition, a subscription was raised among the gentry in order to obtain funds for the care of the orphans. William proved to be energetic as a canvasser, writing to friends such as Francis Wrangham (*M.L.* 211–214) and wealthy merchant associates such as Richard Sharp (*M.L.* 210–211). Wordsworth even composed some elegiac stanzas for the Greens, which he sent to Coleridge on the chance that Coleridge could somehow use the verses to benefit the orphans (*M.L.* 219–220). Eventually £300 was raised for the orphaned Green children and all but one put out to homes in the vale. One boy found a home in Ambleside.

There is no discrepancy between the story of the Greens and the social world Wordsworth created in his own poetry. In "The Brothers," written in 1800, eight years before the deaths of George and Sarah Green, we are told that Leonard and James Ewbank had been left, after the death of their parents, in the care of their paternal grandfather Walter. After Walter Ewbank's death the eldest of the two orphaned boys, Leonard, left Ennerdale to seek his fortune on the seas. The community of Ennerdale took collective responsibility for the care of James.

> He was the child of all the dale—he lived
> Three months with one, and six months with another;
> And he wanted neither food, nor clothes, nor love:
> And many, many happy days were his.
>
> (*P.W.* 2:10)

The activity of the community in coming to the aid of the Green children obviously was a great boon to the needy children, but for Wordsworth the support of the community was, I think, more than a generous aid. For Wordsworth, community support offered as well the protection needed to maintain the fragile hold on being to anyone opposed by the forces of dissolution. The old Cumberland beggar is, though alone, involved in the nexus of community charity. Therefore, the old beggar not only survives, but survives to an almost incredible old age. The fate of the abandoned Indian woman in "The Complaint of a Forsaken Indian Woman" (*P.W.* 2:40–42), written in 1798, is quite different from that of the Cumberland beggar. Her tribe, her community, deserts her and she must die. True, in the poem the tribe leaves her because she is dying, not in order to cause her death. But the symbolic correlation between isolation from a sustaining community and death is effectively established.

But the story of the Greens and what their misfortune reveals about Wordsworth's idea of community is not finished. In a letter to Coleridge written sometime in late May or early June, 1808, Wordsworth attempts to explain why he believes that no more money should be raised for the orphans. What emerges from his explanation is a Tory humanist conception of a community structured by traditional social rank and degree and a belief that such a hierarchic community must be preserved. Wordsworth's first reason for opposing the subscription of additional funds for the Green children is that "a sum considerably exceeding what is already raised, would have excited much envy and unkindly feeling among the poor families of this neighborhood, many of which may deem themselves equally needing and deserving . . ." (*M.L.* 239). That is, it seems likely, nothing should be done that might make the poor restive; especially not something that might make them aspire to greater material well-being than it is their lot to endure. Wordsworth is far more explicit in giving his second reason. He wishes to avoid "much irregular and romantic expectation in distressed persons, an evil which cannot altogether be prevented at present . . ." (*M.L* 239). Finally, there is the risk that if too much is done for the Green children, they might be "puffed up with vanity and pride . . ." (*M.L.* 240). Such feelings would be inappropriate for the social station that it is the children's destined place to inhabit. To be sure, and for that matter, to be fair, this is not the result that Wordsworth explicitly fears from vanity and pride, but it *is* implicit. What Wordsworth expressly fears is that the children will be led to "associate unworthy feelings of complacency with the melancholy end of their parents" (*M.L.* 240).

Wordsworth's concern lest too much be done for the orphaned children reveals that he was part of a social order in which

eveyone is allotted a social rank and a social function. This alloca-
tion of social roles must be maintained. Such a traditional society
is far from the conception of a society in which careers were open
to all talent, or in which there was *egalité des joissances*. The conception of community that led to fears lest the Green children be
helped beyond what was appropriate to their social rank is a traditional conception of community and to some degree even a feudal
conception. In a childhood recollection of a shepherd in Book VIII
of *The Prelude* Wordsworth uses an implicit metaphor that expresses a feudal view of society.

> A rambling Schoolboy, thus
> Have I beheld him, without knowing why
> Have felt his presence in his own domain,
> As of a Lord and Master; or a Power
> Or Genius, under Nature, under God,
> Presiding. . . .
>
> (*Prel.* VIII, 390–395)

The shepherd is independent, is a "Lord and Master" but only "in
his own domain," while at the same time he is even there dependent. He exercises his sovereignty only "under Nature, under
God,/Presiding." He holds his power, but only under fief. In his
domain he is powerful but his domain is sharply limited. This
strongly suggests a hierarchical social ideal.

The implicit metaphor is telling. Each man in society has his
allotted place in which he is free to exercise his will. In his place,
and only in his place, he has dignity and worth. His power is
presided over by one more highly ranked and more powerful than
he. Nor should he be allowed to fall below his station. As with the
Green children, society intervenes to prevent any of its members
from falling lower in the social scale than is their right.

This conception of society is illustrated by an interesting
poem that has received surprisingly little attention in Wordsworth
scholarship. That poem is "A narrow Girdle of rough stones and
crags" (*P.W.* 2:115–117) composed on October 10, 1800. The
poem records an October day when Wordsworth, Dorothy and
Coleridge went for a walk along the lake at Grasmere. It was a day
given to leisure and observation.

> It was our occupation to observe
> Such objects as the waves had tossed ashore—
> Feather, or leaf, or weed, or withered bough,
> Each on the other heaped, along the line
> Of the dry wreck. And, in our vacant mood,
> Not seldom did we stop to watch some tuft
> Of dandelion seed or thistle's beard,
> That skimmed the surface of the dead calm lake,
> Suddenly halting now—a lifeless stand!

They are not, it is clear, industriously engaged. But this does not prevent them from delighting in the sound of the industry of others.

> . . . from the fields,
> Meanwhile, a noise was heard, the busy mirth
> Of reapers, men and women, boys and girls.

While the three are enjoying the lake and the sound of reapers gathering in the corn they see a tall man "Attired in peasant's garb" fishing on the margin of the lake.

> "Improvident and reckless," we exclaimed,
> "The Man must be, who thus can lose a day
> Of the mid harvest, when the labourer's hire
> Is ample, and some little might be stored
> Wherewith to cheer him in the winter time."

For Wordsworth the moral purpose of the poem is the admonition that the three companions are about to receive against the vice of "Rash-Judgment." As they approach the man they see that he is haggard and gaunt, so weak and ill as to be incapable of participating in the harvest. He is, instead, trying to find sustenance by fishing. It had been rash to judge him a slacker on so cursory a view.

What I find interesting in the poem is that it contains an implicit ratification of the traditional social order in which each man has a social role correlative to his social rank. There is nothing immoral or improvident in two gentlemen, formerly of Cambridge, and a female relation idling away on October day sauntering about a lake. But until an excuse is discovered, the same three are distressed at the sight of an idle peasant at harvest time. Without the extenuating circumstance of illness, laborers must work if they are not to suffer deprivation later. Gentlemen may saunter. To be sure, as I have shown, gentlemen have their own responsibilities. They must give to the needy and help the poor in cases of extreme distress.

Lurking behind the initial condemnation of what was presumed to be working-class idleness is unconscious class interest. A laborer who withholds himself from the pool of working people, contributes to the scarcity of labor. This scarcity raises the price of labor, which in turn, all other things remaining equal, raises the cost of commodities. This economic formulation is especially important when the labor withheld is withheld from the production of foodstuffs. As it is necessary for the worker to eat in order to produce and reproduce himself, an elevation of the price of food creates pressure for a corresponding rise in the price of labor, which in turn makes all commodities dearer.

It is not necessary to assume that Wordsworth, Dorothy and Coleridge understood either consciously or fully the economic mechanism by which scarcity of labor results in dearer goods. Without such full and conscious knowledge the three might still, by means of intuitive class interest, recognize that an idle worker undercut their economic and class interest. Coleridge and the Wordsworths maintained their gentility only with difficulty. More expensive food and other goods were a hardship for them. Hence their instantaneous, automatic and premature distress. Nevertheless this argument does not suggest that the three were operating from conscious class self-interest; they were not being selfish and base. I shall return to "A narrow Girdle of rough stones and crags" in my discussion of Wordsworth's unconscious class prejudice and condescension.

The traditional social order that Wordsworth had come to support by 1800 was easily disrupted. It could function where "extreme penury is . . . unknown." Within this context I would like to return to the poem "The Last of the Flock" (P.W. 2:43–46) which portrays the moral disintegration of a shepherd as he becomes increasingly impoverished. To recapitulate, the speaker meets a man on the road who is weeping as he carries a lamb in his arms. On asking what ails the weeping man, the speaker is told that the lamb that he is carrying is the last of a flock of fifty sheep and that the lamb is now being carried away to be sold. The man had fallen upon hard times and been refused relief by the parish. Consequently he had been forced to sell his once-thriving flock one by one in order to sustain himself, his wife, and six children.

What makes this poem significant for my purposes is that it demonstrates that the maintenance of a community of natural and wholesome affection within the traditional social order is contingent upon economic stability. When the shepherd's prosperity ceases he develops an impulse to do evil; he becomes a suspicious, asocial being incapable of participating in the mutual interchange that helps make up community; and, as he becomes progressively more poor, he becomes progressively less capable of loving. That is, he becomes less capable of breaking through the barriers of egoistic self-concern and of generating affection for others, which is the coalescing social power of the traditional community. As a result of his poverty:

> "To wicked deeds I was inclined,
> And wicked fancies crossed my mind;
> And every man I chanced to see,
> I thought he knew some ill of me. . . ."

His capacity to love, which is for Wordsworth the capacity to be a social being, is directly proportional to his prosperity.

> "Sir! 'twas a precious flock to me,
> As dear as my own children be;
> For daily with my growing store
> I loved my children more and more.
> Alas! it was an evil time;
> God cursed me in my sore distress;
> I prayed, yet every day I thought
> I loved my children less. . . ."

Poverty turns the shepherd into an antisocial being.

The poem seems to suggest that men are kept whole by security and property. Economic insecurity creates a situation in which the self receives insufficient support and becomes unstable. This

situation results in evil or in madness or in both. The passage
quoted indicates that economic adversity may drive the self into
madness:

> "No peace, no comfort could I find,
> No ease, within doors or without;
> And crazily and wearily
> I went my work about;
> And oft was moved to flee from home,
> And hide my head where wild beasts roam."

If the traditional social order's ability to maintain a community of mutually sustaining affective ties was contingent upon the
maintenance and prosperity of the natural economy, then the in-
filtration of the newer, more rationalized, more blatantly egotistical and calculating forms of capitalism, as it existed at the
beginning of the nineteenth century, into the natural economy,
could only be destructive of these ties. The bonds of affection between Michael and his son Luke, in the poem "Michael" (*P.W.*,
80–94), composed in 1800, are sundered as a result of the corrosive effect of a trade crisis upon the natural economy of Michael's
household. Michael "had been bound/In surety for his brother's
son," and though his nephew is a man "Of an industrious life, and
ample means . . . unforseen misfortunes suddenly/Had pressed
upon him." This unforseen necessity from another economic
world forces Michael to choose between selling half of "his patrimonial fields" or sending his only and beloved son Luke away to
the city in order to earn enough money to pay off the surety
without alienating the patrimonial heritage. Michael chooses the
latter. Luke is sent off to the city where he eventually

> . . . gave himself
> To evil courses: ignominy and shame
> Fell on him, so that he was driven at last
> To seek a hiding-place beyond the seas.

There is literally no way of conveying old Michael's loss and pain
when his son failed to live up to his paternal expectations and
failed as well to fulfill what Michael himself called "a covenant"
between the two. Many a day Michael went to sheepfold "And

never lifted up a single stone." One has to reach back to Lear's "Pray you, undo this button," to find so simple a line so resonant with power.

As social history "Michael" is relatively accurate. Raymond Williams notes that by "the late eighteenth century we can properly speak of an organized capitalist society, in which what happened to the market, anywhere, whether in industrial or agricultural production, worked its way through to town and country alike, as parts of a single crisis."[12] And according to Bouch and Jones, by the late eighteenth century many people in the Lake District were involved directly or indirectly in commercial ventures, often at great risk. Gentlemen, merchants, mariners, sailmakers, blacksmiths, tanners, tradesmen, shopkeepers and even yeomen all invested in ships (*Lakes* 272). They would put forward a given amount of capital in fitting out a ship in the expectation that through trade the ship would bring home a rich enough cargo to guarantee each investor a handsome profit. Wordsworth and his sister invested heavily in what turned out to be their brother John's last voyage. As captain of the *Earl of Abergavenny*, John Wordsworth was expecting to make a substantial profit on a voyage that was to end in disaster on February 5, 1805 when the *Earl of Abergavenny* foundered and sank off Portland Bill on the southern coast of England, west of Bournemouthe. John drowned. Only insurance preserved the surviving Wordsworths directly from a financial loss such as Michael had suffered indirectly.

Besides economic stability there is one more precondition that must be met before Wordsworth's ideal conception of a rural polity is fully realized. For Wordsworth, the social precondition for human beauty is that man's labor be free and unalienated. No matter how hard a man might work, the product of his labor must be his to dispose of as he chooses. Nor should the rhythm of his work be dictated by any will other than his own. He describes man in the region in which he grew up as

> Man free, man working for himself, with choice
> Of time, and place, and object; by his wants,
> His comforts, native occupations, cares,
> Conducted on to individual ends
> Or social, and still followed by a train

Unwoo'd, unthought-of even, simplicity,
And beauty, and inevitable grace.
(*Prel.* VIII, 153–158)

Not only is man not alienated from the product of his labor, he is so unified with the object of his labor, the land, that it is possible to define the man in terms of the object of his labor. The original published text of "Michael" contains the following lines about Michael and the land he worked upon:

. . . these fields, these hills,
Which were his living Being, even more
Than his own blood. . . .
(*P.W.* 2:82)

This fragment suggests that Michael is virtually interpenetrated with the land he works. A related unity between man and land is suggested in "Home at Grasmere." Grasmere is a place:

. . . where he who tills the field,
He, happy Man! is master of the field,
And treds the mountains which his Fathers trod.
(*P.W.* 5:326)

Earlier, this same passage stresses the importance of being an independent worker. Man is not separated from the conditions or objects of his labor:

. . . Labour here preserves
His rosy face, a Servant only here
Of the fire-side, or of the open field,
A Freeman, therefore, sound and unimpaired. . . .
(*P.W.* 5:325)

Manual labor would be degrading for Wordsworth were it not for the independent status of the worker. A laborer, because he must work excessive hours, is, according to Wordsworth, more self-involved than a gentleman. His spirit is circumscribed by his daily necessity to struggle to support himself. He is continually involved in self-preservation. But labor in Grasmere is unalienated and is graced with Nature's beauty. Therefore, the laborer is not circumscribed in the way that Wordsworth would assume to be otherwise normal. Writing in defense of the significance of the emotions felt by the laboring class of Grasmere, Wordsworth writes:

> Nor deem
> These feelings, though subservient more than ours
> To every day's demand for daily bread,
> And borrowing more their spirit, and their shape
> From self-respecting interests, deem them not
> Unworthy therefore, and unhallowed. . . .
>
> (P.W. 5:328)

If Wordsworth's shepherds are beautiful and free, their beauty and freedom are not based on "the suppression of work in the countryside," a suppression that for Raymond Williams underlies most idealizations of the countryside. The labor of Wordsworth's shepherds is both toilsome and unalienated at one and the same time. The shepherd is a free man not because he has leisure. On the contrary, he works long hours. He is free because, self-employed, he is free of the tyranny of the clock or overseer:

> He feels himself
> In those vast regions where his service is
> A Freeman; wedded to his life of hope
> And hazard, and hard labour interchang'd
> With that majestic indolence so dear
> To native Man.
>
> (Prel. VIII, 385–390)

Wordsworth values the independent statesman, the Cumbrian term for small independent proprietors of land, with difficult but unalienated labor because the statesman represents a traditional, as opposed to a new, social form. He personifies the natural economy. His connection with the land is direct rather than indirect. It is not mediated by the cash nexus.

I have tried to portray Wordsworth's ideal of social community in some detail, having examined the force that bound the community together, the limits of power of each inhabitant, the principles of patriarchal power and patrilineal transmission of land, the structure of the means of distribution of goods and charities, the social hierarchy, the limits of poverty beyond which the system would cease to function, and the ideal conditions of labor. I shall now examine Wordsworth's assumptions, both conscious and unconscious, about the nature and worth of the working inhabitants of this ideal community. For if keeping his eye steadily on the object was a point of pride with Wordsworth (*Prose* 1:132), Blake understood even more profoundly that "the Eye altering alters all." [13] What kind of eye did Wordsworth keep steadily on the dalesman of Cockermouth, Hawkshead and Grasmere? What assumptions underlay his ideal social community, often, perhaps, unbeknownst to Wordsworth himself? The answers to these questions will seem strange and even shocking to the many readers of Wordsworth such as M. H. Abrams who have seen in Wordsworth's apparent solicitude for the poor and the humble a transformation of the republican passion Wordsworth had formerly harbored for the French Revolution. Abrams writes:

> Having given up the hope of revolutionizing the social and political structure, Wordsworth has discovered that his new calling, his divine "mission," condemning him to a period of inevitable neglect and scorn, is to effect through his poetry an egalitarian revolution of spirit. . . .[14]

This is a pleasant notion and it makes matters simple by positing a direct transposition of humanitarian sympathies, but as Jeffrey wrote in the opening of his review of *The Excursion*, "This will not do."[15]

Coleridge, it seems to me, had the most profound insight into Wordsworth's position as an observer of life in the Lake Counties. Wordsworth, as Coleridge saw him, was the observer *ab extra*.[16] Wordsworth's relation to the region of his birth is similar to that of Leonard in "The Brothers." Like Leonard, Wordsworth was born and raised in the Lakes. Like Leonard, Wordsworth left the Lakes for the great world and like Leonard, Wordsworth returned to the Lakes as an adult. When Wordsworth returned to the Lakes, Cambridge, London, and France lay behind him and within him. He was changed from the young Hawkshead student who had gone south to Cambridge. In a sense he had returned to a world that he could never again be part of, never again, that is, return to. His relationship to the Lakes was highly ambivalent. On the one hand, he was indigenous to the country. It was his native region. On the other hand, his personal history—Cambridge, London and France—had uprooted him. He was more aware of other social possibilities than he had been when he first left the Lakes. In the older sense of the word he had become sophisticated, that is, falsified. The relationship he could now establish with the Lakes was a strange one. It was conducive to a self-conscious awareness of himself as an observer. He was, in short, an observer *ab extra*. He was drawn by all his childhood to what he observed, and kept distanced from what he observed by all that he had experienced since adolescence. He was, to quote Walt Whitman, "Both in and out of the game and watching and wondering at it." [17]

Even if his travels had not separated Wordsworth from the dalesmen whom he observed, his adult consciousness of his class status would surely have done so. He was not, as he may have been in childhood or may have wished to believe he was after his return, a fellow with the dalesmen in the fellowship of nature. He was a gentleman. The shepherds and the solitaries were not. His awareness of and his desire to maintain his gentleness created a gulf between him and the common folk he observed. He could observe them. But he would always be an observer apart from them.

Reconsider for a moment "A narrow Girdle of rough stones and crags." The poem is intentionally a didactic poem. Wordsworth has been in error, and the poem calls into question and then rejects the precipitous action that is called into question, hasty judgment. What is more significant are the judgments that the poem makes, and, by not calling them to question, implicitly endorses. It is assumed that it is perfectly appropriate and moral for two gentlemen poets and a gentlewoman to spend a leisurely day investigating the borders of a lake. It is also assumed that a "peasant," provided that he is in good health, is guilty of a breach of the moral and social code if, during harvest time, he spends a day at leisure fishing. The assumption that a laborer has violated the moral and social code if he enjoys his leisure at a time when he could profitably be earning money is based on the prior assumption that such a laborer is guilty of a crime against himself, that he is reckless of the winter ahead. But a man who had taken insufficient care to provide for himself might be forced upon the rates and therefore become an expense to the gentry. These assumptions remain unchallenged in the poem because they are based upon an accepted and internalized code that describes what is appropriate for each social class. This code is taken to be self-evident in its validity. The assumptions of class superiority implicit in this code are not subjected to critical scrutiny. It is powerful testimony to the cultural hegemony of the ruling orders that the ruling orders succeeded, in large part, in gaining working class acceptance of this code. Peasants must labor; gentlemen may leisure. Wordsworth does not see his class preconceptions. He does not see the historical constraints that limit his consciousness, as they limit the consciousnesses of all those subject to history. As a result he is unaware of the assumptions and of the limitations that shape his preconceptions. The reader is left with the same feeling of discomfort that he experiences when, in reading Aristotle's *Politics*, he finds the slave described as a natural instrument of production.[18]

Wordsworth gives direct expression to his class condescension in Book VII of *The Prelude*. He takes in the popular forms of entertainment enjoyed by the London populace. As he observes these entertainments, "Amid the uproar of the rabblement," he finds it no "mean delight/To watch crude nature work in untaught minds . . . (*Prel.* VII, 295–297). He does not even attempt to mask his condescension and contempt. It was not necessary for him to go all the way to London to view the "crude" and often violent pleasures of the ungentle classes. He could have stayed in the Lakes and seen cockfighting, which was widespread there. There was hardly a village in which cockfights were not occasionally held. Within ten miles of Ulverston thousands of cocks perished each year (*Lakes* 343). In her *Journal* entry for June 6, 1800, Dorothy records that she has been kept awake by the sound of cockfighting (*D.W.J.* 24). But Wordsworth with his rentier's vision is intent on idealizing the country in respect to the city. He overlooks or forgets the cockfighting prevalent in his native region and dwells instead on London's "Saw singers, Rope-dancers, Giants and Dwarfs,/Clowns, Conjurors, Posture-masters, Harlequins" (*Prel.* VII, 293–294).

There can be no question but that Wordsworth had an idealized vision of the Lake Country and of the men who inhabited it. Wordsworth saw the most perfect era of Lake Country life as lying in the past. There were social forces at work changing the social and economic structure of the Lakes, so that in some objective sense Wordsworth's native district had changed since his birth and was to continue changing throughout his life. There had been for some time a continuing flow of capital into England's agricultural regions and the consequent rationalization of previous traditional, patriarchal social relations.

Marx regarded the natural economy that Wordsworth valued so highly as an unstable economic form within the context of capitalist development, as "a necessary transitional stage for the development of agriculture itself." In the chapter of volume III of *Capital*, entitled "Genesis of Capitalist Ground-Rent," Marx analyzes in some detail why the natural economy was doomed to be but a "transitional stage."

> The causes which bring about its downfall show its limitations. These are: Destruction of rural domestic industry, which forms its normal supplement as a result of the development of large-scale industry; a gradual impoverishment and exhaustion of the soil subjected to cultivation; usurpation by big land owners of the common lands, which constitute the second supplement of the management of land parcels everywhere and which alone enable it to raise cattle; competition, either of the plantation system or large-scale capitalist agriculture. Improvements in agriculture, which on the one hand cause a fall in agricultural prices and, on the other, require greater outlays and more extensive material conditions of production, also contribute towards this. . . . Usury and a taxation system must impoverish it everywhere. The expenditure of capital in the price of land withdraws this capital from cultivation. An infinite fragmentation of means of production, and isolation of the producers themselves. Monstrous waste of human energy. Progressive deterioration of conditions of production and increased prices of means of production—an inevitable law of proprietorship of parcels. Calamity of seasonal abundance for this mode of production. [19]

Marx's analysis of the disadvantages of "Proprietorship of land parcels" continues for nine pages. Marx points out that the farming of land in small private parcels "by its very nature excludes the development of social productive forces of labour . . . and the progressive application of science." [20]

The economic form, the natural economy, that was the basis of Wordsworth's ideal community, was, along with all other stages in the development of the means of production, a transitional form. Wordsworth was aware that his primary allegiance lay with a social world threatened with extinction unless measures were taken to preserve it.

One little-read poem, "Repentance" (P.W. 2:46–47), written perhaps in 1804 and first published in 1820, illustrates how the influx of new capital subverts and destroys the natural economy as it exists in one parcel of patrilineally inherited land. The poem is narrated by the wife of Allen, a man who succumbs to the "purse" of a "troublesome Tempter," and sells his family's house and fields, for what seemed to be a large quantity of "gold." Perhaps the buyer is a well-to-do capitalist who is systematically buying up adjacent small holdings in order to rationalize and improve them, in which case natural economy would be yielding to capitalist development.

What is significant about the poem is that it attempts to show that while the family was part of the traditional natural economy it was fulfilled, but after it has exchanged the family holding for a sum of gold, it can never again be happy. Before they sold the land:

> There dwelt we, as happy as birds in their bowers;
> Unfettered as bees that in gardens abide;
> We could do what we liked with the land, it was ours;
> And for us the brook murmured that ran by its side.

They could do what they wished with the land. They were free, unregulated by any outside agency. But now they are "strangers" though still living in the same neighborhood. They are outcasts bewildered and depressed. Having been separated from their paternal holding their spirits are broken:

> But now we are strangers, go early or late;
> And often, like one over burthened with sin,

> With my hand on the latch of the half-opened gate,
> I look at the fields, but I cannot go in!

Of the time before their "birthright was lost" the mother can say, "With our pastures about us, we could not be sad. . . ." After having alienated themselves from the land, she says, "Now I cleave to the house and am dull as a snail. . . ." The natural economy is easily destroyed.

Wordsworth can look back to a time when the natural economy was more integrated. He makes this clear in *A Guide through the District of the Lakes*. There are passages in this *Guide*, present in the earliest version of the manuscript, written in 1809 as a preface for a collection of Joseph Wilkinson's engravings of the Lakes, that state clearly Wordsworth's view that the Lakes had previously been an Edenic district whose past was less flawed and less disrupted than its present. He writes of a period "within the last sixty years."

> Towards the head of these Dales was found a perfect Republic of Shepherds and Agriculturists, among whom the plow of each man was confined to the maintenance of his own family, or to the occasional accommodation of his neighbour. . . . The chapel was the only edifice that presided over these dwellings, the supreme head of this pure Commonwealth. . . . (*Prose* 2:206)

Wordsworth emphasizes that each man worked for himself and his family. His labor was not alienated, nor was patriarchal sway threatened. Wordsworth goes on to indicate that this commonwealth was not divided by social distintions; "Neither highborn nobleman, knight, nor esquire was here . . ." (*Prose* 2:206). Further, Wordsworth stresses that the principle of patrilineal inheritance governed the distribution of land: ". . . [M]any of these humble sons of the hills had a consciousness that the land, which they walked over and tilled, had for more than five hundred years been possessed by men of their name and blood . . ." (*Prose* 2:206).

When considering this picture of a now past egalitarian commonwealth it is necessary to bear in mind not only Wordsworth's penchant for glorifying the past, and Marx's critical analysis, but also an observation of Raymond Williams:

> A sanctity of property has to co-exist with violently changing prop-
> erty relations, and an ideal of charity with the harshness of labour
> relations in both the new and the old modes. This is then the . . .
> source of the idea of an ordered and happier past set against the dis-
> turbance and disorder of the present. An idealization, based on a
> temporary situation and on a deep desire for stability, served to
> cover and to evade the actual and bitter contradictions of the
> time.[21]

But when one has given due consideration both to Wordsworth's
psychological peculiarities and to Williams' sharp observation,
there remains, nonetheless, a residuum of truth in Wordsworth's
belief than an ordered and traditional society, capable of producing fully developed and morally admirable human beings, was in
the process of disappearing.

From Wordsworth's poetry a picture emerges of life in the
Lake counties at the beginning of the nineteenth century. Sometimes Wordsworth accurately portrayed this life. At other times he
romanticised it. But at all times he was committed to preserving
intact the social world of the Lakes because he loved and valued
that world. And it is this commitment that explains the apparent
contradiction between, on the one hand, the assertion in the Preface to the *Lyrical Ballads* that it is the function of the poet to give
pleasure (*Prose* 1:139), and, on the other, Wordsworth's repeated
themes of isolation, sorrow, loss, old age and unrequited love. The
Lyrical Ballads were, on one level, political poems designed to educate the governing classes so that they might understand the
necessity of preserving what was for Wordsworth a valuable way of
life. Wordsworth might write about:

> Sorrow that is not sorrow, but delight,
> And miserable love that is not pain
> To hear of, for the glory that redounds
> Therefrom to human kind and what we are.
> <div align="right">(<i>Prel.</i> XII, 245–248)</div>

Wordsworth's argument here and in the 1800 Preface to the
Lyrical Ballads contains a basic contradiction, both sides of which
are closely interrelated, and Wordsworth's movement to a fully developed Tory humanism swings upon the hinge of his contra-

dictory and complex position, present as early as the first edition of *Lyrical Ballads* in 1798. On the one hand, by demonstrating that people of humble station feel intense sorrow and "miserable love," Wordsworth shows the gentle classes that, contrary to the prejudices of the gentry, the humble shepherd or cotter is capable of complete human and spiritual development, of full realization of his species being. To hear of this is "To Hear of . . . the glory that redounds . . . to human kind and what we are." This pole of the dialectic has been sufficiently noted and commented on by critics, from William Hazlitt who suggested of Wordsworth that "the political changes of the day were the model on which he formed and conducted his poetical experiments," and that his "Muse . . . is a levelling one," [22] to M. H. Abrams, whom I have already quoted in this context. But the other pole of the dialectic has been ignored. If such rude and humble men and women are in a significant sense fully developed human beings, then the social system that produced such men and women is both adequate and successful and should, therefore, be preserved from attempts to modify and improve it. The natural economy and hierarchical social order are precious, and one must protect them from social change and from misguided attempts to reform them. No new society will succeed as well in producing developed, fulfilled human beings. Wordsworth's later Tory humanism and conservatism was but the steady development of an aspect of his thought implicit in the *Lyrical Ballads* of 1798. Further, poetry that demonstrated the full humanity of the lower orders would be a source of pleasure, even self-congratulation, for the gentry, as such a demonstration would partially vindicate a social order in which they held a place of privilege. A poetic vision that proclaimed, not "All's right with the world," but rather that all was right with the social world to which the gentry were committed would offer them comfort, and alleviate their anxiety and fear of the possibility that a leveling tumult from the lower orders would destroy the society that they so valued.

According to Wordsworth, the second stage in his discovery of the full humanity of the lower orders was not the result of inspiration or accident. Rather, it was the result of conscious experiment. Having perceived the "utter hollowness" of "the Books/Of

modern Statists" and "of what we name/The wealth of Nations'
(*Prel.* XII, 77–80), alluding perhaps, to Adam Smith's book, *The
Wealth of Nations*, Wordsworth wishes to discover what is the true
source of "The dignity of individual Man" (*Prel.* XII, 83). He
wants to evaluate the correctness of those who make life in high
station the model of what man can be, at his most fully developed.
In making life in high station the measure of full humanity, "the
wealth of nations" is equated with human value. For if Wordsworth can find fully developed men among "those who liv'd/By
bodily labour" then the philosophies that attribute full humanity
only to the gentle classes "vanish into air." Wordsworth finds
human value among those who labor. This is certainly a generous
and humane attribution of full humanity to those without polite
accomplishments and polite manners. By this attribution, Wordsworth refutes the contentions of aristocratic privilege. This interpretation of the passage in Book XII of *The Prelude* that describes
Wordsworth's search for developed humanity among these who
labor is the traditional interpretation of the passage. This reading
seems to support the belief that Wordsworth simply transposed his
humanitarian impulses from France to Cumberland.

This traditional reading is correct as far as it goes, but it does
not go far enough, for if there is an antiaristocratic impulse in
Wordsworth's discovery, there is also its opposite, however latent.
The discovery that Wordsworth makes, at the same time that it denies the assumptions of the gentle classes, also helps to lay the
foundation of Wordsworth's later Tory humanism. If social and
economic inequality are not the "bars . . . thrown/By Nature in
the way of" the hope that all men may at some future time reach
the full measure of their potential human development, then social and economic inequality are not social evils in and of themselves. Traditional England is vindicated, although it may need
some improvements such as the introduction of universal education, and a lessening of the long hours of toil that the working
class must perform.

It is possible, with the discovery of full humanity among
those who live by "bodily labour," to dismiss, once and for all, the
doctrines of the French Revolution, according to which a complete overthrow of the traditional social order, accompanied by

radical social and economic change, would be necessary before all men could reach their full human potential. Here, below, is the passage that Janus-faced looks in two opposite political directions. Until now it has only been read as a refutation of arrogant aristocratic assumptions.

> I could not but inquire,
> Not with less interest than heretofore,
> But greater, though, in spirit more subdued,
> Why is this glorious Creature to be found
> One only in ten thousand? What one is,
> Why may not many be? What bars are thrown
> By Nature in the way of such a hope?
> Our animal wants and the necessities
> Which they impose, are these the obstacles?
> If not, then others vanish into air.
> Such meditations bred an anxious wish
> To ascertain how much of real worth
> And genuine knowledge, and true power of mind
> Did at this day exist in those who liv'd
> By bodily labour, labour far exceeding
> Their due proportion, under all the weight
> Of that injustice which upon ourselves
> By composition of society
> Ourselves entail. To frame such estimate
> I chiefly look'd (what need to look beyond?).
> Among the natural abodes of men,
> Fields with their rural works, recall'd to mind
> My earliest notions, with these compared
> The observations of my later youth,
> Continued downwards to that very day.
> (*Prel*. xii, 87–111)

Something is especially worthy of comment in the passage just quoted—the primitivist assumption. In the Preface to the *Lyrical Ballads* of 1800 and in the tract on the Convention of Cintra Wordsworth exhibits a belief that "the rudiments of nature" are best studied "in the walks of common life . . ." (*Prose* 1, 306). In the Preface to the *Lyrical Ballads* of 1800 Wordsworth wrote:

> Low and rustic life was generally chosen because in that situation the essential passions of the heart find a better soil in which they

can attain their maturity, are less under restraint, and speak a
plainer and more emphatic language; because in that situation our
elementary feelings exist in a state of greater simplicity and consequently may be more accurately contemplated and more forcibly
communicated; because the manners of rural life germinate from
those elementary feelings; and from the necessary character of rural
occupations are more easily comprehended; and are more durable.
. . . (*Prose* 1:124)

Wordsworth chooses to study "low and rustic life," "the natural
abodes of men," as an observer *ab extra* for the same reason that
contemporary students of human nature study primates, infants,
and "primitive" cultures. He believed that in studying rustics he
could more clearly see the invariables of human nature.

Wordsworth may have studied "Low and rustic life" for other
reasons as well. He may have wished to correct the social and political assumptions of the ruling class by educating them in "the
rudiments of nature." As I have suggested Wordsworth may have
wished to demonstrate that revolution was not necessary because
developed humanity was already observable among the common
people produced by traditional society. Finally, Wordsworth may
have wished to confirm his sense of the inadequacy of rationalist
culture, and his belief in the significance of rich and passionate
emotional intensity, by studying emotions in a culture in which
behavior was not freighted by polite encrustations.

That man is most truly human in an organic traditional social
world, not yet penetrated and contaminated by reason, is an Enlightenment assumption derived in part from Rousseau and the
notion of the noble savage. Perhaps this is an example of unconscious retrospective projection on Wordsworth's part, in which the
rustic is equated with the child. The projection could be put into
the following words, "As I was most truly human in the Golden
Age of my youth, so man is most truly human in the yet simple
state of rustic life." Consciously, Wordsworth repeatedly denied
that he saw his youth, while his mother was still alive, as life's
Golden Age.

Wordsworth's great political experiment was successful. He
found examples of fulfilled humanity among those who toiled with
their hands, thereby rendering, within his postulates, revolutionary

social change unnecessary. Of the "lonely roads" (*Prel.* xii, 163) Wordsworth wrote:

> . . . there I found
> Hope to my hope, and to my pleasure peace,
> And steadiness; and healing and repose
> To every angry passion. There I heard,
> From mouths of lowly men and of obscure
> A tale of honour; sounds in unison
> With loftiest promises of good and fair.
>   (*Prel.* xii, 178–184)

Both Betty Foy and Susan Gale of "The Idiot Boy" (*P.W.* 2:67–80), first published in *Lyrical Ballads,* demonstrate through their love and compassion for Betty's idiot son, Johnny, more fully developed humanity than does the socially more respectable doctor who can only think of his disturbed sleep.

There are two exceptions to Wordsworth's belief that realized humanity can be found in any stratum of society. The ability truly to love, that is to be fully human, is not to be found where relentless, grinding poverty reduces man to less than man. And in deforming cities that sicken the human heart, it is not to be expected that man in all his glory is to be found even as frequently as one man in ten thousand (although the artificer lovingly airing his child at the end of Book viii of *The Prelude* is clearly one of the exceptions):

> True is it, where oppression worse than death
> Salutes the Being at his birth, where grace
> Of culture has been utterly unknown,
> And labour in excess and poverty
> From day to day pre-occupy the ground
> Of the affections, and to Nature's self
> Oppose a deeper nature, there indeed,
> Love cannot be; nor does it easily thrive
> In cities, where the human heart is sick,
> And the eye feeds it not, and cannot feed. . . .
>   (*Prel.* xii, 194–203)

Excessive poverty and cities do not belong to nature's self; they are unnatural.

Poems such as "The Idiot Boy," "The Thorn" (*P.W.* 2:240–248), "Michael," and "The Brothers" were all at some level socially didactic. They were meant to correct the false and shallow conceptions that the governing class had of those beneath them. Wordsworth saw it as his task to combat the false consciousness of the governing class. The times made such a task imperative. E. P. Thompson quotes what Frances, Lady Shelley, had written in her diary: "the awakening of the labouring classes, after the first shock of the French Revolution, made the upper classes tremble. . . ." [23]

An understanding of the political purpose of many of the *Lyrical Ballads* makes it far easier to understand why on January 14, 1801 Wordsworth should send a copy of the second edition of the ballads and a covering letter to Charles James Fox, leader of the Whig opposition in the House of Commons. In the letter he writes:

> It appears to me that most calamitous effect, which has followed the measures which have lately been pursued in this country, is a rapid decay of the domestic affections among the lower orders of society. This effect the present rulers of this country are not conscious of, or they disregard it. (*E.L.* 313)

It is the function both of the poems and of this observation to make Fox a more conscious and more morally sensitive legislator. Wordsworth has a similar end in mind when he writes to Fox of the class of men portrayed in "The Brothers" and 'Michael," "small independent *proprietors* of land here called statesmen, men of respectable education who daily labour on their own little properties," that "this class of men is rapidly disappearing" (*E.L.* 314–315). Wordsworth does not make these observations without hoping to gain a practical political effect.

The Prelude itself has a grand social and moral purpose. Wordsworth may be writing when

> This Age fall back to old idolatry,
> Though men return to servitude as fast
> As the tide ebbs, to ignominy and shame
> By nations sink together. . . .
> (*Prel.* XIII, 432–435)

Be that as it may, the wisdom that Coleridge and Wordsworth have achieved may help restore the world to proper moral health. Such wisdom is found in that very poem, as the following passage concludes:

> Prophets of Nature, we to them will speak
> A lasting inspiration, sanctified
> By reason and by truth; what we have loved,
> Others will love; and we may teach them how;
> Instruct them how the mind of man becomes
> A thousand times more beautiful than the earth
> On which he dwells, above this Frame of things
> (Which, 'mid all revolutions in the hopes
> And fears of men, doth still remain unchanged)
> In beauty exalted, as it is itself
> Of substance and fabric more divine.
>
> (*Prel.* XIII, 442–452)

FIVE

A CHALLENGE TO COMMUNITY

NO historical forces could prevent Wordsworth from imaginatively creating and articulating an ideal political community, but
actual political communities that approximated his ideal were not
immune from the corrosive forces of historical change. According
to E. P. Thompson three decisive forces were simultaneously at
work in England at the beginning of the nineteenth century,
changing social structures and social relations. The first was the
tremendous increase in British population, which rose from 10.5
million in 1801 to 18.1 million in 1841. The second was the Industrial Revolution, and the third was the political reaction that
lasted from 1792 to 1832 and that was brought on by the fear on
the part of the English ruling class that the political revolution in
France would be echoed by a revolution in England.[1] It is difficult
to know on what level of conscious awareness Wordsworth perceived these forces.

The ideal of community that Wordsworth cherished was
based upon an actual historical form of community that had come
into being in the Lake counties. This community was, to
Wordsworth's dismay, to suffer mutation from the three forces
noted by Thompson. Indeed these mutations, which I shall outline in this chapter, had begun even before Wordsworth had formulated the conception of community that he was to champion.
His response to the changes that he so grimly noted was not to
reformulate or to abandon his social ideal, but rather to support it

with increasing vigor and even stridency. The result, I believe, was a development that contributed to the decline in Wordsworth's poetic power that he experienced after his great decade, the years 1797 to 1807. Wordsworth's true subject, as Lionel Trilling has observed, both in "Wordsworth and the Iron Time"[2] and *Sincerity and Authenticity*,[3] was *being*. I have suggested that Wordsworth was drawn to this subject in part because of an unbalanced and ill-established sense of his own being. I believe that he became distracted when he saw the erosion of the social form to which he had allied himself. It was precisely in this form of community that he had hoped to establish a more balanced sense of self than he had had. He took his eye off the true subject of his verse, being, and focused, instead, upon maintaining an outmoded and dying *way of being*. It is not my contention that I have discovered the cause of Wordsworth's poetic decline. Wordsworth's shift of attention from being itself to the maintenance of a threatened way of being is only one of the many possible contributing causes of the faltering of his poetic gait. And even the sum of all the possible causes for Wordsworth's loss of poetic force would be insufficient in explanatory power to explain fully the periodicity of Wordsworth's genius. Like its departure, the advent of genius is ultimately inexplicable, and no more can be said. But it is my hope that explanatory contributions such as mine might at least contract, for readers of Wordsworth, the realm of the unknown.

I wish to say a word about the significance of the death of Wordsworth's younger brother, John, by shipwreck on February 5, 1805. Students of Wordsworth will undoubtedly be surprised when, in discussing Wordsworth's poetic decline, I pay scant attention to John's death. Many have dealt with the significance to Wordsworth of John's death, none more memorably than Wordsworth himself in "Peele Castle." I see no need to retread this ground. Rather I have chosen to concentrate on the degree to which disturbing social and political change distracted Wordsworth and weakened him as a poet.

Wordsworth first noted the social change that was taking place in England as early as 1793 or 1794, while he was first composing "Guilt and Sorrow" (P.W. 1:94–127). The female vagrant, the heroine of the poem and character after whom the fragment of the poem published in the *Lyrical Ballads* was named, was driven from her original home, along with her father, by an engrossing landlord who wished to rationalize agricultural production by consolidating small independent land holdings. By unfair use of his power, the landowner gained possession of the estate of the female vagrant and her father. As early as 1797, in "The Reverie of Poor Susan" (*P.W.* 2:217), Wordsworth comments on the wrenching emotional consequences of moving from the country to the city. Even more, the same poem shows that by 1797 Wordsworth had come to see the city as a demographic form uncongenial to the development of the fully realized human spirit.

The Lake counties were doomed to contamination by outside influences. During the eighteenth century the Lakes began to become a fashionable part of Britain to visit. The first guide book to the Lakes appeared in 1779 (*Lakes* 288). The core of what was to become Wordsworth's *Guide to the Lakes* appeared in 1810 as a commentary to Joseph Wilkerson's *Selected Views in Cumberland, Westmoreland, and Lancashire.* The great attraction of the Lakes, a taste for mountain scenery, seems to have developed apace with the Industrial Revolution (*Lakes* 287). Significant tourist traffic to the Lake District did not begin until the second half of the eighteenth century (*Lakes* 283). Innkeepers and carriage-owning gentry exerted their influence to get toll-free stretches of road widened and improved (*Lakes* 281). The growth of coach and carriage traffic brought changes. Kendall, Penrith, Carlisle and Cockermouth, all road junctions, became centers of land traffic in the Lakes. Inns expanded to provide shelter and roads were further improved (*Lakes* 281). Changes in the architecture of the country surrounding the Lakes and even patterns of forestation followed. William and Dorothy Wordsworth followed these changes with indignant attention.

On November 8, 1799 William wrote to Dorothy and told her that he was "much disgusted with the New Erections and objects about Windermere . . ." (*E.L.* 271). Three years later, on March 10, 1802 Dorothy noted in her journal that "They are slashing away in Benson's wood" (*D.W.J.* 99). In June of that year she wrote with disgust about an island on Windermere that had had its groves leveled and an ugly new house built upon it by an "improving" tenant. She had seen "the pleasantest of earthly spots deformed by man" (*D.W.J.* 133). William wrote to Richard Sharp on February 7, 1805:

> Woe to poor Grasmere for ever and ever! A wretched Creature, wretched in name and Nature, of the name of *Crump*, goaded on by his still more wretched wife (for by the bye the man though a Liverpool attorney is, I am told, a very good sort of fellow but the wife as ambitious as Semiramis) this same Wretch has at last begun to put his long impending threats into execution; and when you next enter the sweet paradise of Grasmere you will see staring you in the face upon that beautiful ridge that elbows out into the vale (behind the church and towering far above its steeple) a temple of abomination, in which are to be enshrined Mr. and Mrs. Crump. Seriously this . . . House will stare you in the face from every part of the Vale, and entirely destroy its character of simplicity and seclusion. (*E.L.* 534)

In the story of the Crumps it is possible to see new money made in mercantile Liverpool breaking in on and destroying the "Unity entire" (*P.W.* 5:318) of Grasmere.

In October of the same year Wordsworth wrote to Sir George Beaumont to lament that "the most beautiful specimen of a forest pathway ever seen by human eyes" on Lord Lowther's grounds was about to be replaced by a "manufactured Walk." What is more "many great mansions" were expelling "human creatures from their neighborhood," presumably to make agriculture more profitable by unifying separate parcels of land. This expulsion was painful for Wordsworth who saw people being stripped away from the kind of community that he valued very highly:

> But for my part strip my Neighborhood of human beings and I should think it one of the greatest privations I could undergo. (*E.L.* 626–627)

In November Dorothy complained to Lady Beaumont not only of the Crump house, but of "one offensive object, the house of Mr. Mounsey," and finally of the new imported "Larch plantations, that look like a blotch or scar on the fair surface of the mountain" (*E.L.* 637–638). The larches might be incongruous aesthetically but they made for profitable forestry.

Wordsworth wrote to his benefactor Sir George Beaumont on August 21, 1806 to complain that Applewaite, the estate Beaumont had given Wordsworth in 1803, might be deformed by industrial construction, "a cotton-mill being, I am told, already planted, or to be planted, in the glen" (*M.L.* 76). Dorothy could rejoice to Catherine Clarkson on July 19, 1807 that she had visited "a retired woody winding valley, with steep banks and rocky scars, no manufactures—no horrible Forges. . . ." But in the same letter she noted that "all the trees in Bainriggs are cut down, and even worse, the giant sycamore near the parsonage house . . ." (*M.L.* 158–159). In the same vein Dorothy complained to Thomas De Quincey on May 6, 1809 that Nab Scar was being cleared of trees as Mr. North and Lady Fleming competed to gain the profitable right to cut timber (*M.L.* 338).

Wordsworth's *Guide Through the District of the Lakes* contains many regretful notices of physical changes in the district. I shall quote only from those portions of the text that were written in 1809, with one exception which I shall note. Wordsworth lamented that the natural gradation of shrubbery on fine estates, owned by both new and traditional owners, was being replaced by an impulse mistakenly regarded as an improving one, that is the impulse to be "smitten by formality and harsh contrast." "The hill of Danmallet, at the Port of Ulswater, was once divided into different portions, by avenues of fir trees." Now one must "contrast this quaint appearance with the image of the same hill overgrown with self-planted weed."

> The disfigurement which this country has undergone, has not, however, proceeded wholly from the common feeling of human nature . . . another cause must be added, that has chiefly shown itself in its effect upon buildings. I mean a warping of the natural mind occasioned by a consciousness that, this country being an object of general admiration, every new house would be looked at and commented upon either for approbation or censure. (*Prose* 2:210–211)

This melancholy deformation was the result of what Thorsten Veblen was later to call conspicuous consumption.

Not only were new houses, often built by arriving new

wealth, such as was the case with the Crump house, changing the face of the Lakes, but the mercantile quest for profit was producing ecological havoc. Larches were being grown by those seeking to increase the productivity of forestry on their estates.

> To those who plant for profit, and are thrusting every other tree out of the way, to make room for their favorite, the larch, I would utter first a regret, that they should have selected these lovely vales for their vegetable manufactury. . . . (*Prose* 2:217)

Wordsworth's vegetable love is clearly not the love of profit.

If alien species of trees were being introduced to the Lakes, beautiful stands of traditional trees were being rudely cleared away. Losses had been suffered.

> and scarcely any where has a more grievous loss been sustained than upon the Farm of Blowick. . . . The axe has indiscriminately levelled a rich wood of birches and oaks, which, two or three years ago, varied this favored spot into a thousand pictures. (*Prose* 2:284)

The mercantile spirit destroyed more than the ecological integrity of the Lakes. It destroyed the social fabric of what Wordsworth had referred to in his *Guide to the Lakes* as the ideal republic of the district. It has produced "an unfortunate alteration in the circumstances of the native peasantry." Every family formerly had two sources of income, that produced by the lands and flocks, and that produced by the women and children "spinning their own wool in their own houses (work chiefly done in the winter season), and carrying it to the market for sale." This second source of income became technologically outmoded by the introduction of mechanical spinning devices.

> . . . by the invention and universal application of machinery, this second resource has been cut off; the gains being so far reduced, as not to be sought after but by a few aged persons disabled from other employment. . . . The consequence, then, is—that proprietors and farmers being no longer able to maintain themselves upon small farms, several are united in one, and the buildings go to decay, or are destroyed; and that the lands of the *estatesmen* being mortgaged, and the owners constrained to part with them, they fall into the hands of wealthy purchasers, who in like manner unite and consolidate; and, if they wish to become residents, erect new

mansions out of the ruins of the ancient cottages, whose little enclosures, with all the wild graces that grew out of them, disappear. . . . it is probable, that in a few years the country on the margin of the Lakes will fall almost entirely into the possession of the gentry, either strangers or natives.   (*Prose* 2:223–224)

Commenting on the Vale of Keswick Wordsworth wrote in 1822, "A small Spinning-mill has lately been erected here, and some of the old Cottages, with their picturesque appendages, are fallen into decay" (*Prose* 2:274). In her journal entry of December 7, 1801, Dorothy notes what when she set out from Kendall at dusk "Cotton mills lighted up" (*D.W.J.* 67).

Bouch and Jones substantiate Wordsworth's observations. According to them the ousting of homespun by factory yarn was a calamitous development for the statesmen. By 1837 no domestic manufacture was carried on in the Lakes (*Lakes* 236).

The social structure of the Lakes was breaking up under the combined effects of demographic and economic change. Writing to John Wilson on June 7, 1802 Wordsworth commented that valuable regional distinctions had disappeared "because, even in the most sequestered places, by manufactures, traffic, religion, law, interchange of inhabitants, etc., distinctions are done away which would otherwise have been strong and obvious (*E.L.* 354). Old regional customs and distinctions vanished. On January 20, 1807 Dorothy wrote regretfully to Catherine Clarkson that

We had a letter from Grasmere about a week ago; they have had no fidlers this Christmas, a doleful piece of news to us, seeming to tell of change and the passing away of good times. . . .   (*M.L.* 126)

The Christmas fiddlers were not all that was to pass away from the Lakes. By 1812, as Wordsworth was very likely aware, the hard sark shirt, woven of hemp yarn, had long been regarded as being old fashioned. Increasingly, the growing of flax was no longer practised, especially around Kendal where women were no longer able to spin linen yarn (*Lakes* 244). In Cumberland the old and simple dietary fare was being supplemented, and to some extent replaced, by tea and butcher's meat (*Lakes* 244).

These changes in the customs of the Lakes were reflections of changes in the social order. In this regard, John Fisher's lament to

Dorothy, recorded in the May 19, 1800 entry of her *Journal*, is literally ominous:

> John Fisher overtook me on the other side of Rydale. He talked
> much about the alteration in the times, and observed that in a short
> time there would be only two ranks of people, the very rich and the
> very poor, for all those who have small estates says he are forced to
> sell, and all the land goes into one hand.   (D.W.J. 19)

When consciousness of momentous social change reaches from
the gentry to such common folk as Wordsworth's neighbors, the
Fishers, then one must not be surprised to find that traditional expectations are no longer able to be fulfilled and that traditional
social roles were often abandoned in puzzlement or despair.
Wordsworth's brother-in-law, George Hutchinson, was brought up
to be a gentleman farmer and was disappointed in his expectations.
He was unable to hold on to his property. Wordsworth wrote to his
merchant associate, Richard Sharp, on February 7, 1805 in order
to try to help Hutchinson. He inquired of Sharp,

> Do you know of any Corn or wine Merchant who wants a
> Clerk? Mrs. Wordsworth has a Brother who was brought up to
> farming in the Country, and has been unfortunate, and now wishes
> to try his luck in another line, and let me speak more seriously
> wishes to be in the way of earning his bread, having lost his own
> little property by a series of misfortunes, some of them I know unmerited. (E.L. 230)

Hutchinson's situation was by no means unique. Writing of
statesmen, "small independent *proprietors* of land," Wordsworth
complained to Fox on January 14, 1801 that, "This class of men is
rapidly disappearing" (E.L. 315). The disappearance of small
farms resulted in turn in the disappearance of skilled laborers. A
main cause in the decline of the statesmen was the burdening of
their land with larger families than the land could support. This
was caused in turn by the decline in infant mortality (*Lakes* 237).

Wordsworth may not have fully grasped the significance of
the disappearance of the statesmen. According to Bouch and
Jones, the decline in the number of statesmen meant a rise in
wage labor (*Lakes* 237). That is to say that more and more working
men, women and children were forced to sell their labor within

the expanding framework of the market system. As more and more workers became wage laborers, they entered into an economic world in which all work, no matter how seemingly disparate, was unified by one thing. All work paid wages in return for labor. In such a world, mobility, not only between jobs, but between different kinds of work, increased. Workers left wage labor on the farm for wage labor in the factory. The "country," Dorothy wrote in a letter to Jane Marshall dated June 2, 1806, "is drained by the cotton works and other manufactures, and by the large towns whither they [the rural working class] are tempted to go for great wages" (M.L. 31). By 1801 workers in Howgill pit earned about 3s a day. However unpleasant and dangerous it was, coal mining still lured men away from agricultural labor in Cumberland (Lakes 261).

The increase of wages and of factory labor was epochal in the history of the family, which had been, in the natural economy, the site of all labor. Factories brought about the separation of families and the breakup of households.[4] Indeed, Peter Laslett suggests that the removal of the economic functions of the patriarchal family, as a result of industrialization, created mass society. He further suggests that the end of the system that ensured that man lived and worked at home created large-scale disaffection.[5] Each new stage of industrial differentiation and specialization disrupted the family economy, disturbing customary relations between man and wife, parents and children, while at the same time distinguishing ever more sharply between the categories of "work" and "life." The "family was roughly torn apart each morning by the factory bell, and the mother who was also a wage-earner often felt herself to have the worst of both the domestic and the industrial worlds."[6] In a passage from Book VIII of The Excursion, published in 1814, from which I shall quote extensively later in this chapter, Wordsworth makes it clear that he was aware of the destructive effect that the factory system had on traditional patterns of family life.

Although it is true, as Dorothy suggested, that many workers were lured from the countryside by the promise of higher wages in an industrial town, one must also bear in mind that the old village economy was crumbling behind them as they left.[7] Agricultural improvement that did so much to make traditional small land holdings economically untenable was advanced by large land-owners, first in the Lakes by Dr. Robert Graham and then by Lord Lonsdale who followed his example (*Lakes* 227). The revolution in agriculture antedated the Industrial Revolution. The enclosures of common land, and the consolidation of small separate holdings into compact units, both of which accompanied the new advance in agricultural methods, had an unsettling effect upon the family economy. In his *Guide to the Lakes* Wordsworth had noted the adverse effect of the factory system on the cottage economy. Other destructive forces were at work as well that made it difficult, if not impossible, to supplement earning from cottage industry with agri-cultural products produced both for use and for sale. The war on cottages, the absorption of cottage gardens, the confiscation of rights to the common—all stripped cottage industry of its two main supports, family earnings and agricultural background. Wordsworth's October, 1805 letter to Sir George Beaumont, al-ready cited, indicates a painful awareness that some landowners were indeed waging war on cottages, and stripping neighborhoods of human beings.

> As long as domestic industry was supplemented by the faculties and amenities of a garden plot, a scrap of land, or grazing rights, the dependence of the laborer on money earnings was not absolute.
> . . . The rationalization of agriculture inevitably uprooted the la-bourer and undermined his social security.[8]

The year 1801 was a year of famine and war. Parliament passed the General Enclosure Act, an act that not only simplified the procedure necessary to obtain permission to enclose a parcel of land, but also reduced the costs of enclosure.[9] As a result the rate of enclosure further accelerated. The poor laborer who kept a cow, a sheep, or a pony on the common was pauperized (*Lakes* 239). In village after village, enclosure destroyed "the scratch-as-scratch-can subsistence economy of the poor—the cow or geese, fuel from the common, gleanings, and all the rest." Without legal proof of title the displaced cottager was unlikely to receive any compensa-tion, and even when title could be established he "was left with a parcel of land inadequate for subsistence and a disproportionate share of the very high enclosure costs."[10] Enclosure lowered the status of workers and was one of the causes of the rise of wage labor, as enclosure caused the number of independent cultivators to decline (*Lakes* 235).

As farms increased in size, farmers increasingly adopted a more middle-class mercantile way of life. The old community between masters and servants suffered. Farmers strove to emphasize the gulf between themselves, on the one hand, and their hired servants on the other. Masters stopped eating at the same table with their farm hands. Fewer field laborers lived on the same farm on which they worked. Workers were paid for smaller and smaller time periods. Increasingly the monthly, weekly, and even the daily wage replaced the annual and semiannual contract.[11] It is likely that Wordsworth had some knowledge of these developments.

In the Lakes enclosure became more systematic from the middle of the eighteenth century to the middle of the nineteenth century than it had been in earlier periods. While the eighteenth century saw three enclosures of arable land and eighteen private acts in Cumberland, 200,000 acres of Cumberland soil were enclosed in Cumberland between 1793 and 1816 alone. Forty-seven per cent of all enclosing done in Westmorland was completed by 1820. The process of enclosure in Westmorland was particularly active during the first two decades of the nineteenth century (*Lakes* 232–233). Though enclosure diminished the number of statesmen, yet they persisted. Eight hundred and ninety-nine statesmen could still be found in Westmorland in 1829 (*Lakes* 237).

The immense changes that England, in general, and Grasmere and its environs, in particular, were undergoing, and that I have detailed in the foregoing pages, might well have presented themselves to Wordsworth, to the degree that he was conscious of changes noted by later historians, as a threat to his integrity of self. He had achieved stability by committing himself to a traditional society. Wordsworth expressed the anguish that he felt when he saw what he believed to be a valuable social order battered by forces beyond his control in an unfinished blank verse fragment of almost six hundred lines called "The Tuft of Primroses (*P.W.* 5:348–362), composed in 1808. Unpublished in Wordsworth's lifetime, these verses have until recently received less attention than they merit. "A Tuft of Primroses" seems to show Words-worth's aversion to what he saw to be changes taking place in Grasmere Vale. It is even possible to see in the poem an impulse on Wordsworth's part to flee from perceived change.

This meditative poem opens with a sixty line greeting to the primrose. It would be a

> . . . pity if the faithful Spring beguiled
> By her accustomed hopes had come to breathe
> Upon the bosom of this barren crag
> And found thee not. . . .
>
> (P.W. 5:348)

The primrose, then, is a harbinger of spring, and spring is the season of regeneration. Why is regeneration invoked? For one thing, the vale has come under the baleful sway of mutability, unlike the primrose which "has survived/The lofty band of Firs that overtopp'd/Their antient neighbor the old Steeple Tower . . ." (P.W. 5:350). This grove has been ruthlessly cut down by an "un-feeling Heart" (P.W. 5:350) that would not even spare "that Syca-more high,/The universal glory of the Vale . . ." (P.W. 5:350). Innovation has destroyed

> That incommunicable sanctity
> Which Time and nature only can bestow. . . .
>
> (P.W. 5:351)

Innovation brought about by social and economic changes, brought about by rapidly developing capitalism, has destroyed the sanctity of the vale described in "Home at Grasmere" as a "Unity entire." That which is new has no sanctity, for sanctity can only be bestowed by time and nature. What is new is destructive of all that is organic, natural and traditional. What is new emanates from a world of economic calculation designed to create the "un-feeling Heart." The new capitalist social forces destroying the vale's sacramental value are unnatural, are blasphemous. Sacra-mental value is being replaced by calculable value. Again the words of Marx and Engels seem to echo behind the threnody over the fallen firs. "The bourgeoisie, wherever it has got the upper hand, has put an end to all feudal, patriarchal, idyllic relations." [12]

The related themes of mutability and mortality haunt the poem. It may well have been Wordsworth's intention in "The Tuft of Primroses" to create a traditional meditation on change and death. But whatever Wordsworth's conscious intention may have been, it seems to me that death, as used here, is not only self-referential, but also symbolic of a specific social and historical phenomenon. Wordsworth points to an abandoned cottage near "the vale's northern outlet" (P.W. 5:351). It is empty now. Within sight of it, in the village churchyard, lie the five graves of the former occupants of the cottage. "Death to the happy House in which they dwelt/Had given a long reprieve of fourty years . . ." (P.W. 5:351). Yet within two summers death's "greedy visiting was closed . . ." (P.W. 5:351). Death is personified as being greedy, that is to say driven to accumulate. Nothing in this seems strange at first. Death is traditionally envisioned as a "grim reaper" relentlessly and resistlessly harvesting his crop. But when Wordsworth's personification "greedy" is linked back to the description of the person who cut down the firs and sycamores as being an "unfeeling Heart," a description suggestive of egoism, and then linked forward to a description of death as an unfeeling hoarder of what it has garnered, a suggestion that death signifies something more than the "grim reaper" begins to emerge.

Wordsworth looks at a fallen spray of "jasmine on the ground/Stretching its desolate length" and mourns

> . . . that these works
> Of love and diligence and innocent care
> Are sullied and disgrac'd; or that a gulf
> Hath swallowed them which renders nothing back. . . .
> (P.W. 5:353)

Death by its very nature, "renders nothing back"; it is rapacious and acquisitive, greedy, to use Wordsworth's own word. It hoards without the reciprocity of the system of distributive relations that marks the Tory humanist theory of distribution outlined in my reading of "Stray Pleasures." Here Wordsworth mirrors forth, in imagery traditionally associated with death, a reflection of the new political economy, intruding into the once stable vale, a form of economy in which acquisitiveness is stripped of the responsibility of reciprocity. This new economy dissolves the traditional political economy that implied the duties of reciprocity. Death, mutability, rapaciousness and capitalist development seem to be poetically linked to the latent consciousness of "A Tuft of Primroses." If this is so, then the poem is an implicit critique of capitalism. And if death, mutability, and greed are negative values, then they imply an antithetical set of positive values, vitality, permanence, and generosity or reciprocity.

Wordsworth then wishfully invokes "some band of guardian spirits" (P.W. 5:353) to protect the time-threatened vale from "despoil and wrong" (P.W. 5:354). Significantly, the guardians he evokes are drawn from an image of the fixed, hierarchical, feudal past. He recalls the royal forest wardens of medieval England, who would

> . . . protect from harm
> The wild Beast with her young, and from the touch
> Of waste the green-leav'd thicket
> . . . till the Sovereign comes
> Heading his train. . . .
>
> (P.W. 5:354)

Threatened by social change Wordsworth's imagination goes back to an ordered, aristocratic past so that he may protect the vale from "the deafness of the world" (P.W. 5:354).

More to the point in suggesting the helplessness Wordsworth felt in 1808 when he wrote this poem is his belief that the deaf "world" will press in upon the vale and cause it to "Vanish beneath an unrelenting doom" (P.W. 5:354). Wordsworth sees himself and the only world in which significance is possible for him as being doomed to destruction. He sees the inevitability of this awful change. Rather than indicating enormous rage at the depredation of his beloved vale, he only expresses wistful loss. Although Wordsworth seems to lament only the abstract concept of mutability, the mutability that disturbs him seems to be linked to specific social and historical changes.

It is poignant, then, to read that man's "blissful pleasures live" not in any Yeatsian artifices of eternity, but, rather in "All growth of nature and all frame of Art" (P.W. 5:354), poignant because such growths and frames are subject to change. Pleasure does not exist beyond this world, nor is it a self-contained abstraction. As Wordsworth had already written in *The Prelude*, "in the very world . . . We find our happiness, or not at all" (*Prel*. x, 726–728). But the world in which Wordsworth says that we are to find our happiness is not stable. It is a world subject to change. Wordsworth is faced with a painful difficulty. If pleasure is found in the growth of nature and the frame of art, what happens to pleasure when nature's growth is despoiled and art's frames broken? Pleasure, because it is part of the material world, is subject to historical change and decay. Pleasure may be, at least in part, located in society, also part of the world. But not all forms of society are equally mutable. Some are more mutable than others. Because mutability is inimical to pleasure, highly mutable societies are more destructive of pleasure than others. Capitalism, in the fully developed form it was then achieving in Britain, was the social form most inimical to pleasure as Wordsworth defined and experienced pleasure. Marx and Engels in the "Manifesto of the Communist Party" explain why this should be so;

> The bourgeoisie cannot exist without constantly revolutionizing the instruments of production, and thereby the relations of production, and with them the whole relations of society. Conservation of old modes of production in unaltered form was, on the contrary, the first condition of existence for all earlier industrial classes. Constant revolutionizing of production, uninterrupted disturbance of all social conditions, ever-lasting uncertainty and agitation distinguish the bourgeois epoch from all earlier ones. All fixed, fast-frozen relations, with their train of ancient and venerable prejudices and opinions, are swept away, all new-formed ones become antiquated before they can ossify. All that is solid melts into air, all that is holy is profaned, and man is at last compelled to face with sober senses his real conditions of life and his relations with his kind. [13]

It is precisely after noting that pleasure lives in nature and in art, and that it seems the fate of the vale to "Vanish beneath an unrelenting doom," that Wordsworth, some thirteen years before writing the early "Ecclesiastical Sonnets" in praise of early Catholicism and monasteries and nunneries, launches into a two-hundred-line hymn in praise of the monastic life and ideal. He praises and seems to envy a life withdrawn from the shocks that flesh is heir to, shocks that industrialization may well have made more painful. If the vale had become infected with the "world" and its concomitant changes, Wordsworth mentally retreated to a realm as free from the world and its mutability as possible, free of "Getting and spending" (*P.W.* 3:18). Wordsworth describes a hermit spending his life "Fast anchored in the desert" (P.W. 5:354). Perhaps the desert is representative of the sequestered vale. Here motionless in space seems to become the metaphoric equivalent of changelessness in time.

Against the innovations and incursions of the new society Wordsworth stood as a poet committed to upholding and preserving the traditional social order. The poet "is the rock of defence for human nature; an upholder and preserver, carrying everywhere with him relationship and love" (*Prose* 1:141). Further, in his struggle against change "the Poet binds together by passion and knowledge the vast empire of human society, as it is spread over the whole earth, and over all time" (*Prose* 1:141). And as a poet in his mature poetry, Wordsworth attacks, often only implicitly, the new social order. There is, I believe, an implicit protest at the end of "Michael" (*P.W.* 2:80–94), when after Isabel, Michael's widow, dies, their cottage, The Evening Star, scene and witness of so much human suffering, rejoicing, and being, is leveled and the ground beneath it plowed under by someone in search of larger profits making war upon the cottages that prevented the plough from going the shortest distance between two points.

> The Cottage which was named the EVENING STAR
> Is gone—the ploughshare has been through the ground
> On which it stood. . . .
>
> (*P.W.* 2:94)

The destruction of the cottage by someone adding to the capital value of the land is, for Wordsworth, something to lament, as his October 17, 1805 letter to Sir George Beaumont indicates.

In "The Brothers" (*P.W.* 2:1–13) old Walter Ewbank "sank/And went into his grave before his time," because he had been "buffeted with bond/Interest, and mortgages . . ." (P.W. 2:7). The financial complexities of the new economic order are worrisome and destructive to the older patriarchal order. Benjamin, the good-hearted drover of "The Wagonner" (P.W. 2:176–205), written in 1805, is fired by his master, the type of the prideful egoistic capitalist, "Sour and surly as the north" (P.W. 2:201), because the Master's pride is wounded when he sees Benjamin come into view with his master's prize mastiff "Tethered to the waggon's tail" (P.W. 2:202) beside an ass. "Benjamin the good/The patient, and the tender hearted" (P.W. 2:203) is fired because he had had the charity to take a family—man, woman, and child—into his wagon from a raging storm. The master, who is one of the monied worldlings, is unable to be compassionate. As a result, his pridefulness destroys the natural, social harmony of Grasmere Vale. When Benjamin had been wagoner:

> A living almanack had we;
> We had a speaking diary,
> That in this uneventful place,
> Gave to the days a mark and name
> By which we knew them when they came.
> (P.W. 2:204)

And now the community can no longer be sure that

> The lame, the sickly, and the old:
> Men, women, heartless with the cold;
> And babes in wet and starveling plight . . .
> (P.W. 2:205)

will find kind shelter from the elements if they are on the road when one of Benjamin's replacements passes by. The master, symbol of the new social order, has caused the community loss of continuity and charity.

So far I have attempted to portray the forces that brought change into Wordsworth's sacred vale and to record Wordsworth's response to these changes. Now I wish to describe two formations, the factory and the city, that developed outside the vale but which cast shadows that Wordsworth, to the degree that he was aware of them—and I shall show that he was—could only watch with horror and disgust. First I shall discuss the factory.

I have referred and shall frequently refer to the work of E. P. Thompson, a Marxist labor historian whose book, *The Making of the English Working Class*, is in accord both with the traditional Whig historians from Macaulay to G. M. Trevelyan, and with the Fabian Socialist historians such as Beatrice and Sidney Webb. Approaching the subject from distinctly different perspectives, the Whigs, the Fabians, and the contemporary Marxists such as Thompson and E. J. Hobsbaum agree that the Industrial Revolution brought about a rapid growth of the factory system, urbanization, and the enclosure movement. They further agree that these developments created large-scale misery, at least in the short run, among the laboring class. It was not merely the recovery of fresh and relevant source material that made Thompson's work necessary. The tradition that Thompson shared with the Whigs, the Fabians, and his fellow Marxists had been challenged by a revisionist school of English historiography founded by Sir Lewis Namier and supported by such historians as T. S. Ashton and David S. Landes. The revisionists denied that the industrialization of Britain caused major suffering among the laboring class, and even went so far as to assert that industrialization brought about a rise in the standard of living for the workers who were affected by it.

I choose to cite Thompson because I believe that he effectively refutes the claims of the revisionists, that his work is in accord with a great tradition of British historiography, and that his work is more recent and fresh than that of Macaulay, Trevelyan, and the Webbs.

Thompson has noted that "The classic exploitive relationship of the Industrial Revolution is depersonalized, in the sense that no lingering obligations of mutuality—of paternalism or deference . . . are admitted." [14] This was brought about by many causes; the rise of a master-class without traditional authority or obligation, the increasing separation between master and man, the new transparency with which exploitation could be seen as the source of the master's wealth, the worker's loss of status and independence as he became totally dependent on his master's instruments of production, and the reduction of the man himself to a mere instrument of production.[15]

To the emergence of a distinctive exploitative relationship was added the rapid abrogation of paternalist legislation. "Between 1803 and 1808 the regulations covering the woolen trade were suspended." They were repealed in 1809.[16] The capitalist made war upon the customs of traditional trades by introducing new machinery, by the factory system itself, by employing unrestricted competition among producers, by forcing down wages, and by mass-producing cheap goods shoddier than the traditional standards of craftsmanship would have permitted.[17]

During the Wars, although Wordsworth might not have been consciously aware of this, the doctrine that labor was but another commodity that discovered its natural price by means of the law of supply and demand was energetically propagated in order to oppose the traditional notion of a just wage.[18] According to Polanyi the self-regulating market made no less a demand than that of the institutional separation of society into a social sphere, on the one hand, and an economic and political sphere, on the other.[19] The increasing supply of cheap labor reserves in agriculture was a growing contradiction of the paternalist tradition of earnings based on need.[20]

To the voice of Tory paternalism, now on the defensive, was added the voice of disappointed Romanticism. "In their recoil from the Enlightenment, Wordsworth, Coleridge, Southey, had reaffirmed traditional sanctities, 'the instincts of natural and social man'."[21] Not only radical craftsmen, but also Romantics "opposed the annunciation of Acquisitive Man."[22] I believe that to Wordsworth the social relations that were replacing Tory paternalism threatened to break what appeared to be an organic society into an aggregate of monads relating to one another only through competition.

At the center of the new exploitative relationship and the repeal of paternalist legislation was the factory, a form of social organization for production that was inconsistent with the values of the old Tory paternalism. "The mill appeared as a symbol of social energies which were destroying the very 'course of Nature'."

It threatened the traditional order in several ways. To the land-owners whose incomes were tied to their rent rolls, the new indus-trialists were ambitious upstarts whose increasing wealth threat-ened the established power of the gentry. Second, the mill seemed to the gentry to create an undisciplined, licentious working class, devoid of the habits of deference.[23] Traditional interests were hos-tile to the effects that the new wealth of new manufacturers had in influencing Parliament through bribery.[24] Indeed, in 1809 Lowther's main opponent, J. G. Curwen, introduced a bill to re-strict the activity of merchants and wealthy cnadidates in order to allow more landed gentlemen to become M.P.s. Curwen's idea was similar to one that Wordsworth later expressed to Lord Lons-dale in 1818 (*Lakes* 329).

In November, 1799, John Thelwall, still to some degree a member of the Wordsworth circle, wrote, "What is a huge manu-factury, but a common prison-house, in which a hapless multi-tude are sentenced to profligacy and hard labour, that an individ-ual may rise to unwieldy opulence."[25] Wordsworth, writing to his college friend, Francis Wrangham, on June 5, 1808, about the same time that he composed "A Tuft of Primroses," wrote about the conditions of factory workers, commonly called "Manufac-turers" at the time. He stressed how sharply the conditions of the factory workers differed from that of the agricultural workers of Westmorland and Cumberland:

> The situation of Manufacturers is deplorably different. The monotony of their employments renders some sort of stimulus, in-tellectual or bodily, absolutely necessary for them. Their work is carried on in clusters, Men from different parts of the world, and perpetually changing; so that every individual is constantly in the way of being brought into contact with new notions and feelings, and of being unsettled in his own accordingly. (*M.L.* 248–249).

Factory workers are by their very condition denied the possibility of avoiding change. And change empties human life of happiness and stability. And, if this were not bad enough, the development of factories to the south in Lancashire was adversely affecting the Lakes. In the November 9, 1809 issue of *The Friend* Coleridge wrote, ". . . the vaste Machines of Lanchashire have overwhelmed and rendered helpless the domestic Industry of the Females in the Cottages and small Farmhouses of Westmorland and Cumberland."[26]

The history of the stocking industry in the Lakes is one index of the calamitous decay of cottage industry. In 1770 approximately 28,600 dozen pairs of stockings were knitted in the Lakes. By 1801 the number had fallen to 10,000 dozen pairs. This long-protracted decay of rural craft knitting was disastrous to the Lakes, where knitting instruments were inexpensive and men, women and children all could practice knitting (*Lakes* 265). Wordsworth had written in his *Guide to the Lakes* of the "universal application of machinery," had written, in part, that is, of the factory.

Further, the development of factories in Lancashire helped to bring about the physical deterioration, not only of the factory workers, but also of the workers in the cottage industries that were adversely affected by the growth of the factory system. Evidence suggests that the living and working conditions of artisans and of some rural workers were healthier in the second half of the eighteenth century than the living and working conditions of factory hands and outworkers in the first half of the nineteenth century.[27] According to E. P. Thompson, to observers in the second quarter of the nineteenth century, old workers in the mills seemed to be inferior in strength and appearance to the old "peasants."[28] Between 1800 and 1830 the consumption of beer, which the workers felt was necessary to their labor, declined, while the per capita consumption of tea and sugar went up.[29]

Wordsworth came to loathe the factory system. He saw it as a threat to every social value that he cherished. In *The Excursion*, published in 1814, Wordsworth has the Wanderer denounce that system. The Wanderer exclaims with particular bitterness against the psychological and physical deformities that factories inflicted on the children who worked in them.

> The Father, if perchance he still retain
> His old employments, goes to field or wood,
> No longer led or followed by the Sons;
> Idlers perchance they were,—but in *his* sight;
> Breathing fresh air, and treading the green earth;
> Till their short holiday of childhood ceased,

Ne'er to return! The birthright now is lost.
Economists will tell you that the State
Thrives by the forefeiture—unfeeling thought,
And false as monstrous! Can the mother thrive
By the destruction of her innocent sons
In whom premature necessity
Blocks out the forms of nature, preconsumes
The reason, famishes the heart, shuts up
The infant Being in itself, and makes
Its very spring a season of decay!
The lot is wretched, the condition sad,
Whether a pining discontent survive,
And thirst for change; or habit hath subdued
The soul deprest, dejected—even to love
Of her close tasks, and long captivity.

. . . The boy, where'er he turns,
Is still a prisoner. . . .

. . . Behold him—in the school
Of his attainments? No; but with the air
Fanning his temples under heaven's blue arch.
His raiment, whitened o'er with cotton-flakes
Or locks of wool, announces that he comes.
Creeping his gait and cowering, his lip pale,
His respiration quick and audible. . . .

(P.W. 5:274–275)

Whether or not Wordsworth was aware of the precise evidence marshaled by some modern historians of the Industrial Revolution, Wordsworth saw enough to know that industrialization as it was being carried out in Britain was a moral evil that destroyed, both physically and emotionally, the laborers who were drawn into the factory system.

Wordsworth despised no less than the factory the form of community associated with the factory, the city. Raymond Williams observed that:

> . . . a real conflict of interest, between those settled on the land and those settled in the city, which continually defined itself in the shifting economy of the time, could be made the basis of an ideology, in which an innocent and traditional order was being invaded and destroyed by a new and more ruthless order.[30]

Wordsworth adopted such an ideology. He condemned the "deformities of crowded life" as being "self-pleasing" (*Prel.* VIII, 465–467), that is to say egoistic. Stating the same matter more abstractly, Wordsworth notes in a rejected manuscript to Book XI, that though

> The love of order is a sentiment
> Inherent in the mind, yet does it seem
> That each access of strength this passion gains
> From human labours, by a course direct
> Or sinuous, is productive evermore
> Of littleness and pride.
>
> (*Prel.*, 612–613)

A humanly created social order, as opposed to a Burkean natural social growth, produces "littleness and pride." This barb seems to be directed, in the main, against rationalist, utopian schemes at creating a new or improved social order, but it hits, at least glancingly, the social world that man builds for himself in the city. The city breeds "littleness and pride" in the form of "self pleasing" deformities.

The city seemed, to Wordsworth, to be a type of anticommunity, an aggregation of people unconnected by emotional links. As a child, he tells us, "one thought"

> Baffled my understanding, how men lived
> Even next-door neighbours, as we say, yet still
> Strangers, and knowing not each other's names.
>
> (*Prel.* VII, 117–120)

The same lack of feeling, the same littleness and pride is demonstrated by those so involved in mean worldly pursuits that they pass untouched through the binding net of music cast by the blind fiddler in "The Power of Music." Those who unheedingly pass the knot of the fiddler's listeners, have, unbeknownst to themselves, placed themselves outside of a vital community:

> Now, coaches and chariots! Roar on like a stream;
> Here are twenty souls happy as souls in a dream:
> They are deaf to your murmurs—they care not for you,
> Nor what ye are flying, nor what ye pursue.
>
> (*P.W.* 2:219)

The dissonant roar that envelops the anticommunal worldlings may be compared with the beautiful fiddle melody that suffuses the community of twenty happy souls.

Perhaps Wordsworth's most intense expression of revulsion at urban life is his denunciation of Bartholomew Fair at the close of Book VII of *The Prelude*. The fair is described as a hell

> For eyes and ears! what anarchy and din
> Barbarian and infernal! 'tis a dream,
> Monstrous in colour, motion, shape, sight, sound.
> (*Prel.* VII, 658–661)

Readers have traditionally read this expression of disgust as Wordsworth's rejection of urban life in favor of the ordered and meaningful life lived as part of nature. This reading is certainly true as far as it goes, and is given support by Wordsworth's deliberate juxtaposition of this Boschean vision with the following Claudian scene of a rural fair under the shadow of Helvellyn. It has not been read, I think, as an expression of ruling class hatred and fear of the unruly lower orders. But when this passage from *The Prelude* is placed alongside passages from Thompson's *The Making of the English Working Class*, it becomes at least plausible to read Wordsworth's treatment of London's most popular fair as an expression not only of a nature-lover's disgust, but also as an expression of ruling-class alarm.

It is important that the reader not confuse the tone of disgust and anxiety that characterize Wordsworth's description of Bartholomew Fair, with the sardonic and somewhat mincing tone that characterizes Wordsworth's attempts at satire when he describes Parliamentary orators and dandified London preachers. In Wordsworth's description of the great fair, men, women and children are vomited forth from tents and booths (*Prel.* VII, 691–694). Clowns are seen "Grimacing, writhing, screaming" (*Prel.* VII, 672) in cries that seem to record Wordsworth's revulsion, fear, and even suffering, as he views the Fair.

If one compares the tone of the description of the Fair with Wordsworth's description of the London clergyman, a description at once mannered and arch, I think that it becomes clear that Wordsworth's description of the fair is too filled with rage and terror to be thought of as merely another one of Wordsworth's satires of London life. The preacher is "a comely Bachelor/Fresh from a toilette of two hours" who after an upward "seraphic glance" leads

> . . . his voice through many a maze,
> A minuet course, and winding up his mouth,
> From time to time into an oriface
> Most delicate, a lurking eyelet, small
> And only not invisible, again
> Open it out, diffusing thence a smile
> Of rapt irradiation exquisite.
>
> (*Prel.* VII, 544–556)

In the anxiety following the French Revolution, the humanitarian conscience of the ruling class became infected by class hatred and fear.[31] There was among the ruling class a conviction that there was a correlation between moral levity among the lower orders on the one hand and political sedition on the other. The opening of the new century saw an increase in prosecutions for drunkenness and lewd behavior.[32] In 1795 the London crowd seemed to be in a revolutionary mood,[33] and in 1798 wealthy merchants complained that performances at the Royal Theater, near the Tower, encouraged "habits of dissipation and profligacy" among "their numerous Manufacturers, Workmen, Servants, & C."[34] Authorities viewed "taverns, fairs, any large congregations of people as a nuisance—sources of idleness, brawls, sedition or contagion."[35] The amusements of the poor came to be regarded in a lurid light, and were continually preached and legislated against.[36] The ruling order assaulted, in particular, traditional holidays and fairs.[37] Bartholomew Fair, London's largest, eventually came to be feared as "the general rendezvous for sedition and the signal for insurrection."[38] In light of this historical background, it beomes difficult to avoid the conclusion that Wordsworth's vituperative attack on Bartholomew Fair was, at least overdetermined, and that on one level it was an expression of class solidarity with the fearful and vengeful ruling orders. Speaking of the occasions like the Fair, Wordsworth asks

> What say you then,
> To times, when half the City shall break out

> Full of one passion, vengeance, rage, or fear,
> To executions, to a Street on fire,
> Mobs, riots, or rejoicings. . . .
> (Prel. VII, 644–648)

For Wordsworth the Fair is a "blank confusion" and being that, it is

> a type not false
> Of what the mighty City is itself
> To all except a Straggler here and there,
> To the whole Swarm of its inhabitants. . . .
> (Prel. VII, 695–698)

Wordsworth, that is, sees the Fair as a "type" of the chaos and lack of human coherence and connection of the city. There is no meaning inherent in the city. It is "blank confusion." For Wordsworth the city is not, like nature, a text in which it is possible to find profound significance; it cannot teach. To be brought up in such a meaningless environment is to be stunted, to be one of many

> . . . slaves unrespited of low pursuits,
> Living amid the same perpetual flow
> Of trivial objects, melted and reduced
> To one identity, by differences
> That have no law, no meaning, and no end. . . .
> (Prel. VII, 700–704)

Like nature the city can produce oneness. But the oneness it produces is a ghastly caricature of the sentiment of being. There is no presence that disturbs one

> with the joy
> Of elevated thoughts; a sense sublime
> Of something far more deeply interfused,
> Whose dwelling is the light of setting suns,
> And the round ocean and the living air,
> And the blue sky, and in the mind of man:
> A motion and a spirit, that impels
> All thinking things, all objects of all thought,
> And rolls through all things.
> (P.W. 2:291–292)

Rather there is the oneness of reduction, of all things brought low, the oneness of "trivial objects, melted and reduced/To one identity. . . ." The sentiment of being offers the oneness of transcendence. The sentiment of blank urban confusion offers the oneness of contraction and reduction. The former leads to infinite expansion, the latter to infinite contraction. The oneness of Wordsworth's city is correlative with Blake's condition of single vision or with Blake's state of Ulro. If the oneness of the sentiment of being is filled with significance, connected with "All thinking things, all objects of all thought," the oneness of the urban experience is unintelligible and insignificant, the oneness of "no law, no meaning, and no end. . . ." This city offers an alternative form of infinity, meaninglessness and lawlessness without end.

Being can find no support in this terrible reduced condition, and being is, therefore, threatened with dissolution. Life in the city forces one to accept

> Oppression under which even highest minds
> Must labour, whence the strongest are not free. . . .
> (*Prel*. VII, 705–706)

Wordsworth writes of

> . . . a hell
> For eyes and ears! What anarchy and din
> Barbarian and infernal!
> (*Prel*. VII, 658–660)

of "blank confusion" and

> An undistinguishable world to Men,
> The slaves unrespited of low pursuits,
> Living amid the same perpetual flow
> Of trivial objects, melted and reduced
> To one identity, by differences
> That have no law, no meaning, and no end,
> Oppression under which even highest minds
> Must labour. . . .
> (*Prel*. VII, 699–706)

From this catalogue of denunciation, I believe that it is possible to derive a group of values that repelled Wordsworth and that were reduced and melted into a constellation of related and rejected concepts. The urban, the chaotic, the infernal, the unintelligible, and the oppressive form a constellation of related ideas in the matrix of Wordsworth's indignant verse. This constellation of negative values implies, in its turn, an opposite constellation of positive values, the rural, the ordered, the sacred, the significant, and the liberating. Freedom, order and significance seem to be linked as are their opposites, oppression, chaos, and meaninglessness. These relationships supply a new perspective from which to view Wordsworth's apostasy from the French Revolution. He came to reject the French Revolution because freedom was impossible without order, and the revolution produced not order but chaos, linked in the constellation of ideas to tyranny.

Wordsworth concludes his horrified description of Bartholomew Fair by observing that even in such a hell, "The Spirit of Nature was upon me here . . ." as was "The Soul of Beauty." Both were present even amid "the press/Of self-destroying, transitory things . . ." (*Prel.* VII, 735–739). The phrase "self-destroying, transitory things" is rich with significance. It suggests that transitory things, as opposed to the permanent forms of nature, destroy not only themselves, but also the self that dwells among them and links its being to them. The ideal society should be stable, rather than transitory. In such a society the self would not be destroyed and brought to nonbeing, but rather would be preserved. Capitalism, if Marx and Engels are correct, is a form of society that by its very nature produces transitory economic and social relations, replacing each relation in its turn by a new one. It is a set of social and economic productive relationships that must create new productive relations and, therefore, new social forms. Capitalism creates a world of "self-destroying transitory things" and is therefore inimical to the stability of the self, as Wordsworth conceives it. In a realm dominated by the spirit of capitalism Wordsworth would be threatened with nonbeing. His self would lack both any permanent referent, and any stabilizing affective ties. Chaos in the outer world is, then, linked to chaos within the self, and not by means of any form of pathetic fallacy. The self needs permanent and unchanging forms if it is to survive. The dual revolution and its associated demographic form, the city, and the economic links between the dual revolutions are all associated with instability, with "self-destroying, transitory things."

On another level, it is possible to see the tumult of Bartholomew Fair as a symbol of Wordsworth's own tumultuous repressed desires. The Fair, that is, may represent the chaotic realm of the psyche, that which Freud would call the id. Note that Wordsworth describes the Fair as being everything that his conscious moral judgment would reject. It is "a hell/For eyes and ears," that is, everything that eyes should not see and ears should not hear. It is "Barbarian," which is to say that it conforms to moral and cultural norms other than those that Wordsworth consciously obeyed. Further, the Fair is "a dream/Monstrous in colour, motion, shape, sight, sound." Now dreams, according to Freud, regularly present the dreamer with pictures of his own egoistic wishes, often, though not exclusively, sexual. Such wishes may be distorted by the dream censorship until they become monstrous in appearance and action. Moreover, to the degree that the wish appears in a relatively undistorted form, or to the degree that the dreamer's conscience intuits the hidden significance of the forbidden wish, he is likely to be repelled by what seems to his waking, moral judgment monstrous and abhorrent. So the tumult and welter of the fair may represent Wordsworth's forbidden and repressed desires struggling to obtain at least consciousness, if not fulfillment. It is significant in this regard that the crowd at the fair is described in terms that are also terms of erotic disgust. The crowd is "Inviting." The buffoons are described as "Grimacing, writhing, screaming . . ." (*Prel.* VII, 671–672).

If the fair is seen as an outlet for otherwise repressed sexuality, then it becomes clear how such an opportunity for license can lay "The whole creative powers of man asleep!" (*Prel.* VII, 654). Bartholomew Fair enervates creativity because for Wordsworth creativity results from sublimating brutal egoistic desires, transforming them into the imaginative faculty. The fair would directly discharge egoistic impulses, depriving the imaginative faculty of part of the energy that the imagination needed to function.

The results obtained from treating Bartholomew Fair as a symbol of Wordsworth's repressed desires are consonant with both the previous readings of the passage. Whether one reads the pas-

sage as an expression of the ruling classes' fear and hatred of the
lower orders, or as a rejection of the city as a social form capable
of supporting being, or finally as a symbol of repressed desires,
what is rejected in all three cases is the possibility of chaos, the
breakdown of established norms of conduct, and the possible release of pent-up egoism.

Because it may be true, as I suggest, that Wordsworth, in his
denunciation of Bartholomew Fair, joined himself to a ruling-class
withdrawal of sympathy from the often boisterous pleasures of the
lower orders (for Wordsworth, of the urban lower orders) at a time
when the ruling class feared the lower orders to be in a revolutionary mood, it is possible to misunderstand Wordsworth. Wordsworth was not, and never became, a mean-spirited Tory who had
contempt for the poor and those who toiled. Wordsworth was certainly by 1808, and, if my argument is correct, had been since
1800, a Tory humanist. He was to remain a Tory humanist for the
rest of his life. All subsequent political change on Wordsworth's
part was merely a gradual evolution of his Tory humanism. He
cared deeply about the condition of the poor not only in 1793,
when, as a republican supporter of the French Revolution, he
wrote his unpublished letter to Bishop Llandaff. But he still cared
about the poor in 1834, when, as a Tory supporter of the established English social order, he wrote, and had published a year
later as a postscript to the 1835 edition of his poems, an indignant
and humane attack on a Parliamentary report recommending re-
forms of the Poor Laws. The report Wordsworth attacked recom-
mended, in the words of the editors of the most recent collection
of Wordsworth's prose, "the abolition within two years of all relief
to the 'able-bodied' and their families, except that offered in 'well-
regulated' workhouses . . ." (*Prose* 3:234). The idea was to make
the conditions under which public relief was administered so unpleasant that few would ask for public assistance. Wordsworth's
humanitarian sensibility was outraged.

Increasingly as the war with revolutionary France continued,
and markedly after Bonaparte's rise to power on the eighteenth
Brumaire, Wordsworth's hostility to the forces that were disrupting
Grasmere's traditional order and his hostility to the two antitypes
of traditional society, the factory and the city, became focused,

symbolically, in antipathy to the French, now become aggressors in their turn. All Wordsworth's revulsion against the new social and economic order became caught up in his patriotic ardor, and in his hopes that iniquitous France would be conquered. To some extent this symbolic antipathy is quite understandable. The French were inspired by a revolutionary ideal dedicated to social change, however perverted that ideal had become. As Burke had early recognized, the Revolution had served the interests of the commercial and industrial interests of French society, and representatives of these interests were partisans of the Revolution. It was these same interests that Wordsworth now opposed in England. Most dramatically, England was literally making war upon the armies that fought for French commercial and industrial capital. It was actually, not figuratively, a life or death struggle, and Wordsworth became committed to France's defeat with all his soul. The battlefield of ideas had been supplemented, and to some extent replaced for him, by the bloody field of battle itself.

Wordsworth was not unique in his anxiety and commitment. Alarmed by the French example, and stimulated by the nationalist patriotic fervor brought on by the war, the English aristocracy and the English manufacturers became allies.[39] Sir Samuel Romilly later recalled that the French Revolution created "among the higher orders . . . a horror of every kind of innovation."[40] Wordsworth, it seems, was not alone in combining a hatred of the French Revolution (as it had evolved), with hatred of domestic innovation. Thompson notes that "The Evangelicals exhorted the upper classes to reform their own manners as an example to the poor."[41] And as a result of the invasion scare, a spate of patriotic broadsides and ballads became common fare. This popular literature provides a context for Wordsworth's patriotic sonnets. In the name of preserving British liberty "freedom of the press, of public meeting, of trade union organization and of election, were either severely limited or in abeyance."[42]

The panic-stricken gentry organized volunteer militia to help repel the threatened French invasion, should it take place. The gentry used its power to encourage and even to intimidate members of their community to join. William joined the Grasmere volunteer force, but in eagerness, not out of coercion, as

Dorothy makes clear in her October 9, 1803 letter to Mrs. Clarkson:

> William had gone to volunteer his services with the greatest part of
> the men of Grasmere—alas! alas! Mary and I have no other hope
> than that they will not be called upon out of these quiet far off
> places except in the case of the French being *successful* after their
> landing, and in that case what matter? We may all go together. But
> we want him to wait till the Body of *the people* should be called.
> For my part I thought much of the inconvenience and fatigue of
> going to be exercised twice or thrive a week, however if he really
> enters into it heart and soul and likes it, that will do him good, *and*
> *surely there never was a more determined hater of the French nor*
> *one more willing to do his utmost to destroy them if they really do*
> *come.*

[Final emphasis mine]
(*E.L.* 403)

One way that Wordsworth expressed his hatred of the French
revolutionaries was to link them associatively with Satan's host. At
one point in *The Prelude,* describing French revolutionaries, he
refers to "hissing Factionists with ardent eyes" (*Prel.* IX 57),
thereby evoking the line in *Paradise Lost,* when, turned into serpents to their chagrin, the fallen host utter "A dismal universal
hiss,"[43] rather than the "universal shout and high applause"[44]
with which they had intended to welcome Satan. Later Wordsworth refers to Robespierre and his fellow Montagnards as a "foul
tribe of Moloch" (*Prel.* X, 469). It is even remotely possible that
when Wordsworth refers to the revolutionary French nation as
being "a People risen up/ Fresh as the morning Star" (*Prel.* IX,
390–391) that this is a subtle indictment, as Lucifer is a name of
the morning star as well as being one of Satan's appellations. It is,
I hope, clear that I have not attempted to discuss exhaustively the
Miltonic influence on *The Prelude,* a task far beyond my present
purpose. *The Prelude* was, in a sense, written as a response to *Paradise Lost,* and opens, in its fifteenth line, with a deliberate echo
of the close of Paradise Lost, "The earth is all before me . . ."
(*Prel.* I, 15).

It is possible that Wordsworth evoked Milton in these Satanic
references in *The Prelude.* It is certain that Wordsworth con-

sciously attempted to follow Milton in reviving the passionate political sonnet and adopting the difficult Miltonic sonnet form. In
these sonnets Wordsworth alternately denounced France for its in-
iquity, and England for its lack of fervor. In the sonnet, "To Toussaint L'Ouverture" (P.W. 3:112–113), written in 1802, Wordsworth voices sympathy with a victim of French tyranny and
expresses some basic Wordsworthian beliefs about freedom. For
Wordsworth, freedom's ultimate emergence is ineluctable, because it is allied to the eternal aspects of nature, "air, earth, and
skies." Toussaint, though imprisoned by the French, has

> Powers that will work for thee; air, earth and skies;
> There's not a breathing in the common wind
> That will forget thee. . . .

Further, all that is innate in human nature, man's natural affections, his joys and sorrows, all work in the cause of liberty. Liberty
is man's birthright, his proper condition. Toussaint

> has great allies;
> Thy friends are exultatious, agonies,
> And love, and man's unconquerable mind.

In another sonnet written in 1802, "I Grieved for Buonaparté" (P.W. 3:110–111), Wordsworth finds Bonaparte pitiable
precisely because Bonaparte lacks those natural affections that are
forever allied with freedom. For all his transient worldly power,
Bonaparte is but a base, pitiable slave.

> The tenderest mood
> Of that Man's mind—what can it be? what food
> Fed his first hopes? what knowledge could *he* gain?

But Britain likewise has much to fear if it fails to live up to
the fullest potential of its humanity. Failure of full humanity risks
loss of freedom. Wordsworth expresses this fear in a series of sonnets written in 1802 and 1803, most directly, though not most
magnificently, in the sonnet "Written in London, September,
1802" (P.W. 3:115–116). He is distraught. Where can he find
comfort when wealth is more highly regarded in England than
"Plain living and high thinking" and "The homely beauty of the

good old cause. . . ." "Rapine, avarice, expense" are the subjects
of the new "idolatry."

> O! Friend I know not which way I must look
> For comfort, being, as I am, opprest,
> To think that now our life is only drest
> For show; mean handy-work of craftsman, cook,
> Or groom!—We must run glittering like a brook
> In the open sunshine, or we are unblest:
> The wealthiest man among us is the best:
> No grandeur now in nature or in book
> Delights us. Rapine, avarice, expense,
> This is idolatry; and these we adore:
> Plain living and high thinking are no more:
> The homely beauty of the good old cause
> Is gone; our peace, our fearful innocence,
> And pure religion breathing household laws.

Here Wordsworth clearly expresses his fear that the traditional
order may be dead. The good old values seem to have been replaced by the egoistic attributes of rapine and avarice. The new
social order and the new political economy seem to have reduced
England's full humanity. England's freedom is, therefore, in
jeopardy.

The sonnet "London, 1802" (P.W. 3:116) echoes these
themes. Would that Milton were alive. England is in need of such
a great spirit. Traditional English "manners, virtue, freedom,
power" have been lost. Wordsworth's contemporaries "Have forfeited their ancient English dower" because "We are selfish men.
. . ." Selfishness, again, has corrupted freedom. The same fear
that greed is enervating England's manliness and capacity for freedom is expressed in "When I have borne in memory what has
tamed" (P.W. 3:117–118), composed in 1802 or 1803. Wordsworth is aware that once-great nations have been brought low by
exaggerated concern for, and love of, money.

> When I have borne in memory what has tamed
> Great Nations, how ennobling thoughts depart
> When men change swords for ledgers, and desert
> The student's bower for gold, some fears unnamed
> I had, my country!

For England is "a bulwark for the cause of men . . ." and if England should grow weak from moral turpitude, all mankind's freedom would be threatened by French tyranny. England is mankind's "bulwark," its protector. It must maintain the probity proper for such a paternalistic force.

Wordsworth takes up the theme of the enervating effects of wealth again in the sonnet of 1803, "These times strike monied worldlings with dismay" (P.W. 3:119). Again he insists that the social fabric of a society is weakened when a social class dedicated to acquiring and accumulating wealth is allowed to exist and grow in power in that society. Wordsworth, in 1803, is writing of times when England struggled against a seemingly invincible Napoleonic France. Other countries joined the struggle, but only England unswervingly persisted, except for the brief and mutually convenient Peace of Amiens in 1802. It is of such times of trial that Wordsworth wrote:

> These times strike monied wordlings with dismay:
> Even rich men, brave by nature, taint the air
> With words of apprehension and despair. . . .

Men who are by nature brave are rendered cowards by the possession of that universal use-value, money. "Riches," Wordsworth asserts, "are akin/To fear, to change, to cowardice, and death." While in opposition to the "monied wordlings" are

> . . . the tens of thousands thinking on the affray,
> Men unto whom sufficient for the day
> And minds not stinted or unfilled are given,
> Sound, healthy, children of the God of heaven,
> Are cheerful as the rising sun in May.

These men sufficient for the struggle against Napoleon have what the monied worldlings do not, what man must have if his days are to be bound together by natural piety, that is, hope.

> . . . every gift of noble origin
> Is breathed upon by Hope's perpetual breath. . . .

To have natural piety, man's present must not only form a continuity with his past, but also with his future. And it is hope that allows man to break through "dismay" and "apprehension" and unite his present being with the future.

Riches destroy "virtue and the faculties within" because riches are "akin . . . to change." Change, as I have attempted to show, destroys pleasure; it makes the world forbidding. Hope cannot grow in a despairing world. Riches make even brave men cowards by impairing their capacity to hope. Further, the possession of riches causes the rich man to become absorbed in the concern for maintaining his riches intact. This diverts his attention from the communal good and channels it into egoistic self-concern. As I shall show in the next chapter, Wordsworth believed that a contraction of the sympathy into oneself is a failure of imaginative power, and the maintenance of hope requires an expenditure of imaginative power. So both because of the connection between riches and change, and because of the tendency of riches to increase self-concern, riches destroy man's capacity to hope, and without hope, courage, the faith in the possibilities of the future, perishes. A self-involved man has withdrawn his sympathy into himself. He is a contracted spirit, threatened with further contraction, dissolution, and ultimately nonbeing. Wordsworth had previously connected the capitalist spirit with several negative values, but in "These times strike monied wordlings with dismay" he indicts the capitalist spirit with effeminacy for the first time.

But if Wordsworth laments England's falling away from full humanity, he is still fully human and can hope, and his hope is validated by the moral condition of the French. The French have not only fallen away from full humanity, they are actively at war with what is truly valuable in human life; liberty, community, sanity, wisdom, sobriety, and patience. Wordsworth expresses this view of the French in another sonnet of 1803, "One might believe that natural miseries" (P.W. 3:118). The French have established an anticommunity. The community of natural affections is shattered in France. Rather than being bound in reciprocal relations of charity, "Whole myriads should unite/To work against themselves such fell despite." They unite, not to aid one another, but to thwart one another in a hideous parody of community. Out of the lack of harmony comes a blight so serious that:

> One might believe that natural miseries
> Had blasted France, and made of it a land
> Unfit for men. . . .

But such is not the case:

> But 'tis a chosen soil, where sun and breeze
> Shed gentle favours: rural works are there,
> And ordinary business without care;
> Spot rich in all things that can soothe and please!

Nor is it enough that the French should have destroyed their own precious community. In their "phrensy and in drunken mirth" they are

> Impatient to put out the only light
> Of Liberty that yet remains on earth!

The French with their "dearth/Of knowledge," their inability to work together in the works of peace, their "phrensy," their "drunken mirth," their impatience and their hatred of liberty, have made themselves contemptible. They no longer possess the attributes of fully realized, fully developed humanity that are necessary for true freedom. No longer truly human, no longer free, they are bestial slaves who, incapable of sustaining true community themselves, seek to destroy the community that Wordsworth values, that gives Wordsworth's self stability.

Wordsworth could not and did not patiently await the destruction of his precious community. His community was threatened not only by the French, but by the factory, and the city, and the whole new, calculating, egotistical order of rapidly maturing capitalism. When he opposed the Napoleonic French, he symbolically opposed the new economic system and its hated creations as well. So Wordsworth joined the Grasmere volunteers and drilled. He wrote a series of patriotic sonnets for newspaper publications, in order to help brace the national spirit. And, when the proper moment came, he issued, after much labor, a powerful defense of the England that he loved.

SIX

COMMUNITY DEFENDED

THE proper moment did come. It came in September, 1808, when news reached Wordsworth of the convention between the British expeditionary force, that had been sent to fight the French occupying the Iberian Peninsula, and the occupying French force. The convention had been signed at Cintra, in Portugal, and bore the town's name.

I shall only give a brief outline of the events leading up to the Convention of Cintra, using Owen and Smyser's general introduction to Wordsworth's essay as my source (*Prose* 1:193–217). Napoleon attempted to bring Portugal into his Continental System by demanding in August, 1807, that Portugal should declare war on Britain. Failing to receive a satisfactory reply, Napoleon concluded the Treaty of Fontainebleau with Spain on October 27, 1807. Spain was to permit French troops to pass through Spain on their way to occupy Portugal, and in return Spain was to participate with France in the partition of Portugal. French troops, under General Junot, entered Lisbon on November 30. By the beginning of January 1808, over 55,000 French troops had entered Spain, and it soon became apparent that, rather than marching to support Junot, they were, in fact, beginning a French occupation of Spain. By the middle of February the French threw aside all pretense that they were acting in accord with the Treaty of Fontainbleau and advanced on Madrid.

On May 2, riots broke out in Madrid, occupied by General

Murat. The riots were brutally suppressed, and news of their suppression sparked a general revolt in Spain, breaking out first in Asturias on May 24. The Spanish revolt not only cut the line of communications to Junot's force in Portugal, but induced a Portuguese revolt as well. By the middle of June, the entire Iberian Peninsula was in active rebellion against French occupation.

On August 1 a British expeditionary force, under Wellesley, landed at Mondego Bay on the Portuguese coast. Wellesley began his advance on Lisbon. He defeated a small French force at Rolica on August 17. Junot attacked Wellesley at Vimiero on August 21. Wellesley repulsed Junot's attack and succeeded in throwing Junot's forces into disorder. Though Wellesley wanted to pursue and harry the retreating French force, he was prevented by the arrival of his overcautious successor, Sir Harry Burrard on August 22. The policy of caution was reconfirmed by Sir Hew Dalrymple who replaced Burrard almost immediately. Before any British offensive could be resumed, Junot's subordinate, General Kellermann, arrived in the British camp and requested that a convention be negotiated. The convention was negotiated between August 23 and August 30 and signed on the last day of the negotiations. British newspapers published news of the Convention of Cintra on September 16.

The terms of the convention were repellent to many Englishmen. For one thing, the convention provided that the British evacuate the French troops, horse, artillery and supplies and deposit them at a French port near the Spanish border. That seemed to many to be generous treatment to mete out to an enemy already defeated twice on the field of battle, once signally. The enemy was to be moved from a spot where it was surrounded by an armed and hostile populace and confronted by a successful, reinforced enemy army and navy. It was then to be removed to the safety of its own land, placed where it could soon resume the attack. Despite the fact that the French had pillaged Portugal they were, according to the convention, to "be at liberty to dispose of their private property of every description; with full security hereafter for the purchasers" (*Prose* 1:353). Who was to say that crime did not pay? Not only did the treaty legitimatize looting but, while supposedly a military treaty, it bound the Portuguese government from restoring stolen property to its rightful owners. It also bound the British forces to protect Portuguese collaborators from the full force of Portuguese justice. An army that had been brought into Portugal as an ally entered into an agreement with the French without consulting the Portuguese government and forces, and also failed to limit the agreement to a purely military one, and by failing to do so arrogated to itself civilian authority over Portugal. The convention contained many more of what seemed to be disgraceful clauses. The British ministry, far from showing disapprobation, ordered the cannons of London be fired as a signal of victory, thereby implicating itself in the Convention of Cintra.

Public meetings took place first in London, and then elsewhere in England in order to petition the King to persuade him to refuse to honor the convention and to prosecute those responsible for betraying the public trust by drawing up and signing such a convention. The first known response that Wordsworth made to the convention came on September 27 in a letter to Richard Sharp, "We are all here cut to the heart by the conduct of Sir Hew and his Brother Knight in Portugal" (M.L. 267). Wordsworth wanted to organize a public meeting in Cumberland and to speak out at it against the abhorred convention, but Lord Londsdale threw his powerful political weight against the plan, effectively blocking any public protest.

Thwarted in his first attempt to reach the public Wordsworth set out to reach an audience through the printed word. In November Wordsworth undertook to write a prose tract denouncing the Convention of Cintra and expressing what he believed to be the true principles of polity. This task was to be one to which Wordsworth would dedicate six months of difficult, often anxiety-provoking labor. Originally Wordsworth intended his tract to be published in Daniel Stuart's newspaper, The Courier. And indeed the first two installments appeared in the December 27, 1808, and January 13, 1809, issues of The Courier, but what Wordsworth referred to as "the pressure of public business" (Prose 1:223)* made the protracted appearance in installments of a long and often quite abstract political tract unlikely. The public business to which Wordsworth referred was probably the scandal involving the Duke of York's mistress, who was accused of taking bribes in order to influence the Duke's decisions about promotions in the Army. The scandal broke at the end of January. But even in late December Wordsworth was negotiating with Daniel Stuart about Stuart's bringing out the completed text as a published pamphlet. Towards the end of February DeQuincey arrived in London, commissioned by Wordsworth, to supervise the printing of the tract. It was DeQuincey who had to deal with the continual stream of additions, revisions, and alarms about possible libelous matter that flowed to London from Grasmere. The printing was finally finished on May 18, after much delay.

During December, 1808, when Wordsworth was working on his pamphlet, he wrote two sonnets inspired by his work on the tract. The first of these, "Composed while the Author was engaged in writing a Tract occasioned by the Convention of Cintra" (P.W. 3:128), adumbrates several themes taken up in the tract itself. The sonnet suggests that the soul of man is born free, but only conditionally so. The "World's vain objects . . . enslave/The free-born Soul," just as "selfish interest perverts the will. . . ." Vanity and selfish interest engender thoughts that "bondage can restrain." But if the social world of egoism and vanity, of calculated policy and "factions," the world, perhaps, of the capitalistic monied worldlings, can bind the soul, the world of "mighty Nature" is a "school sublime" in which Wordsworth can "weigh the hopes and fears of suffering Spain. . . ." Nature is the world of

> . . . dark wood and rocky cave,
> And hollow vale which foaming torrents fill
> With omnipresent murmur as they rave
> Down their steep beds, that never shall be still. . . .

Here the unbound mind is free to "consult the auguries of time" for "Triumph, and thoughts no bondage can restrain." The reader might profitably contrast the bound world of "vain objects that enslave" with the ever-active world of Nature in which "foaming torrents . . . never shall be still. . . ."

The free soul is not fettered, not solipsistically locked in on itself. It can move out of the limited present and explore "the auguries of time." But this freedom is conditioned. If the soul cleaves to the world of eternal forms, the world of nature, it is free;

it has access to highest reason. But if the soul enters into the world of "factions" and "selfish interest," the bourgeois world of calculation, then the soul is bound in the present without access to time's auguries. It may use only the perverted, limited reason of bare utilitarian counters. So the social world to which the soul has access can help to determine the soul's bondage or freedom.

The tract over which Wordsworth labored for six months was first advertised in *The Courier* on May 27, 1809. The formidable complete title of this tract is *Concerning The Relations of Great Britain, Spain, and Portugal, To Each Other, And To The Common Enemy, At This Crisis; And Specifically As Affected By the Convention Of Cintra: The whole brought to the test of those Principles, by which alone the Independence and Freedom of Nations can be Preserved or Recovered.*

Though Wordsworth was not a rigorously systematic thinker, Wordsworth's thought is, nevertheless, so highly integrated that it is not possible, in reading the Cintra tract, to separate Wordsworth's political theory from his ethics, epistemology, psychology, and aesthetics. The consonance among these areas of his thought is great, connected as they are by Wordsworth's concepts of the imagination and the passions. Because it is so difficult to extract the purely political and social ideas in the Cintra tract from ideas about aesthetics, or psychology, I have found it necessary to subject the Cintra tract to a close reading. In doing so, I hope that I make it possible to see the relations between Wordsworth's Tory humanism and the rest of his thought, particularly his aesthetic thought.

Wordsworth's Cintra tract is by any measure an aesthetic oddity. Its prose lacks the semblance of clarity and simplicity that leads the unwary reader of Wordsworth's Preface to the *Lyrical Ballads* to premature certitude. The prose is dense, tangled and resistant. Moreover, on first reading, the tract seems formless, and, perhaps, void. No obvious structural pattern emerges. The reader is apt to be bored by what appears to be endless repetition. One thing is soon apparent; the form, whatever it may be, is not linear.

Upon examination a form can be found, but it is a form that seems closer to ballad structure, or even musical structure, than to more familiar modes of prose discourse. A refrain, or theme, is stated, but rather than progressing in a linear fashion to following themes, the text circles back again and again to the same point from different angles, here expanding, there emphasizing a hitherto undeveloped aspect of the theme. As in a ballad when a refrain is repeated, or as in musical form when a melodic sequence is repeated, every repetition is changed by that which came between the two thematic statements. It is in this fashion, and in this fashion only, that the Cintra tract progresses. And when Wordsworth falters, the structure is reduced to dull repetition.

Wordsworth opens the tract with the assertion that the Convention of Cintra "is one of the most important events of our time" (224). Further reading will demonstrate that Wordsworth is earnest rather than hyperbolic here. News of the convention rocked England like an "earthquake." Wherever news of the convention reached it produced sorrow.

> . . . [Y]et, through force of scorn, impatience, hope, and indignation, and through the universal participation in passions so complex, and the sense of power which this necessarily included— the whole partook of the energy and activity of congratulation and joy. (224)

Here on the very threshold of his essay Wordsworth produces the first of several seeming paradoxes that penetrate into the center of Wordworth's social thought. A piece of news that immediately produces sorrow ultimately effects congratulation and joy. How is it that congratulation and joy can be the direct products of sorrow? The answer is that England is a morally healthy commonwealth. It is capable of hope and indignation. Hope indicates that the community is not confined to the present. It is capable of projecting its spirit into the future. Where an individual or community is morally sound even intense suffering will bring forth good. Despair is a failure of hope. Joy is the product of hope.

But this emergence of hope from despair is overdetermined in the closely woven texture of the Cintra tract. Later, in a passage that I shall examine in some detail, Wordsworth suggests that the true sorrow of life is that reality offers so few experiences that are correlative "to the dignity and intensity of human desires . . ."

(339). Now the Convention of Cintra, an object truly worthy of shame and sorrow, offered an opportunity for the release of emotions that would not be beneath the dignity and intensity of human desires. The sorrow of human life would be overcome in the experience of true shame and sorrow. A catharsis would have been achieved. If an occasion in the affairs of men is equal to the worth and strength of human emotion, that occasion, even if as a thing in and of itself it be sorrowful, may produce pleasure, because by affording an opportunity for the expression of sorrow, it is affording an opportunity for the discharge of pent-up emotion. The discharge of emotion may well lessen the emotional tension in the sorrowing individual's psychic economy. The diminution of psychic tension is felt as a form of pleasure.

The greater part of the British people had opposed its leaders in England's initial declaration of war against the French. But when France came to embody "the spirit of selfish tyranny and lawless ambition" (226), the English nation united in support of the war. It is significant that "selfish tyranny and lawless ambition" should be the moral crimes that, in Wordsworth's eyes, turned England against France. Selfishness and ambition are manifestations of uncontrolled egoism. Lawlessness is a failure to impose discipline upon the self, while tyranny is an unwarranted imposition of discipline upon others. These two moral failures violate two of Wordsworth's highest values, self-control, a virtue he dedicates himself to in "Peele Castle" and "Ode to Duty," and the virtues of gentleness and kindness to others, a value that so pervades Wordsworth's work that it is difficult to isolate a *locus classicus*.

Wordsworth says that the tide of English feeling began to turn against France "after the subjugation of Switzerland . . ." (226). In saying this Wordsworth seems to be projecting his own feelings onto the English people. For Wordsworth to do this so early in the tract suggests that consciously or unconsciously he is assuming the voice of the English people.

The people entered the war not with valorous determination, but out of the negative desire that they not seem to acquiesce to French tyranny. They strove to avoid "the guilt of seeming to approve what they had not power to prevent, and out of a consciousness of the danger that such guilt would otherwise actually steal upon them . . ." (226). For Wordsworth the moral probity of a community cannot be achieved passively. Virtue inert is in danger of becoming vice. The people wished, then, for war, because "the sword, in the hands of the good and the virtuous, is the most intelligible symbol of abhorrence" (226). War, then, when just, cannot be chaotic. It is, rather, "intelligible," or meaningful.

Some statesmen counciled peace, but the people demanded a just war. There "are promptings of wisdom from the penetralia of human nature, which a people can hear, though the wisest of their practical Statesmen be deaf toward them" (227). There is a suggestion here of a folk wisdom stemming from the collective consciousness of the people. The wisdom of the people emanates directly from their natural domestic affections. Their vision is not blocked by the cultural superstructure that sometimes obscures the statesman's vision. Yet, as the English fought to avoid subjugation rather than to achieve positive moral good, their struggle "had too much of fear, and therefore of selfishness, not to be contemplated in the main with rueful emotion" (227). Fear is equated with selfishness because fear demonstrates an inability to hope, demonstrates that the ego is imprisoned in a cage of present circumstances, drawn in upon itself and unable to flow with the possible future. An ego drawn in upon itself is close to the state of selfishness. The fearful self is, in my terminology, contracted. This is a theme to which Wordsworth will return fugally, again and again.

The Iberian uprising disturbed British self-involvement, and allowed hope. Instead of being frozen in the present moment, the British were free to range backward and forward in time:

> . . . we looked backward upon the records of the human race with pride, and, instead of being afraid, we delighted to look forward to futurity. (228).

If the British were to act to aid the Spanish, then the British must have steady "PRINCIPLES to confront and direct us (without which we may do much harm, and can do no good) . . ." (p. 230). For Wordsworth the only effective guarantee that a social end will be achieved is that the means be moral. If good is to be sought, it must be sought with good. Action not based on sound principles is likely to be self-defeating.

The Spanish had been defeated in the field but not in the spirit. "The Spaniards . . . have been loath to depart from established laws, forms, and practices." This shows "a thoughtfulness most hopeful for" (232) their cause. Just as British policy can only thrive if it is morally sound, so it is necessary that "the Chiefs of the Spanish Nation be men of wise and strong minds . . ." (233). Both British and Spanish must be wise and principled. Though the tract started out as an attack on the Convention of Cintra, it is beginning to take the form of a statesman's manual. This is underscored by Wordsworth's explicit separation of the Spanish people, on the one hand, and their government on another. Speaking of the Spaniards Wordsworth says that those Spanish people who would work with government "would rely more confidently upon a Government which thus proved that it had confidence in itself" (233). One of the great questions of the Cintra tract is how may the governing class be instructed so as to compensate for the loss of wisdom it inflicts upon itself by separating itself from the people.

The Spaniards were never expected to succeed in and through their army: "if by their *army* be meant anything but the people. The whole people is their army . . ." (233). In following up this point Wordsworth uses a telling simile. He writes, "A military spirit should be there," amid the Spanish people, "and a military action, not confined like an ordinary river in one channel, but spreading like the Nile over the whole face of the land" (234). The alert Wordsworthian should be reminded of the image of the overflowing Nile that concludes the "'Imagination" passage in Book VI of *The Prelude* that follows Wordsworth's discovery that he had crossed the Alps:

> The mind beneath such banners militant
> Thinks not of spoils or trophies, nor of aught
> That may attest its prowess, blest in thoughts
> That are their own perfection and reward,
> Strong in itself, and in the access of joy
> Which hides it like the overflowing Nile.
> (*Prel.* VI, 543–548)

The same image that is used in *The Prelude* to describe the excess of joy produced by an intense imaginative experience is here used to describe the spirit of an armed partisan uprising. Implicitly the imaginative experience and partisan warfare are, I think, linked. And if they are linked, the linkage provides evidence that the imaginative experience was not only, for Wordsworth, the response to nature of a passive solitary. A populous armed mass could, if morally elevated, achieve the beatification that is traditionally ascribed to Wordsworth's intercourse with nature. If this is true then social life and activity can be a source of imaginative fulfillment for Wordsworth. Other passages of the Cintra tract, as I read it, support this conjecture.

Wordsworth here envisions an affective community with effective power, in this case military power. Spain may realize, he says, "the civic and the military spirit united in one people, and in enduring harmony with each other" (234). The Spaniards have been raised to "an elevated mood" by "indignant passions . . ." (234). It is this elevated mood that makes possible the seeming anomaly of Wordsworth giving his approbation to a community possessing both affective and effective power. The people have been elevated to a moral plane above the egoism that normally makes the combination of material and emotional power dangerous. Their effective military power is to be used not for self-aggrandizement but for the restoration and protection of their original community in which affective power was balanced by lack of effective power. Evidence for this construction may be found in Wordsworth's suggestion that the Spanish "seek additional aid from affections, which . . . exclude all individual interests" (234). Again, in the same vein, Wordsworth asserts, "In the moral virtues and qualities of passion which belong to a people, must the ultimate salvation of a people be sought for" (235). The emotional power of the people is able to coexist with physical force because the former is the source and cause of the latter. Without these virtues and qualities of passion, the Spaniards would be but an armed band, despondent, incapable of hope, like the monied worldings. Strength comes from moral virtues because these virtues "are more permanent in their nature" (235).

Wordsworth then makes an epistemological assertion that bears not only upon his argument, but also upon his theory of how poetry functions. He says without qualification that "all knowledge of human nature leads ultimately to repose . . ." (237). He makes this claim in order to protect himself from the charge of having written many words so far with little matter about the convention itself. It is necessary, he says, to deepen his readers' knowledge of human nature in order to allow his "readers to form an estimate of the grounds of hope and fear in the present effort of liberty against oppression . . ." (237). Wordsworth's assertion that all knowledge of human nature leads to repose bears significantly upon his theory of the function of poetry. In his Preface to *Lyrical Ballads* Wordsworth makes traditional assertions about the function of poetry. Good poetry teaches and delights. As to the educative function Wordsworth wrote in the 1800 version that his poetry was "well adapted to interest mankind" because of the "multiplicity and . . . the quality of its moral relations . . ." (*Prose* 1:120). Wordsworth interprets in a new way the traditional requirement that poetry instruct when he writes that the poems have been chosen so that they might "illustrate the manner in which our feelings and our ideas are associated in a state of excitement" (*Prose* 1:126). As to the necessity that poetry give delight Wordsworth added in 1802 that the "particular purpose" of a poet was "that of giving pleasure" (*Prose* 1:138). Now in making these two demands upon poetry Wordsworth is scarcely breaking new ground. That poetry should instruct and delight is traditional poetic theory going back to Sidney and, even further, to Horace.

However, if "all knowledge of human nature leads ultimately to repose," then all poetry that deepens our understanding of human nature leads ultimately to repose, and if I may be allowed to describe repose as a form of delight or pleasure, then all poetry that deepens our knowledge of human nature gives at least one form of pleasure, if not more. So for Wordsworth, poetry written insightfully about men, whether about himself, as in *The Prelude*, "Tintern Abbey" or the "Intimations Ode," or about others, as in "The Idiot Boy," "Peter Bell," or "The Waggoner," fulfills both demands made of poetry. Such poems instruct and give pleasure. If human nature is Wordsworth's subject he can delight by giving instruction. His two tasks become, by his definition of human knowledge, one.

There is a political corollary to the assertion that knowledge of human nature leads to repose. Such knowledge could lead to repose and composure only if man were "naturally" good, and evil an unnatural distortion of the human essence. This presupposes, to be sure, that Wordsworth would not find repose in the belief that men were naturally vicious. Assertions that man is naturally good, later in the tract, support this presupposition. The belief that men are, on balance, naturally good and that there is little radical evil is a holdover from the days of Wordsworth's revolutionary radicalism. The belief in man's natural depravity has been a cornerstone of Western conservative political thought since St. Augustine.

Wordsworth then sets out to show that there was a deep antipathy between the Spaniards and the Portuguese on the one hand, and the French, on the other. The purpose of this demonstration is to show that had the British expeditionary force not proved itself unworthy, it would have found a great natural ally in the inhabitants of the Iberian Peninsula. Wordsworth attempts to show the enormity of the tyranny under which the Peninsula labored. "Such tyranny," he says, "is, in the strictest sense, intolerable; not because it aims at the extinction of life, but of every thing which gives life its value—of virtue, of reason, of repose in God, or in truth" (241). The forces of contraction can take the form of all that destroys the significance of life. If life is rendered chaotic and morally meaningless, it becomes unendurable, verging on annihilation. Virtue, reason, trust in God, and truth are all ordering, stabilizing principles. Everything that renders life significant is, for Wordsworth, due honor, while all forces that render life meaningless are to be opposed. Let me quote again a portion of a text cited in an earlier chapter, "The Communist Manifesto":

> Constant revolutionizing of production, uninterrupted disturbance of all social conditions, everlasting uncertainty and agitation distinguish the bourgeois epoch from all earlier ones. All fixed fast-frozen relations, with their train of ancient and venerable prejudices and opinions, are swept away. . . . All that is solid melts into air, all that is holy profaned. . . .[1]

Would it be surprising if, in light of this observation, Wordsworth came to find bourgeois development, and with it capitalist development, destructive of virtue, reason, repose in God, and truth, and therefore destructive of order and of significance?

The destruction that Napoleon has unleashed in Spain, "the carnage and devastation spread over their land have not afflicted this noble people so deeply" as "the arrogant assumptions of beneficence made by him from whose order that blood has flowed" (242). Napoleon in his arrogance still believes that he is Spain's benefactor. Wordworth writes:

> Still to be talking of bestowing and conferring, and to be happy in the sight of nothing but what he thinks he has bestowed or conferred, this, in a man to whom the weakness of his fellows has given great power, is a madness of pride more hideous than cruelty itself. (242)

Wordsworth abhors Napoleon's egotism. Napoleon, as Wordsworth sees him, can be content only in a world in which every object or institution bears his own imprint, has somehow been affected by him. Such a desire to control the world is inimical to the community hymned in "Home at Grasmere." It is, perhaps, an aggressive impulse that Wordsworth had felt in himself, in his princely experience of himself, and had consequently repudiated. An egotism so intense that it can conceive of things outside the self only as emanations of the self, presses towards narcissism and megalomania. All affect, previously projected onto the world, seems to have withdrawn back into a self that conceives that it and it alone can give, for it and it alone contains all. Wordsworth, who in *The Prelude* proclaimed that he gave the setting sun new splendor, was, perhaps, oversensitive to a self that announced its power to give and change everything. Bonaparte could change actively in the real world that which Wordsworth could change only in fantasy. And a potency such as Bonaprte's might be repellent to Wordsworth. Wordsworth may well have been reacting against a now rejected, previously valued element of his own mental life.

The Spanish do not "murmur or repine" (243) in their suffering. Rather they see the French occupation as a divine visitation sent first to punish and then to arouse them. They call to their

minds Pelayo and the Cid that they may be worthy of their ances-
tors:

> And surely to a people thus united in their minds with the heroism
> of years which have been long departed, and living under such
> obligation of gratitude to their ancestors, it is not difficult, nay it is
> natural, to take upon themselves the highest obligations of duty to
> their posterity; to enjoy in the holiness of imagination the happiness
> of unborn ages to which they shall have eminently contributed.
> . . . (244)

Wordsworth here adopts Burke's conservative conception of a society that survives by reason of its organic and diachronic wholeness.
Society is kept sound by being linked backward in time to its an-
cestors and forward to its posterity in order to create a wholesome
state of natural piety. There is a backward continuity of reverence
for one's forefathers. One does not seek to be a Promethean rebellious son, but, rather, to be a father in one's turn who may hope
to be looked back upon with due respect.

Again echoing Burke, Wordsworth describes a commitment
towards "re-constructing out of the materials of their ancient institutions, customs, and laws, a better frame of civil government
. . ." (247–248). The new will be organically continuous with the
structure of government left by the forefathers.

Wordsworth then apologizes for having dwelt on the sufferings of the Spanish, the cruel madness of Bonaparte, and the high
moral plane on which the Spanish have borne themselves. He
knows that the reader is aware of all this.

> It is not from any thought that I am communicating new informa-
> tion, that I have dwelt thus long upon this subject, but to recall to
> the reader his own knowledge, and to re-infuse into that knowledge
> a breath and life of appropriate feeling; because the bare sense of
> wisdom is nothing without its powers, and it is only in these feel-
> ings that the powers of wisdom exist. (248)

Wordsworth stands outside of the Baconian tradition. Knowledge
in and of itself does not and cannot communicate power. Knowledge can only add to power when it is united with "appropriate
feeling." The poet unites feeling with knowledge, and the result is

power. A limited rationalism that ignores the richness of the emotions is dry and impotent.

Given the intensity of both the British and the Spanish people's hatred of Bonaparte, what was the response of the British people to this convention, which failed to mete out condign punishment to Bonaparte's representatives and army? The British people "with one voice" (248) decided the matter by reprobating the Convention of Cintra. The "People were compelled by . . . the very constitution of man as a moral Being . . ." (249) to take this action. Man in his uncorrupted natural state is, for Wordsworth, a moral being. But the convention had destroyed the only power against Bonaparte "which ever afforded a glimpse of hope to a sane mind, the power of popular resistance rising out of universal reason, and from the heart of human nature . . ." (253). Such a power arose from fully developed man, devoid of self-hood, united collectively with others into a militant affective community. Only such emotional unity, rooted in what was fundamentally human—defense of home, loved ones, country, and traditions—could oppose the ardor of the French, an ardor of which Wordsworth had had some firsthand knowledge during the time he spent in revolutionary France. To the extent that the community had to transcend its selfish interests in order to put forward popular resistance, such resistance was an act of imaginative fulfillment.

At the time Wordsworth wrote "Home at Grasmere," beginning in 1800, he felt that he had found a refuge from the world outside the vale. Further, as I have shown, Wordsworth was conscious of a restraint upon the sterner, more angry aspect of his being, a restraint imposed, perhaps, in reaction to his failed attempt at rebellion against father and fatherland. By June, 1808, in "A Tuft of Primroses," Wordsworth expressed pained resignation, rather than rage, at what he saw as the "unrelenting doom" (*P.W.* 5:354) that the vale faced from worldly forces from outside the vale. But in the Cintra tract, begun not six months after "A Tuft of Primroses," Wordsworth is able to express his rage at those who destroy and those who fail to protect community. Later he will denounce the disruptive forces that he calls "Manufacture and Commerce" (332). Further, throughout the tract Wordsworth seems hopeful of the ultimate victory of the form of community that he

values. Rage and violence are not forbidden him as he calls for
guerilla uprising because they are linked to the defense of traditional community. Nevertheless, the expression of rage was still
something so linked to the forbidden in Wordsworth that he was
haunted by fears that he would be clapped into Newgate for libel,
in retaliation for his denunciation of the ministry, Wellesley, and
Dalrymple—fears that Dorothy and Mary correctly dismissed as
exaggerations.

After justifying anger and condemnation in defense of worthy
values, Wordsworth goes on to assert that "government was from
the beginning ordained" in order "to support" preserve and cherish
the "benign elementary feelings of society" (267). Society is prior
to and more natural than the state, which is a secondary organization created to protect and foster society. So "benign and elementary feelings" generate society which in its turn generates government. Society is founded not by a contract nor by a collective
rational calculation of the greatest good of the greatest number.
Nor is society the a priori given without which and outside of
which man cannot exist as man, as it is for Aristotle. Society is
generated by man's basic and natural impulse to love. If government exists to protect these tender feelings, then the British, in ig-
noring the rights and desires of the Portuguese government, and in
offending the deepest feelings of the Portuguese people, dealt a terrible blow to the very fabric of their ally's society.

Wordsworth tries to show that the convention is so worded
that it allows the French to leave Portugal with the booty that they
had been able to seize by force of arms. The governor of Cadiz, on
the other hand, refused to allow General Dupont's army to carry
off its plunder. If the Spanish government had acted differently to
General Dupont it would have lost the confidence of the Spanish
people, for "These are sympathies which prove that a government
is paternal . . ." (271), and only a government with these sympathies can gain the loyalty of its subjects. Such a government
"makes one family with the people . . ." (271–272). The familial
model of government was widely thought, by Wordsworth and his
contemporaries, to be the best model of the state. Here is further
evidence, however indirect, that Wordsworth's advocacy of the
doctrines of the French Revolution constituted in part a symbolic

rebellion against the father, and his abandonment of revolutionary doctrines a resubmission to the father, for the established government and the father are here metaphorically and conventionally equated.

Wordsworth speaks out against the British government for condemning a group of Londoners who called for punishment of those responsible for the Convention of Cintra. The government insisted that such condemnation constituted a prejudging of the matter and a denial of a constitutional right to a fair trial.

> Actions and agents like these, exhibited in this connection with each other, must of necessity be condemned the moment they are known: and to assert the contrary, is to maintain that man is a being without understanding, and that morality is an empty dream. (274)

This is an implicit statement that man does have understanding and that morality is not a dream, nor is morality a relative historical construction. It is something absolute and definite that man will recognize if he is truly human. Men who have no moral sense are not representative of fully developed humanity; nor are men who lack understanding so developed. Moral sense and developed understanding are natural human characteristics. They do not require wealth, leisure, or advanced education for their cultivation. Here again is that Janus-faced aspect of Wordsworth's political thought. Even the socially humble man is, by his nature, fully human. Wordsworth excepts from this statement about the nature of the socially humble only those men who have suffered greatly from poverty, and those whose faculties have been stunted by being forced to develop "In cities where, the human heart is sick . . ." (*Prel.* xii, 194–202). This is, on the one hand, a compliment to those of low social station, and, on the other hand, a salve to the conscience of the ruling orders, as it assures them that the existing social order successfully produces fully developed men.

Those who continue to insist that condemnation of those guilty in the matter of Cintra should await "the formal sanction of a court of judicature" are guilty of nothing less than "selfishness" which has "cut them off from fellowship with the species" (274). They have failed to unite with the species because they are underdeveloped in their understanding and their moral sense. For self-ishness is an imaginative failure to break free of the self that leads to an inability to conceive of any being other than oneself, and is therefore a failure to understand anyone else. Such a failure of understanding leaves one an isolate, cut off from any collective moral sensibility.

Wordsworth says of the convention:

> it was not done in a remote corner by persons of obscure rank; but in the eyes of Europe and of all mankind; by the leading authorities, military and civil, of a mighty empire. It did not relate to a petty immunity, or a local and insulated privilege—but to the highest feelings of honour to which a nation may either be calmly and gradually raised by a long course of independence, liberty, and glory; or to the level of which it may be lifted up at once, from a fallen state, by a sudden and extreme pressure of violence and tyranny. (288)

Nations may be raised to high feelings of honor either by a tradition of independence, or by being "lifted up at once from a fallen state, by a sudden and extreme pressure of violence and tyranny." For Wordsworth suffering may be a redemptive force not only for an individual, as "The White Doe of Rylstone," composed from 1807 to 1808, with its epigraph from *The Borderers*, suggests. But also suffering, "violence and tyranny," may act as a redemptive power on a nation as well, literally as an uplifting force.

In responding to the news of the convention Britain reacted as a united affective community. Wordsworth writes that "Every human being in these islands was unsettled . . ." (289). This leads Wordsworth to observe that "when the people speak loudly, it is from being strongly possessed either by the Godhead or the Demon" (290). Wordsworth takes it for granted that a people quiet or at rest will not speak loudly unless acted upon by an external spiritual force, either divine or Satanic. The natural state of the people is, then, silence, so that one way or another their utterances were literally ominous. They were expected, under normal circumstances, to be quiet, lending their passive consent to virtual representation. Beyond their community they were not expected to have a determining voice in civil affairs.

Now the people could at times speak loudly. If they were influenced by a diabolic force, then the voice of the collective multitude could be a source of terror. This was the insurrectionary voice of the *menu peuple,* the leveling mob of redressors, the "swinish multitude," that the ruling orders feared. If the people were influenced by a divine force, then the voice of one collective people would be a vast chant hymning patriotic utterances of despair or joy, reaffirming traditional morality and community. This voice, far from having anarchistic, leveling tonalities, would express loyalty and virtue.

Again Wordsworth's highly ambivalent view of the people, that elsewhere grants them full species being, with both progressive and regressive implications, expresses itself. If the people speak loudly, they are divinely or demonically inspired. No intermediate causal possibility is allowed. The people's speech can either be blessed or evil.

The Spanish had been done an evil and they rose with the active and divine aim of ridding the world of an evil:

> Riddance, mere riddance—safety, mere safety—are objects far too defined, too inert and passive in their own nature, to have ability either to rouze or to sustain . . . for the mind gains consciousness of its strength to undergo only by exercise among materials which admit the impression of its power,—which grows under it, which bends under it,—which resist,—which change under its influence,—which alter either through its might or in its presence, by it or before it. (291)

The mind comes to understand its own strength to undergo, to endure, only by actively working upon, effecting, and projecting itself outward upon the world. This same active interchange—this dialogue of mind and world—is the essence of the creative imagination as Wordsworth describes it in many passages of *The Prelude,* particularly the Mt. Snowdon passage of the last book. This interchange is the opposite of the narcissistic state in which the mind draws in upon itself, refusing to enter dialogue with the phenomenal world. Here is part of the Mt. Snowdon passage from *The Prelude:*

A meditation rose in me that night
Upon the lonely Mountain when the scene
Had pass'd away, and it appear'd to me
The perfect image of a mighty Mind,
Of one that feeds upon infinity,
That is exalted by an under-presence,
The sense of God, or whatsoe'er is dim
Or vast in its own being, above all
One function of such mind had Nature there
Exhibited by putting forth, and that
With circumstance most awful and sublime,
That domination which she oftentimes
Exerts upon the outward face of things,
So molds them, and endues, abstracts, combines,
Or by abrupt and unhabitual influence
Doth make one object so impress itself
Upon all others, and pervade them so
That even the grossest minds must see and hear
And cannot chuse but feel. The Power which these
Acknowledge when thus moved, which Nature thus
Thrusts forth upon the senses, is the express
Resemblance, in the fulness of its strength
Made visible, a genuine Counterpart
And Brother of the glorious faculty
Which higher minds bear with them as their own.
That is the very spirit in which they deal
With all the objects of the universe;
They from their native selves can send abroad
Like transformation. . . .

(*Prel.* XIII, 66–94)

Not only does consciousness become capable of contemplating and understanding itself by reaching, not inward into consciousness itself, but outward into the world as object, transformed
in the process into subject, but the movement of consciousness
outside the self, the refusal of consciousness to take itself *directly* as
object, this alone makes courage possible. "All courage," Wordsworth writes, "is a projection from ourselves; however short-
lived, it is a motion of hope" (292). When the consciousness
breaks through its own barriers, when consciousness becomes conscious of something other than itself, other than consciousness, it

unites with futurity. And this motion constitutes both hope and courage and is pleasurable.

Painful "thoughts bind too closely to something inward—to the present or to the past,—that is to the self which is or has been."

> . . . the vigour of the human soul is from without and from futurity,—in breaking down limit, and losing and forgetting herself in the sensation and image of Country and of the human race; and, when she returns and is most restricted and confined, her dignity consists in the contemplation of a better and more exalted being, which, though proceeding from herself, she loves and is devoted to as to another. (292)

When the self is broken through, and consciousness unites with futurity, the experience gives pleasure even after the self returns to its normal limits. The pleasure that a moment of patriotic courage yields to after reflection is like the experience of pleasure that Wordsworth claims a beautiful landscape can give long after its image has passed through the outer eye:

> These beauteous forms,
> Through a long absence, have not been to me
> As is a landscape to a blind man's eye:
> But oft, in lonely rooms, and 'mid the din
> Of towns and cities, I have owed to them,
> In hours of weariness, sensations sweet,
> Felt in the blood, and felt along the heart;
> And passing even into my purer mind,
> With tranquil restoration. . . .
> (P.W. 2:260)

Similar, too, are the revivifying spots of time, referred to in *The Prelude,* to which the mind repairs to drink as at a fountain. These are moments of intense past experience that have healing, soothing, restorative powers. For Wordsworth man's life continually resonates pleasurably with the past. The madeleine is always there to be tasted. And as this passage in the Cintra tract demonstrates, this resonance with the past is true not only of aesthetic man, and introspective man, but also of political man. Interestingly, the self that has flowed outward and broken down limits is pleasurably contemplated by the quotidian self as something other, not part of self, something that has left the self and consequently returned, but as object. Perhaps what Wordsworth is suggesting here is that the subject that breaks free of the limits of the self, by virtue of its freedom and the consequent heightened consciousness, becomes alienated through an upward mobility, so that this elevated consciousness becomes object in relation to the original subject. If this conjecture is sound then it would seem to follow that for Wordsworth the goal of consciousness or spirit, in the imaginative act as described here or in the Mt. Snowdon passage, would be to transcend itself, to alienate itself from itself, and thereby raise consciousness as subject into consciousness as object. The passage seems to concede that this process can never complete itself, that some portion of consciousness will remain subject contemplating alienated spirit as object, but the goal towards which consciousness aspires seems to be clear.

Wordsworth says that his countrymen "forbid that their noble aim should be frustrated by measuring against each other things which are incommensurate—mechanic against moral power—body against soul" (292). In his rejection of attempting to measure the spiritual by the gross and palpable Wordsworth seems to be saying, along with Blake, "Bring out number weight & measure in a year of dearth."[2] Wordsworth articulates a series of antitheses. On the one hand the government employs "mechanic" power, the "body," "purblind calculation," "the tools and impliments of policy," "might," and "selfish power." All these ignore the spiritual and are base and weak. To these Wordsworth opposes the spiritual tools on which, and on which alone, the government should depend: "moral power," the "soul," "purest hopes," the "mighty engines of Nature," "Justice," and "moral law" (292). It becomes clear through these carefully balanced antitheses that the Convention of Cintra and the debate it triggered were for Wordsworth a morality play with the British ministry and general staff allied to the forces of evil and the Portuguese, Spanish and British people allied to the forces of good.

Wordsworth returns once more to the relationship between the suffering of the Spanish people and their spiritual power. The circling back to the same subject to make the same point is typical of Cintra's form. And, as is frequently the case, the argument develops in complexity and significance in the repetition. The quotation is long, but it is so significant that I must quote it in its entirety. It follows several accounts of the prodigious and powerful exertions that men can be raised to by moral passion despite religious superstition.

> But, if the object contended for be worthy and truly great (as, in the instance of the Spaniards, we have seen that it is); if cruelties have been committed upon an ancient and venerable people, which "shake the human frame with horror"; if not alone the life which is sustained by the bread of the mouth, but that—without which there is no life—the life in the soul, has been directly and mortally warred against; if reason has had abominations to endure in her most inmost sanctuary;—then does intense passion, consecrated by a sudden revelation of justice, give birth to those higher and better wonders which I have described; and exhibit true miracles in the eyes of men, and the noblest which can be seen. It may be added that,—as this union brings back to the right road the faculty of the imagination, where it is prone to err, and has gone furthest astray; as it corrects those qualities which (being in their essence indifferent), and cleanses those affections which (not being inherent in the constitution of man, nor necessarily determined to their object) are more immediately dependent upon the imagination, and which may have received from it a thorough taint of dishonour;—so the domestic loves and sanctities which are in their nature less liable to be stained,—so these, wherever they have flowed with a pure and placid stream, do instantly, under the same influence, put forth their strength as in a flood; and, without being sullied or polluted, pursue—exultingly and with song—a course which leads the contemplative reason to the ocean of eternal love. (294–295)

Wordsworth first expands upon the mechanism by which suffering may lead to power. Suffering, when there is the ability to hope, leads to "intense passion" and to "a sudden revelation of justice." These are the catalysts in the reaction that lead to the release of moral power, in the form of the ability to perform almost superhuman "wonders." This moral power "brings back to the right road the faculty of the imagination" where that faculty has been brought to error by religious superstition, and "cleanses those affections . . . dependent upon the imagination, and which may have received from it a thorough taint of dishonour. . . ."

What happens next is crucial. After the rectification and purification of the imagination have taken place, "domestic loves and sanctities" which are by nature not likely to be corrupted, "put forth their strength as in a flood" and lead "contemplative reason to the ocean of eternal love." Again the release of power is contingent, this time upon domestic love and sanctities having "flowed with a pure and placid stream. . . ." The key to reaching "the ocean of eternal love" is the purity of domestic love. Domestic love is the alpha and the omega. Both the imagination and the reflexive community presuppose domestic love. Wordsworth's aesthetics, epistemology, and political theory all predicate domestic love, without which one cannot imagine, know, or form communities. In seeing domestic love as the basis of sound polity Wordsworth was not introducing a new idea to British Romanticism. On this point he was in full agreement with his friend Coleridge who had been insisting on the importance of domestic love since he had published *The Watchman* of 1796. Hazlitt had also made the same point in his philosophical work.

In one passage of *The Prelude* Wordsworth hypothesizes that the genesis of the ability to know and of the ability to create poetry is found in the loving relationship between mother and infant. This relationship is, certainly, a significant aspect of domestic love.

> Bless'd the infant Babe,
> (For with my best conjectures I would trace
> The progress of our being) blest the Babe,
> Nurs'd in his Mother's arms, the Babe who sleeps
> Upon his Mother's breast, who, when his soul
> Claims manifest kindred with an earthly soul,
> Doth gather passion from his Mother's eye!
> Such feelings pass into his torpid life
> Like an awakening breeze, and hence his mind
> Even [in the first trial of its powers]
> Is prompt and watchful, eager to combine
> In one appearance, all the elements
> And parts of the same object, else detach'd

And loath to coalesce. Thus day by day,
Subjected to the discipline of love,
His organs and recipient faculties
Are quicken'd, are more vigorous, his mind spreads,
Tenacious of the forms which it receives.

(*Prel.* II, 237–254)

And the poetic faculty is born in the stimulation of the infant by its mother's love.

From nature largely he receives; nor so
Is satisfied, but largely gives again,
For feeling has to him imparted strength,
And powerful in all sentiments of grief,
Of exhaltation, fear, and joy, his mind,
Even as an agent of the one great mind,
Creates, creator and receiver both,
Working but in alliance with the works
Which it beholds.—Such, verily, is the first
Poetic spirit of our human life;
By uniform controul of after years
In most abated or suppress'd, in some,
Through every change of growth or of decay,
Pre-eminent till death.

(*Prel.* II, 267–280)

The same force, nurtured by the loving mother, generates relationship between subject and object and therefore makes knowledge possible. The reciprocity by which this force acts on subject and on object, enabling them to coalesce, creates the poetic spirit. By creating relationship between subjects, by drawing them together, it is the force that generates community. It is "the great social principle of life/Coercing all things into sympathy . . ." (*Prel.* II, 408–409).

Love between mother and child is but one aspect of pure domestic love. Patriarchy is another. The wife and the children must accept the father's authority, if all is to be well. Egoistic childhood strivings that would repudiate both the father's authority and sexual control of the mother must be repressed. If the family is irradiated by the mother's love and accepts paternal sway, then the domestic affections are pure and may generate the power to propel the contemplative mind to the ocean of eternal love. But if social forces, such as economic change and development, stimulate egoism, the flow of maternal love is limited, and rebellion against patriarchy is encouraged. Such familial developments make knowledge, imagination, community, and access to eternal love impossible. Upon the purity of the family unit depend both the fulfilled humanity of every member of society, and the possibility of true community.

Suffering induces intense passion and a revelation of justice which in their turn liberate human power and energy. This liberated energy in turn works on domestic loves and sanctities, which, if pure, "put forth their strength as in a flood" that propels "contemplative reason to the ocean of eternal love." This elaborate process that begins in suffering and moves through energetic collective armed struggle and resistance leads to contemplative union with eternal and loving forces, a union that seems to me to be similar to the imaginative epiphanies described in *The Prelude*, in the Mt. Snowdon passage, for example. If this is so then it seems that Wordsworth's conception of the imagination might have been far more deeply interfused with society, social change, and social struggle than the epiphany of Mt. Snowdon, experienced in retreat from society and politics, has suggested to many readers.

Wordsworth continues his argument with an attempt to show that evil, here exemplified by Bonaparte, destroys itself. It is incapable of deriving power from pure affections.

Bonaparte himself, in spite of his intentions, worked to facilitate the allied cause:

> The government which had been exercised under the name of the old Monarchy of Spain—this government, imbecile even to dotage, whose very selfishness was destitute of vigour, had been removed; taken laboriously and foolishly by the plotting Corsican to his own bosom. . . . (298)

This action afforded an opportunity to see "to what a narrow domain of knowledge the intellect of a Tyrant must be confined . . ." (298). Wordsworth goes on to write that

> . . . a Tyrant's domain of knowledge is narrow, but melancholy as narrow; inasmuch as—from all that is lovely, dignified, or

exhilarating in the prospect of human nature—he is inexorably cut off; and therefore he is inwardly helpless and forlorn. (298)

These observations are in keeping with thoughts Wordsworth had already expressed in the sonnet of 1802 "I Grieved for Buonaparté." Bonaparte uses narrow policy rather than wisdom, which is beyond his reach. Bonaparte is cut off from affective power, from imaginative power. As a result "he is inwardly helpless and forlorn." That is to say that effective power, stripped of affective power, results in psychic impotence, a maimed incapacity to extend beyond the self. Such an incapacity results in psychic pain.

Here, it seems to me, Wordsworth, intentionally or not, comes close to restating the claim made by Plato in the *Gorgias* and *The Republic*. A tyrant, no matter how powerful, no matter how able to have his every desire fulfilled, cannot be happy because he is not good. It is far better to be deprived of the ability to control the phenomenal world, than it is to be deprived of the ability to feel, for the ability to feel includes the ability to feel pleasure.

Pursuit of naked power used in order to coerce may bring about a punitive response on the part of the limiting paternal powers. Be that as it may, such a pursuit results in painful contraction and a resulting inability to participate fully in being. Napoleon is like the monied worldlings in having traded emotional richness for worldly power, a sordid boon.

After lamenting the ignorance of the British leaders, which it is his purpose to help dispel, and after saying that he is compelled to write by the "power of conscience" which is "a perception of justice united with strength of feeling" (303), Wordsworth seeks to clear himself from the charge of presumption in offering counsel to generals and ministers.

> For there can be no presumption, upon a call so affecting as the present, in an attempt to assert the sanctity and to display the efficacy of principles and passions which are the natural birth-right of man; to some share of which all are born; but an inheritance which may be alienated or consumed. . . . (303)

Man as man has natural principles and passions. These principles and passions are his species endowment, but they are not integral to man as a mere living creature. They are integral only to man as fully developed man.

After having defended his right to instruct statesmen, Wordsworth delivers his first axiom of statesmanship,

> —we may confidently affirm that nothing, but a knowledge of human nature directing the operations of our government, can give it a right to an intimate association with a cause which is that of human nature. (p. 304)

The corollary that Wordsworth draws from this first principle is one that would seem to make the task of writing a statesman's manual useless before it was even undertaken. "It is plain *a priori*," Wordsworth writes, "that the minds of Statesmen and Courtiers are unfavourable to the growth of this knowledge. For they are in a situation exclusive and artificial . . ." (304). Further Wordsworth writes of the ruling orders, that their "situation therefore must be eminently unfavorable for the reception and establishment of that knowledge which is founded not upon things but upon sensations,—sensations which are general, and under general influences (and this it is which makes them what they are, and gives them their importance) . . ." (304–305). So not only are the ruling orders cut off from human nature, but they are cut off from those general sensations which alone could convey that missing knowledge. If this is so then a stateman's manual would seem to be a contradiction in terms. Statesmen and courtiers are deracinated. They have been cut off from true experience of and knowledge of human nature, so that human existence, as they experience it and know of it, is artificial. It is interesting to call attention to the similarities between this argument and the line of reasoning Wordsworth propounded in 1800 and 1802 in the Preface to the *Lyrical Ballads*. There Wordsworth argued that the poetic taste of the educated, gentle classes had become vicious and corrupted because they had lost touch with the simple language of real men, spoken in a state of emotional stress, and from the direct experience of life, unmediated by cultural superstructures and assumptions. Polite readers had become unable to recognize and to enjoy true poetry because these readers had lost touch with human nature. Wordsworth's assumptions, whether he was arguing politics or poetic theory, were remarkably consistent. In *Lyrical Ballads* and its preface Wordsworth hopes to educate his audience in the liberating principles of poetic judgment. In the Cintra tract he hopes to teach his audience the liberating principles of governance. In both cases the same knowledge must be conveyed, a true knowledge of human nature. It is Wordsworth's constant task to teach the polite culture the true principles of human nature, and to the degree that this knowledge is necessary in order to rule, the *Lyrical Ballads* may be seen as being, at least in part, politically programmatic.

A "ruling minister of a long-established government" (306) has little familiarity with the deep passions associated with the love of country and the desire for liberty, passions that in a struggle against an oppressor transform and elevate the emotional life. These grand passions, "these—elements as it were of a universe, functions of a living body—are so opposite, in their mode of action, to the formal machine which it has been his pride to manage;—that he has but a faint perception of their immediate efficacy . . ." (306). The minister is separated from passions, which are natural, and deals familiarly with the artificial and mechanical. The minister neither feels nor sees that which is natural. To it, he is insentient; he is removed from a significant aspect of life and located on the verge of insentience, of nonbeing. Wordsworth's aim is to teach the minister how to feel and see. His aim in relation to the minister is that of the poet in relation to his audience.

The world would certainly be improved "if Governors better understood the rudiments of nature as studied in the walks of common life . . ." (306). Again Wordsworth's primitivist assumption that the rudiments of nature are best studied in the walks of common life is evident. Wordsworth believed that that which was most truly human would be more accessible to scrutiny among the walks of common life than in polished society, because common life was less encrusted with a false, mannered and highly rationalized surface than was polite society. If, as Marx said, Jeremy Bentham "takes the modern shopkeeper, especially the English shopkeeper, as the normal man," [3] then it might with some truth be said that Wordsworth takes the free- or copyholder, especially the Cumbrian statesman, as the normal man.

If Wordsworth creates an obstacle for the creation of a man-ual of statesmanship by asserting that courtiers and ministers lack both the knowledge of human nature necessary to govern, and the means of acquiring such knowledge, he creates a further obstacle by rejecting Plato's notion of philosopher kings. "Nor," he writes, ". . . is it so desirable as might at first sight be imagined, much less is it desirable as an absolute good, that men of comprehensive sensibility and tutored genius—either for the interests of mankind or for their own—should, in ordinary times, have vested in them political power" (307). Wordsworth does not further develop his seeming qualification, "in ordinary times," so he leaves the reader in a quandary. Those who rule do not, and seemingly cannot, know, while those who know should not rule. Wordsworth is not rigorous enough to realize the logical box he has placed himself in. He gets out of the box, as I shall show, by qualifying himself. Statesmen turn out to be more educable that he first shows them to be.

In part Wordsworth means that a virtuous and free people require no special qualities in their leaders other than strength of honesty in carrying out the will of the people. In "ordinary times" a society can continue to be guided by public servants of ordinary ability. But Britain has in the past thirty years twice waged wars "against Liberty," once in America and once "against the French People in the early stages of their Revolution" (308). During this time British leaders have exhibited "the same presumptuous ir-reverence of the principles of justice, and blank insensibility to the affections of human nature, which determined the conduct of our government in those two wars *against* liberty . . . (308). In this case the logical box Wordsworth has constructed is the necessity of explaining how a people whose instincts can be trusted could have allowed such perverse governors to gain power and to remain in power for thirty years.

The qualities that lead to "comprehensive sensibility and tu-tored genius" are perishable, especially in the world of public af-fairs:

> But whatever may be the cause, the fact is certain—that there is an unconquerable tendency in all power, save that of knowledge act-

ing by and through knowledge, to injure the mind of him who exercises that power; so much so, that best natures cannot escape the evil of such alliance. Nor is it less certain that things of soundest quality, issuing through a medium to which they have only an arbitrary relation, are vitiated: and it is inevitable that there should be a reäscent of unkindly influence to the heart of him from whom the gift, thus unfairly dealt with, proceeded. (308)

Wordsworth says that when any natures are placed in positions of political power, and are given the power to dispense and therefore be the object of admiration and of toadying, "it is inevitable that there should be a reäscent of unkindly influence to the heart." Notice that Wordsworth says "reäscent." He takes it for granted that all men pass through a period of egoism, that must be conquered before one can become a man of great spirit and tutored genius. (Wordsworth demonstrates this belief in "The Two Thieves" and to some extent in "Nutting.")

In using the term "reäscent," then, Wordsworth admits not only the necessity of rulers subduing pride and arrogance, but the existence of these or similar feelings in himself at some earlier date. Such had been the case with Wordsworth himself, as he knew, so that this passage affords the reader with a bit of autobiographical insight. Wordsworth had assumed a tone of contempt, arrogance, and condescension in his "Letter to Bishop Llandaff," and Wordsworth had repudiated such contemptuous feelings in "Lines Left upon a Seat in a Yew-tree," completed in 1797, approximately four years after "Llandaff." In these "Lines" Wordsworth writes "that he who feels contempt/For any living thing, hath faculties/Which he has never used . . ." (P.W. 1:94). Wordsworth's inclination to feel contempt was linked to the princely, masterful conception of himself. In a struggle, discussed earlier in my examination of The Borderers, Wordsworth was forced to renounce the power over the external world that was one component of the ego state that I have designated "princely." Such power over external things was linked, as I have tried to show, with sadistic and patricidal impulses, impulses that were vigorously repressed.

So Wordsworth believed that effective power, however necessary to the statesman, is ineluctably related to egoism, and is therefore a regressive force for the fully developed man become statesman. The fully developed man has fought against, and repressed, egoism at least once before, but the force of the repression is weakened by the worldly power attendant upon political office.

In the beginning, for Wordsworth, is the natural affectively bound society. This society delegates its effective power to a governing class that precipitates out of and rises above society. But effective power by its nature erodes the full humanity of the governing class and fosters egoism that results in a tendency to govern by false mechanical policy. Though effective power had been separated from affective society in order to preserve society, this very separation endangers society as government becomes deracinated from the soil of human passion and human nature, thereby endangering the society it was created to preserve.

Wordsworth attempted to diminish the destructive effects caused by the possession of governing power by infusing the governing class with the wisdom of the human heart so that the governors would not totally lose touch with their full humanity and thereby err. It is noteworthy that Wordsworth has rejected the solution to this problem that he put forward in his "Letter to Bishop Llandaff," which would be to diffuse the concentration of effective power so that it was no longer held solely by a governing class alone but, rather, by all of the people. Such a distribution of power would lessen the destructive effects of governing power, because the destructive effects would not act on one individual or one group, but would be diluted by being shared by all. Such a solution is, however, radically democratic, in that all members of society would share the responsibility of governing, no one alone having enough responsibility to corrupt him. Wordsworth did not believe in what he might have called a purely numerical democracy in which fifty-one percent of the population could exercise a tyranny of the majority. For Wordsworth an elected representative should never be reduced to the state of a mere delegate, but should act in accordance with his idea of the common welfare, rather than do nothing more than express the wishes of a mathematical majority of his constituents.[4]

Wordsworth sees a central problem of political philosophy quite differently from the way in which Plato saw it. For both men the ideal society must be governed by philosopher-rulers. For Plato the problem is how to make the wise rule, while for Wordsworth the difficulty is how to make the already existing rulers wise.

If the current struggle against France is to be successful, then Britain must "employ the true means of liberty and virtue for the ends of liberty and virtue" (309). Wordsworth gives an example of how a failure to employ the true means of liberty is counterproductive. The ministers at the time of Britain's war with her American colonies

> found it an easy task to hire a band of Hessians, and to send it across the Atlantic. . . . The force, with which these troops would attack, was gross—tangible,—and might be calculated; but the spirit of resistance, which their presence would create, was subtle—ethereal—mighty—and incalculable. (309)

The ministers chose the physical rather than the spiritual force, and from that moment on "the success of the British was . . . impossible" (309). The word "ethereal," when used to describe the spirit of resistance, the spiritual force, may connote the angelic and the divine, although it may have reference to the theoretical chemistry of Wordsworth's day.

In a similar way the British government chose to depend on physical force in the Iberian Peninsula, because "moral energy" was a material "too fine for their calculation" (309). Still more seriously "the English army was made an instrument of injustice, and was dishonoured" in the support of "a cause which could have no life but by justice and honour" (309). In such circumstances, "Our rulers . . . must begin with their own minds" (310). And it was in order to help them with this task that Wordsworth wrote his Cintra tract.

After suggesting that Britain choose between two policies, either to send a massive force of two hundred thousand men into the Peninsula, or to limit aid to material support only, Wordsworth examines Bonaparte in order to ascertain whether or not the French ruler's successes might be due to genius and superior talent. Wordsworth denies Bonaparte any claim to genius or superior talent, and attributes all of his success to his moral depravity. The key to Bonaparte's success lies "in his utter rejection of the restraints of morality—in wickedness which acknowledges no limit but the extent of its own power." "Let any one," Wordsworth writes, "reflect a moment; and he will feel that a new world of forces is opened to a Being who has made this desperate leap" (312). It is, I believe, more than coincidence that the immense forces unleashed by Napoleon's rejection of any traditional moral value coincide in time, in power, and, for Wordsworth, in evil with the immense forces that the new economy of the Industrial Revolution unleashed in the English social order. The power released by this momentous phase of capitalist development was similar to Napoleon's power. Like Napoleon, the Industrial Revolution did not govern itself by traditional values. Instead, it destroyed traditional values and institutions. Like Napoleon, the supreme egotist, the Industrial Revolution was guided by unrestrained egotistical calculation.

But what of the fate of Spain, a nation unwilling to take such a desperate leap? Wordsworth says that when a nation keeps the fundamental passions of love, hate, and pride alive, it does not matter if some are not zealous in their country's cause. It does not even matter if some are actually traitorous. "Never are a people so livelily admonished of the love they bear their country, and of the pride which they have in their common parent, as when they hear of some patricidal attempt of a false brother" (p. 321). Here Wordsworth consciously and specifically identifies country and father. The father and his country now have his love, which was not always so. He too had once patricidally rebelled. Now his intense ambivalence about his father seems to have been resolved by unconsciously splitting the father into two separate entities, each the conscious object of one pole of the ambivalence. Bonaparte, who as a rebel could be admired, but only unconsciously, is the powerful figure who is the object of hostility whose source is, in part, repressed hostility against Wordsworth's father. England, and the abstract conception of a free nation state as fatherland, such as he hopes both Portugal and Spain to become, are the objects of the profound and now sublimated love that he bore his father. Through the mechanism of displacement each pole of the highly charged ambivalence towards his father finds its own symbolic object, onto which can be consciously directed both his love and his hate.

Wordworth, while discussing the suspicion with which the patriot maintains his vigilance against the destructive and patricidal traitor, makes a statement that shows how complete was his rejection of egoism. The spirit of suspicion, "which has grown out of the instinct for self-preservation," which is in normal times productive of "dire and pitiable effects" is "in times of national danger . . . elevated into a wakeful and affectionate apprehension of the whole, and ennobling its private and baser ways by the generous use to which they are converted" (321). Because of the generous use to which it is put, the instinct of self-preservation, when directed at saving the country, or, pretty much the same thing, saving the father, has its baser, more selfish aspects ennobled. Here is a statement that says, in effect, that the ego instincts of self-preservation are, in and of themselves, base when they act only to preserve the self. These instincts only become respectable when they are put in the service of something outside of and larger than the self, here the fatherland and beyond it the father. The instinct of self-preservation is not, in and of itself, unworthy. But it must, for Wordsworth, be subordinated to an aim or a cause beyond the self.

Following his discussion of suspicion and self-preservation Wordsworth asserts that one never has as clear a perception of the power of virtue as at the moment of the reflux of faith following an ebb caused by "some atrocious act of perfidy . . ." (321).

Nor ever has a good and loyal man such a swell of mind, such a clear insight into the constitution of virtue, and such a sublime sense of its power, as at the first tidings of some atrocious act of perfidy; when, having taken the alarm for human nature, a second thought recovers him; and his faith returns—gladsome from what has been revealed within himself, and awful from participation of the secrets in the profaner grove of humanity which that momentary blast laid open to his view. (321)

First, the Wordsworthian should notice the similarity between the intensity of faith in human nature following initial disappointment of expectations, and the intensity with which Wordsworth was capable of experiencing a sensation after an initial disappointment in his quest for sensation. Wordsworth gives an example of this in the "There Was a Boy" passage of Book v of *The Prelude*, written in the first person in early manuscripts. The boy, originally Wordsworth himself, would blow mimic owl cries through his clasped palms in eager anticipation of teasing the real owls into response.

> And when it chanced
> That pauses of deep silence mock'd his skill,
> Then sometimes, in that silence, while he hung
> Listening, a gentle shock of mild surprize
> Has carried far into his heart the voice
> Of mountain torrents; or the visible scene
> Would enter unawares into his mind
> With all its solemn imagery, its rocks,
> Its woods, and that uncertain Heaven, receiv'd
> Into the bosom of the steady Lake.
>   (*Prel*. v, 404–413)

There seems to be a common denominator to both of the experiences just described. Both begin with a painfully thwarted expectation. In neither case does the discomfort caused by the disappointment disappear of its own accord. Instead, Wordsworth restores equilibrium to the pleasure-pain economy by having the subject of the disappointment experience a compensatory pleasure. It is significant that in the Cintra passage the second and reassuring thought is supplied by the imagined self that experiences the initial disappointment in human nature:

> a second thought recovers him; and his faith returns—gladsome from what has been revealed within himself. . . .

It is possible that the intense experience of perceived harmony was a mechanism that Wordsworth devised, consciously or no, to cope with the otherwise ineluctable pain of disappointed expectations. In any event it is significant that as a part of his fundamental belief in human goodness Wordsworth does acknowledge the existence of a "profaner grove of humanity" that may be momentarily laid open to view.

There is no reason to doubt that Spain will ultimately be free, but this "cannot be accomplished (scarcely can it be aimed at) without an accompanying and an inseparable resolution, in the souls of the Spaniards, to be and remain their own masters; that is, to preserve themselves in the rank of Men; and not become as the Brute that is driven to the pasture, and cares not who owns him." (322) That is to say that men can sink below the level of full manhood if they cease to have regard for their own freedom. Political freedom, and the desire for it, are conditions for full humanity.

Wordsworth discusses the question of whether it is worse to be enslaved by domestic tyranny or foreign tyranny. Wordsworth decides, ultimately, that foreign tyranny is more odious, but he comes up with several justifications for foreign conquest. This passage is of enormous importance because, among the great English Romantics, little is said about the British Empire, and even less in defense of empire:

> Where indeed there is an indisputable and immeasurable superiority in one nation over another; to be conquered may, in course of time, be a benefit to the inferior nation: and, upon this principle, some of the conquests of the Greeks and Romans may be justified. (322)

But the French are in no "really useful or honourable" way superior to the Spanish, so that Spain cannot benefit in this way from such a conquest.

England is now developing "Mechanic Arts, Manufactures, Agriculture, Commerce, and all those products of knowledge which are confined to gross—definite—and tangible objects. . . ." These have been created "with the aid of Experimental Philosophy" (324-325), but works of imagination and sensibility have been languishing:

> the splendour of the Imagination has been fading: Sensibility, which was formerly a generous nurseling of rude Nature, has been chased from its ancient range in the wide domain of patriotism and religion with the weapons of derision by a shadow calling itself Good Sense: calculations of presumptuous Expediency—groping its way among partial and temporary consequences—have been substi-

tuted for the dictates of paramount and infallible Conscience, the supreme embracer of consequences: lifeless and circumspect Decencies have banished the graceful negligence and unsuspicious dignity of Virtue. (325).

Parts of the passage seem almost Blakean in tone. By calling "Good Sense" a shadow Wordsworth is metaphorically linking this limited form of rationality with death, by way of Milton's Death in *Paradise Lost*. The first description of Death that Milton gives the reader, and the image that controls all that come after, culminates with likening Death to a shadow:

> The other shape,
> If shape it might be call'd that shape had none
> Distinguishable in member, joint, or limb,
> Or substance might be call'd that shadow seem'd,
> For each seem'd either.[5]

Good sense, a faculty allied with "calculations of presumptuous Expediency" is linked with death. These calculations may be of the same sort that Marx and Engels refer to when they describe the "egotistical calculation" of the self-asserting bourgeoisie. In this constellation of related ideas, capitalism and industrial enterprise are causally linked to the destruction of imagination and of virtue. The spirit of calculation is linked to industrial endeavor and is seen to be inimical to the imagination. Things "gross—definite—and tangible" are opposed to things of the spirit. Men have been "picking up things about their feet, when thoughts were perishing in their minds" (324).

Wordsworth then refines his point. Material advances in culture are not evil in and of themselves but because the seeming impressiveness of these advances "has misled the higher orders of society in their more disinterested exertions for the service of the lower" (326). Here again it is Wordsworth's task to educate and to correct the erring ruling orders. Wordsworth is at pains to instruct them not to make war, unaware, on the traditional virtues of the lower orders. If material improvements serve to hide the fact that "the Peasant or Artisan . . . be a slave in mind" then such improvements "are worse than worthless" (326). It is worth noting Wordsworth's concern, or perhaps perception, that the spiritual well-being of the lower orders may suffer from a profound malaise, despite advances (or perhaps because of them) in material culture. Of the "Peasant or Artisan" Wordsworth writes, "The springs of emotion may be relaxed or destroyed in him; he may have little thought of the past, and less interest in the future" (326). If the springs of emotion are relaxed or destroyed, the laborer is rendered affectively powerless and dead, and if he care neither for the past nor the future then he is bound in upon himself, cut off from imaginative power and consquently from hope. Perhaps, then, Wordsworth is, after a certain point has been reached, against material progress because it focuses attention on the gross and palpable and deflects attention from the spiritual. Were this the case such progress would be ultimately destructive. Such a view would be consistent with the passage in the Preface to the *Lyrical Ballads* that animadverts against the effects of gross emotional stimulants. Wordsworth emerges, by implication, as an opposer of innovation and as a defender of traditional Tory England.

Wordsworth continues his argument by making an astonishing statement. "The great end and difficulty of life," he writes, "for men of all classes, and especially difficult for those who live by manual labour, is a union of peace with innocent and laudable animation" (326). Here, concisely stated, is the contradiction posed by the confrontation of the princely sense of self with the contracted sense of self. How is it possible to reconcile the impulse toward animated activity, that emanates from the princely desire to master, with the peace that comes from repressing, sublimating and turning into their opposite, egoistic self-asserting impulses? How are we to be at once active vigorous human agents and at the same time not be driven by guilty, egoistic emotions that emanate from aggressiveness and even from sadism?

"By," says Wordsworth, "the genial and vernal inmate of the breast, which at once pushes forth and cherishes" (326), by, that is, the power of the imagination—thus is the contradiction to be resolved. Just as the imagination can solve the dilemma between personal freedom, on the one hand, and social necessity, on the other, by creating community through its social power while leaving each individual free to create his own world for himself, so the imagination can solve the dilemma between animation and peace.

The imagination "pushes forth." It projects us outside of ourselves and thereby concerns us with what is outside ourselves, impelling us to "laudable animation." At the same time the imagination "cherishes." That is, it stands opposed to the destructive and rapacious "calculations of presumptuous Experience. . . ."

But Wordsworth says that the "great end and difficulty of life" is "especially difficult for those who live by manual labour." If the end of life is so difficult to attain for those who live by manual labor, does this not contradict my previous observation, that as the English shopkeeper was Bentham's normal man, the Cumbrian statesman was Wordsworth's? That Wordsworth affirmed the full humanity of the simple people described in Lyrical Ballads? No. It is precisely because Wordsworth sees the end of life as being more unattainable for the laborers than for the gentlemen that their existence as developed human beings is so significant. Wordsworth could point with patriotic pride to the Cumbrian shepherds who, despite the added barrier of physical labor, attained the full human development that the French in their myopic rashness believed could only be reached by a complete and revolutionary transformation of society. The English gentry were asked to look at these shepherds in order to learn the "rudiments of nature."

But, and upon this but everything depends, the attainment of the end of life by manual laborers was precarious. It depended upon the existence—and increasingly the preservation—of a delicate world of social relations. Wordsworth looked with horror, despair, and finally rage at changes introduced by the well-meaning but misguided "higher orders of society." These changes were gross and material such as those brought on by the wave of agricultural improvement that swept England in the last quarter of the eighteenth century

Now I must address myself to the question of why Wordsworth believed that manual labor rendered the attainment of the end of life so difficult. What made it so difficult for the laborer to maintain the "springs of emotion" and to unite "peace with innocent and laudable animation"? The answer is complex. First, Wordsworth's belief may have been influenced by the class prejudice and condescension that he exhibited in poems such as "A narrow Girdle of rough stones and crags." To a gentleman manual labor, however much he might defend its dignity, is implicitly degrading. It is the actual and at the same time highly symbolic activity that marks the extinction of gentility. The condition of being a member of the lower orders was, on one level, frightening for Wordsworth, because his own fears of annihilation were represented, in his conscious mind, by the fear of being declassed. Wordsworth shows his intense anxiety about the life of and among the lower orders in "Resolution and Independence." And that which will induce fear will often induce, on some other level of consciousness, rage and hatred, resentment against being made to feel anxious.

Secondly, the idea that it is more difficult for a manual laborer to attain the end of life was a correct social perception, shared by Marx, among others. The dependence on the exchange of labor power for the means of sustenance in precapitalist society, and its outright sale as a commodity in capitalist society, made the worker vulnerable to being overworked and sweated. Such a burden of overwork was dehumanizing, inimical to the development of full species being. It was inimical to moral, spiritual, and aesthetic growth.

Thirdly, if the spiritual and imaginative capacity were crushed under the burden of excess toil, the force that made it possible to bring together animation and peace would have been destroyed. The destruction of the spiritual and imaginative capacity would leave only the egoistic calculations of expediency as guides to behavior, causing the coarse, revolting behavior Wordsworth found at Bartholomew Fair, and the failure of fundamental maternal affection that allowed the prostitute, in the London book of *The Prelude*, to dandle her beautiful infant son amid the ruffian curses of a tavern table.

Finally, Wordsworth lived through a period that E. P. Thompson describes as one of counterrevolution. The ruling orders, frightened by the French example, looked with alarm and anger at the British lower orders. There was reason to fear that at least some manual laborers would not combine animation with peace, but would rather combine animation with aggression and animatedly rebel against established political and property relations. So Wordsworth's class bias, caused by fears of revolutionary unrest among the lower orders, might have led him to believe that animation and peace, although possible and highly to be desired, were not often found together among the lower orders.

Next, of "the feeling of being self-governed," Wordsworth says that "where this feeling has no place, a people are not a society, but a herd . . ." (327). Wordsworth then describes Britain as being free, so that it is clear that by freedom Wordsworth does not mean political democracy, either direct or indirect, but rather the negative right of the free-born Englishman not to be arbitrarily interfered with, and the system of virtual Parliamentary representation. The English laborer does not have, in the terms I have been using, effective power or freedom. Rather Wordsworth would seem to mean that he has affective power and freedom. Wordsworth writes of the emotions of pride and hope that "The poorest Peasant, in an unsubdued land, feels this pride" (327).

Wordsworth pursues his argument that the feeling of freedom is necessary to man by a seeming non sequitur intended perhaps to emphasize the freedom of even the poor in "a sound polity." The wealthy in such a society are far more dependent upon society than the laborers, who are relatively independent—

> . . . there is no more certain mark of a sound frame of polity than this; that, in all individual instances (and it is upon these generalized that this position is laid down), the dependence is in reality far more strict on the side of the wealthy; and the labouring man leans less upon others than any man in the community. (327)

Wordsworth accepts as a "sound frame of polity" a social system with an inequitable distribution of wealth in which a wealthy class exists and enjoys its wealth while at the same time remaining dependent upon the laboring class. It is outside the realm of possibility, in the world of Wordsworth's social thought, to ask a leveling question, to envision or desire a world devoid of distinctions of wealth. Wordworth was hardly unique in this respect in his time, or even, for that matter, in our own time. But all the same the observation must be made because so many readers of Wordsworth share his acceptance of a society divided into economic classes and are therefore incapable of becoming conscious of the political and social choices implicit in such a vision.

It is possible and even to some extent suggested that the inequitable distribution of wealth is justified as being the result of an
equitable exchange of values in Wordsworth's chimerical political
economy. Wealth, in this exchange of values, would be exchanged for independence. One could have one or the other, but
not both. The poor man, having given up his claim to wealth,
possesses independence. He has no fear of being declassed, and he
is not disgraced by manual labor, so he is free to provide for himself, depending only on his own efforts. The wealthy man, having
given up his claim to independence, has his wealth and the ability
to transform his wealth into any gratifying use-value that has entered the realm of commodity exchange. The wealthy man is,
however, dependent upon the laboring classes for his sustenance.
Without them he would perish or suffer the humiliation of being
declassed.

This symmetrical exchange of Wordsworth's is a myth, in the
sense that Claude Lévi-Strauss uses the term myth. It is a structure
of thought whose function is to rationalize social reality, and more
significantly create a symmetry on the level of mythic thought that
serves to disguise a radical asymmetry in social reality. In Wordsworth's myth, wealth belongs to those who have forfeited their independence. No notion of brutal and asymmetrical exploitation is
allowed to enter this mythic and chimerical world. Nor is the
suggestion that the control of wealth conveys a power that limits
the independence of the laborer allowed to enter either. Wordsworth's myth is little more than a mystification of existing property
relations.

Wordsworth continues to elaborate his mythic structure.
Speaking of the pleasure of patriotism he writes,

> In fact: the Peasant, and he who lives by the fair reward of his
> manual labor, has ordinarily a larger proportion of his gratifications
> dependent upon these thoughts—than, for the most part, men in
> other classes have. For he is in his person attached, by stronger
> roots, to the soil of which he is the growth. . . . (328)

Patriotism and its pleasures are a 'social inheritance" (328) for the
peasant. He is thought to be more naturally connected to, rooted
to, the land. His mind has not been weakened "by false philoso-

phy" (328). As "his intellectual notices are generally confined within narrow bounds . . . no partial or antipatriotic interests counteract the force of those nobler sympathies and antipathies . . ." (328). There is an exchange. Since little of his quantum of pleasure comes from wealth, a reciprocally larger share comes from the pleasure of patriotism. Freedom is a more important possession to the peasant because he possesses so little else. If his great love of freedom is based upon his lack of possessions, then implicitly, if he comes to possess too much wealth he will love freedom less. It is therefore in the interests of society to keep a poor and sturdy peasantry as a bulwark of fredom. Again the myth of reciprocal exchange is evident. The rich exchange some of the pleasure of freedom and patriotism for the greater use of wealth, while the peasant exchanges some of the pleasure of wealth for the greater pleasure in the experience of freedom and patriotism. The seeming reciprocity of the myth again disguises a real social inequity.

It is now possible to see one of the major points that I have developed in a different, perhaps even in a larger, framework. I have asserted that Wordsworth's attribution of full humanity to the humble has conservative implications, in that such an attribution is an implicit endorsement of existing society. But I think that it is evident that such an attribution is the largest symmetrical exchange in the mythic structure embedded in Wordsworth's thought, a mythic structure that serves to disguise the radical asymmetry and inequality in Tory England. In exchange for wealth, the humble are given full humanity, and a direct experience of all that is eternally valauable in life, unmediated by the cultural superstructure of the wealthy.

Wordsworth then attempts to explore the psychological roots of patriotism:

> Love and admiration must push themselves out towards some quarter: otherwise the moral man is killed. Collaterally they advance with great vigour to a certain extent—and they are checked: in that direction, limits hard to pass are perpetually encountered: but upwards and downwards, to ancestry and to posterity, they meet with gladsome help and no obstacles; the tract is interminable. (328)

Love and admiration are linked to imagination. Man can love and admire only if he breaks through the limits of the self. The emotional path of least resistance for this love is a channel of affection often praised by Burke, the love of the wholeness of one's line and one's country, their past and future, one's ancestry and one's posterity. This sense of continuity is important for Wordsworth for other reasons than it is important for Burke. For Burke it is a necessary guarantee to a sound and organic polity. It has a social and political function. For Wordsworth, however, this diachronic affective bond has a private rather than a public function, or at most only an indirectly public function. It is "salutory to the moral nature of Man" (328).

Wordsworth says that "In the conduct of this argument I am not speaking *to* the humbler ranks of society," but rather "to the worldlings of our own country" because the "failure was with those who stood higher in the scale" (328–329). This is an overt declaration that the tract is meant to educate the ruling orders. It is a statesman's manual. He wishes the worldlings to know that "there is no true wisdom without imagination" (329)—and "that the man, who in this age feels no regret for the ruined honour of other Nations, must be poor, in sympathy for the honour of his own Country . . ." (329). If a man is "wanting here towards that which circumscribes the whole" then how can he be expected to have "a social regard" (329) for his own community, contained within that country, or properly defend his family contained within that community?

Wordsworth then turns his attention, and his advice, to the leaders of the Spanish people. He cautions them that the Spanish ruling orders have nothing to fear from the people and should therefore accept their help:

> Spain has nothing to dread from Jacobinism. Manufacturers and Commerce have there in far less degree than elsewhere—by unnaturally clustering the people together—enfeebled their bodies, inflamed their passions by intemperance, vitiated from childhood their moral affections, and destroyed their imaginations. Madrid is no enormous city, like Paris; overgrown, and disproportionate; sickening and bowing down, by its corrupt humors, the frame of the

body politic. Nor has the pestilential philosophism of France made
any progress in Spain. (332)

This passage is critical because of the linkages that it makes explicit. Spain is not threatened by political unrest by the lower
orders because the imagination and moral affections of the lower
orders are intact. Why is this so? Because bodies of the lower
orders have not become enfeebled; their passions have not become
inflamed. Why? Because they have not been unnaturally clustered
together in cities that sicken and corrupt the body politic. And, finally, what has prevented this unnatural and enfeebling population density? Manufacturer and commerce have not, in Spain,
taken the form that requires the concentration of laborers into
single work places, the concentration of any army of surplus laborers into an area of concentrated industrial production, where
the presence of such a pitiful army can serve to reduce wages, and
finally manufactures and commernce have not destroyed the natural economy in Spain. Cottage industry still thrives in Spanish agricultural households. In other words, Spanish manufactures and
commerce have not yet entered the momentous phase of capitalist
development called the Industrial Revolution. The Industrial Revolution, as Wordsworth sees it, is the father of Jacobinism. By unnaturally concentrating laborers in urban settings, and thereby
weakening their bodies, inflaming their passions, vitiating their
moral affections, and destroying their imaginations, the Industrial
Revolution breaks down traditional forms of behavior, such as deference to one's social betters and stoic acceptance of one's earthly
lot. When deference and acceptance of place, integral to the traditional social order, have given way, the laborer is left subordinate
and dissatisfied. He is a potential Jacobin.

The passage demonstrates that Wordsworth was consciously
aware of the relationship between the economic base and the ideological superstructure. Wordsworth sees the relationship between
the development of large manufacturing and commercial cities
such as Paris, on the one hand, and the development of modes of
thought that rationalize the interests of the commercial classes, on
the other. Unnatural, skeptical, mechanical materialism, a form
of thought that denies the transcendent and synthetic power of the

imagination, has developed in France, but cannot develop in Spain. This observation directly follows and is connected to Wordsworth's observation that "Manufactures and Commerce" have not created heart-deforming cities in Spain, cities that destroy the imagination.

> The Spaniards are a people with imagination: and the paradoxical reveries of Rousseau, and the flippancies of Voltaire, are plants which will not naturalise in the country of Calderon and Cervantes. (352)

Men of sound mind have more reason to be confident of the future of Spain than to fear the lack of a predisposition to Jacobinism among the lower orders, because "every thing which is desperately immoral, being in its constitution monstrous, is of itself perishable: decay it cannot escape . . ." (333). So the Napoleonic yoke cannot hold. But this statement is larger in its reference than the French occupation of the Iberian Peninsula, and is indicative of greater hope than Wordsworth felt when he consigned Grasmere to unrelenting doom in "A Tuft of Primroses." The pestilential cities and the new forces in manufacture and commerce are in their constitution monstrous and therefore perishable. Industrial capitalism, at least at this point in Wordsworth's life, is seen as being a transient phenomenon that can be fought and destroyed. The corollary is that the "moral" and traditional social and economic order will prevail.

Saragossa valorously, but unsuccessfully, resisted a French siege. If Spain hopes to become free, 'The Government of Spain must never forget Saragossa for a moment," because "Nothing is wanting, to produce the same effects everywhere, but a leading mind such as that city was blessed with" (336). Spain is in need of one leading mind to help effect its deliverance. The salvational and decisive effect of the great leader was one of Wordsworth's most profound beliefs, a belief which antedates the Cintra tract. In the 1805 *Prelude* Wordsworth wrote, referring to France, that he could not believe

> But that the virtue of one paramount mind
> Would have
> . . . clear'd a passage for just government,

> And left a solid birthright to the State,
> Redeem'd according to the example given
> By ancient Lawgivers.
>
> (*Prel*. x, 180–189)

More than traditional Plutarchian influence is at work in making this idea so important to Wordsworth. I believe that the idea of the great political leader was another refraction of Wordsworth's princely conception of himself as hero, the image of his own perfect self, or ego-ideal.

There are despairing men who believe that "the hearts of the many *are* constitutionally weak" (338) and that Wordsworth is overly optimistic when he encourages men to be of good cheer and to base their faith in the Spanish people's ability to become a mighty force in their own liberation. Wordsworth believes that no "resistance can be prosperous which does not look, for its chief support, to these principles and feelings" (p. 338)—referring here to "the grand and disinterested passions, and . . . the laws of universal morality" (338). French tyranny will call forth and create these spiritual forces in abundance:

> Oppression, its own blind and predestined enemy, has poured this of blessedness upon Spain,—that the enormity of the outrages, of which she has been the victim, has created an object of love and of hatred—of apprehensions and of wishes—adequate (if that be possible) to the utmost demands of the spirit. (338)

Those who question Wordsworth's faith are ignorant of human nature. In one sense the Spanish are fortunate in having such a worthy object of their passion because:

> The true sorrow of humanity consists in this;—not that the mind of man fails; but that the course and demands of action and of life so rarely correspond with the dignity and intensity of human desires: and hence that, which is slow to languish, is too easily turned aside and abused. (339)

Wordsworth has already stated what he believes to be the true end of life; now he identifies life's true tragedy. Daily life does not afford the self with worthy correlatives to the human passions. To understand the depth of this tragedy in Wordsworth's eyes, it is necessary to remember that man is made capable of extending himself beyond himself not through his intellectual faculties, but through his emotional faculties. Daily life, Wordsworth is saying, generally leaves us locked up within the narrow circuit of the self. If this is the true sorrow of life, it is possible to come to a new understanding of what Wordsworth understood to be the vocation of the poet. The poet creates a fictive world in which men can find objects and circumstances that correspond "with the dignity and intensity of human desires," and thereby transcend the tragedy of life. What is more, Wordsworth's desire to take "subjects . . . chosen from ordinary life" and apply to them "the power of giving the interest of novelty by the modifying colours of imagination"[6] becomes more understandable. Wordsworth strove to show that to a mind sufficiently vital with imaginative power even quotidian existence could correspond to the richness and intensity of human passion. To a mind sufficiently attentive there is "A tale in every thing" (P.W. 4:63), as the prosaic narrator of "Simon Lee" puts it. If this is so then it becomes clear that Wordsworth is a poet at war with the tragic vision.

If "the surviving chiefs of the Spanish people . . . prove worthy" there is much work to be done:

> Young scions of polity must be engrafted on the time-worn trunk: a new fortress must be reared upon the ancient and living rock of justice. Then it would be seen, while the superstructure stands inwardly immoveable, in how short a space of time the ivy and the wild plant would climb up from the base, and clasp the naked wall. . . . (342)

The trunk of polity is not cut down and replaced but rather is engrafted with young shoots; the new fortress is not built upon a new foundation but on the traditional and somehow organically living original rock of justice; the superstructure will remain intact despite changes. Here Wordsworth echoes the principal note of Burkean conservatism. All reform must be in harmony with existing patterns. The future of a society must bear a continuous relation to its past without any radical breaks, because society is organic and living like a tree. It must grow and change naturally and gradually. Radical change is literally change that strikes at the roots of society and such change would be fatal to the organic structure of the social plant.

Wordsworth concludes the Cintra tract by reminding his British readers that they must "look to ourselves" (342). They must expiate the guilt of the Convention of Cintra. He closes with a quotation from Milton's *History of Britain* to the effect that martial victories are of little benefit to those so injudicious and unwise as not to know the end and reason of winning.

So ends Wordsworth's repetitive, curious, but ultimately marvelous polemic. It is a critique of the Convention of Cintra; it is a statesman's manual; and it is a powerful defense of traditional society, a society bound together by emotional ties, and the natural economy threatened by the Industrial Revolution. As a defense of traditional society it cannot be said to be consecutively reasoned. The argument must be pieced together as it is put forth in hints and digressions. But it is a brilliantly argued piece and if one had to summarize it one would, finally, have to emphasize first the practical efficacy of the morally good, and second the power and the moral necessity of the passions, both great and small, that link man to his home, his neighbors, his community, his country, his past and his posterity. A community that fosters such passions will be good, will be valid, and will endure, for Wordsworth insists that the ethically good, the true, and the permanent cannot be separated and that many of the errors of statecraft stem from a failure to understand how closely the grand passions of human nature are related to the good, the true and right, and the permanent. Wordsworth takes his argument further and asserts that all that fosters egotism is inimical to valid community, to all moral good, to truth and sound policy, and to all that would endure.

It is almost impossible to read Wordsworth's Cintra tract both attentively and with an open mind without having one's understanding of Wordsworth both deepen and change. For Wordsworth says here many things that he says nowhere else, many things of great importance that bear either directly or by implication on Wordsworth's practice and intention as a poet. Even were this not so, the document would still be of special importance for this study of the development of the idea of community in Wordsworth. The Cintra tract is Wordsworth's first and most profound full articulation of the value, the necessity even, of the rural community of Tory England, the community already being visibly dissolved in the poisonous and acid waste of the Industrial Revolution. The tract is a testament to Wordsworth's commitment to a community bound together by affective and moral ties rather than by the exchanges and conveniences brought about by ruthless, egotistical, rational calculation.

CONCLUSION

IN this study I have attempted to demonstrate how a profound division of Wordsworth's sense of himself into two polar potential identities, one grandiose, the other stunted, intensified for him the human impulse to find security in human community. Human community would, Wordsworth hoped, free his own ego from the strain of painful oscillations between its polar conceptions of itself. He looked to community to provide stability.

The French Revolution offered Wordsworth the exciting possibility of a community which would be both stabilizing, in the support he would gain by being one with the enormous community of universal brotherhood, and liberating to the grandiose conception of himself that would be imperiously free to destroy an old social order and to replace it with a new one. But the opportunities that the Revolution offered Wordsworth's egoism were heavily conflicted. For him to strike out against an established social order may well have been unconsciously perceived by him as striking out against the established authority of his father, still alive in his timeless unconscious, though dead since 1783. Indeed, on the evidence of *The Borderers*, it seems as though the paternal authority that Wordsworth had internalized, and that restrained his ego, responded savagely to Wordsworth's rebellious attachment to the Gironde, punishing Wordsworth's ego remorselessly with guilt, self-reproaches and confusional depression.

Wordsworth freed himself from this painful onslaught by

295

abandoning the cause of the French Revolution, and in addition
abandoning all claims to what I have called effective power, accepting, instead of control over the physical world, control over
the imaginative world, or what I have called affective power.
Wordsworth shifted to a new ideal of community congruent with
these emotional developments. The new community was really
the traditional community of the Lakes. Characteristically its inhabitants had great affective power, but little effective power (save
for the sanctified power of patriarchal sway). Therefore egoism was
kept within check while the community was bound by intense and
reciprocally acting affective bonds. Because of these bonds every
individual was assured that his identity could be spared the anomic
ravages that could work on it in a community (or anticommunity)
in which the self received no reflexive support from others. Labor
in this community was unalienated, and the land labored on
passed from father to son. Laborers were expected to work hard
both in the fields and at the loom. The ideal was a natural economy, independent of the market and of commodity relationships.
It was not expected that this ideal would be fully realized, but it
was, nonetheless, a goal to be striven for. If the rewards of labor
could not, for some reason, be realized, or if the community
member was too old or infirm to work, he or she could expect to
be carefully looked after and supported by the rest of the community, especially by the gentry who shared the excess of their wealth
with those in need. The exploitative relationship was alien to such
a community. The accumulation of great wealth was a social boon
that made the squire's largesse possible.

But Wordsworth formulated this ideal of a polity at a time
when the social and economic forces generated by the Industrial
Revolution were already destroying the type of society he most valued. Wordsworth was quite aware of the changes taking place in
the social fabric of Grasmere and the region about it. He resented
these changes, sometimes reacting with despair and loss, sometimes with bitterness and outrage. I have attempted to suggest that
Wordsworth's commitment to an already decaying set of social
forms so distracted him that he took his eye off the object, that is
he ceased to write about his true subject, being, and concerned
himself instead with preserving a moribund way of being. Further,

I have suggested that this distraction contributed to the remarkable diminution of Wordsworth's poetic power after 1808.

Finally, I have attempted to show that Wordsworth's growing concern with the humble classes as a usable subject for serious verse, after his disillusionment with the French Revolution, was not the simple transposition of humanitarian concern from revolutionary politics to Lake Country rustics that it is commonly taken to be. Rather, it was a complex and contradictory gesture with distinct humanitarian significance, on the one hand, but a gesture that also signified a ratification of the established social structure on the other. The development of Wordsworth's Tory humanism was, from this perspective, a protracted resolution of the contradiction, as the Tory significance of his high valuation of the rural poor (in order to ratify existing society) came more and more to the fore. Indeed, I have tentatively suggested that the entire structure of social relations, as described in Wordsworth's poetry and prose, constituted a mythic structure whose function was to disguise social inequity and show, in its stead, a false social symmetry.

This study began with a psychological examination of William Wordsworth, and if it had ended there, or had continued in the same vein, perhaps all would have been well, and this study would have taken its place in an established genre of Wordsworth criticism among the biographical and psychological studies of Wordsworth and his poetry. But my psychological examination of the poet was a means to an end, a way of approaching Wordsworth's social and political ideals from a fresh perspective, and it is precisely here that my study breaks with the major tendencies in Wordsworth studies today.

Following the brilliant, and I fear overly seductive work of David Ferry, who sees Wordsworth turning his back on man and his works in favor of eternity, and of Geoffrey Hartman, who sees Wordsworth repudiating a desired apocalyptic vision which both obliterates and transcends time, modern critics of Wordsworth have, with the notable exceptions of David Erdman, E. P. Thompson, and Carl Woodring, turned their backs on the political and social implications of Wordsworth's poetry.

It is not, I think, fashionable any longer to see works of art as moral and political statements that implicitly or explicitly call upon those who respond to them to change their lives, and to change, especially, the way their lives impinge upon those of their fellow men. But to see a work of art in this fashion is to recognize in art a social act. Wordsworth's great contemporary, William Blake, did not question the social life of a work of art, and I deliberately use the phrase social life which on one level of meaning attributes to a work of art a peculiarly human activity. For Blake, each work of art contributed to the building of Jerusalem, the city of fully realized human potentiality, the city that defined the fully realized life as being social life. Every beautiful or cleverly wrought artifact contributed to the task of making man fully human.

And going back to Plato and the first fully articulated Western theory of the function of art, one finds that Plato was convinced that poetic and dramatic works of art were so inescapably social and political in their function that he found it necessary to ban poets from any republic expected to produce good men. However adversely Plato finally came to view poetry, he took it as his premise that poetry bore heavily on the moral and the social life.

One would think, since literature is created in the uniquely human medium of communication, language, that it would be commonly recognized that all literature is either implicitly or explicitly a social act. But our culture does not find this truth to be evident. The density of human connection exists in our culture, as it does in others, but it is neither seen nor felt. The fully social nature of art is no more seen than the fully social nature of man himself. Free market economic and social relationships have acted to make it appear that objects of human production and exchange relate to one another reciprocally and organically as subjects through the seemingly ideal and eternal "laws of supply and demand." Marx called the state of consciousness, which sees these objects of production and exchange apparently relate to one another as subjects, "commodity fetishism." Because of the illusion created by commodity fetishism, "the social character of labour appears to us as an objective character of the products themselves."[1] In other words, "a definite social relation between men . . . assumes, in their eyes, the fantasic form of a relation be-

tween things."[2] Just as Marx first diagnosed this disorder of consciousness, so it was he who first analyzed the processes that
brought about this disorder:

> The equality of all sorts of human labour is expressed objec-
> tively by their products all being equally values; the measure of the
> expenditure of labour-power by the duration of that expenditure,
> takes the form of the quantity of value of the products of labour;
> and finally, the mutual relations of the producers, within which the
> social character of their labour affirms itself, takes the form of a
> social relation between the products.
>
> A commodity is therefore a mysterious thing, simply because
> in it the social character of men's labour appears to them as an ob-
> jective character stamped upon the product of that labour; because
> the relation of the producers to the sum total of their own labour is
> presented to them as a social relation, existing not between them-
> selves, but between the products of their labour. This is the reason
> why the products of labour become commodities, social things
> whose qualities are at the same time perceptible and imperceptible
> by the senses.[3]

But the more commodities are seen as acting and relating, the
more are the true underlying relationships of the human producers, exchangers, and consumers hidden in a veil of mystification. Human consciousness denies itself as subject, recognizing itself only as object, while at the same time endowing objects of
consciousness with the very subjectivity it denies itself. Consciousness alienates its own subjectivity, leaving itself reduced and impoverished, a deformed and isolated caricature of its fully subjective whole. Meanwhile consciousness in the same act reifies the
objects of human production, exchange, and consumption. It is at
this point in the history of the social means of production and
reproduction that men, in the thrall of the very social organization
by which they produce and reproduce themselves, "discover" in
isolation, weightlessness, and abject helplessness and despair, what
is most authentic in "human nature." The history of human consciousness is revised accordingly, or as the victims of self-alienated
consciousness would have it, corrected.

With the density of human connection hidden from the collective consciousness of our culture, man appears most fully human as an isolated individual. What appeared self-evident to Aristotle, that man was truly human only in his social existence and social relationships, is no longer self-evident to a society that cannot penetrate the mystification that disguises the full nexus of its human relationships. And in this historical circumstance man as alienated being replaces man as social being.

It is not to be wondered at that literary critics of such a culture have lost the hard truths of Aristotle and Plato—that man is social and that art, to the degree that it is humanly significant, participates in the moral and social life of society. Hence the phenomenon, harmless in itself, that Wordsworth scholarship is largely preoccupied with almost every aspect of Wordsworth and his work but the social and political concerns of the man and his work.

Much good has come from the diversity of critical approaches to Wordsworth, and I would not wish to be understood as suggesting that there is but one true way to approach Wordsworth, and no other. But perhaps I went too far when I suggested that the tendency to ignore the social and political aspects of Wordsworth and his work was harmless. It is not; and such ignorance may result in a failure to understand Wordsworth precisely where he wanted most to be understood, and consequently in a failure to respond to the full and enormous power of his best work. It is my conviction that Wordsworth was, before anything else, a moralist. He wrote with a moral purpose, and the idea of an art devoid of moral purpose would most likely have been both alien and rebarbative to him. In the Preface to *The Lyrical Ballads* of 1800 Wordsworth wrote that "the Poems in these volumes will be found distinguished at least by one mark of difference, that each of them has a worthy *purpose*" (*Prose* 1:124). On June 14, 1802, in a postscript to a letter that William had written to Mary and Sara Hutchinson admonishing them on their inability to appreciate his poem "Resolution and Independence," Dorothy wrote:

> Dear Sara
> When you happen to be displeased with what you suppose to be the tendency or moral of any poem which William writes, ask yourself whether you have hit upon the real tendency and true

moral, and above all never think that he writes for no reason but
merely because a thing happened. . . .   (E.L. 367)

It seems likely that Dorothy understood her brother's conception of
poetry's function.

But if a reader of Wordsworth's poetry is not alive to its explicit social and political meaning, then much of the poetry's
moral content and force will be missed when the reader does
respond to Wordsworth's moral vision, and all of the poetry's
moral content and force will be missed in those poems and passages where the reader finds no moral and assumes that Wordsworth wrote "merely because a thing happened."

In order to respond fully to Wordsworth it is necessary to recognize that he is first and foremost a moral poet. And in order to
respond fully to his moral vision it is necessary to recognize that
social and political tendencies occupied a significant place in his
moral vision. Wordsworth took seriously the idea that he and the
other great Romantics inherited from Milton, that the poet was a
public figure with a social role. He wrote to a generation that had
experienced the shock of the French Revolution and to many,
including himself, who had experienced the "melancholy waste of
hopes o'erthrown" (Prel. II, 449). Wordsworth believed that, as a
result of his painful encounter with the French Revolution, he
had discovered important and sanative moral truths that could
help restore a generation led astray by false political philosophy.
Wordsworth believed that he and Coleridge could play a restorative role to a generation so misled. He and Coleridge were to be:

> United helpers forward of a day
> Of firmer trust, joint-labourers; in a work
> (Should Providence such grace to us vouchsafe)
> Of their redemption, surely yet to come.
> Prophets of Nature, we to them will speak
> A lasting inspiration, sanctified
> By reason and by truth; what we have loved,
> Others will love; and we may teach them how;
> Instruct them how the mind of man becomes
> A thousand times more beautiful than the earth
> On which he dwells, above this Frame of things
> (Which, 'mid all revolutions in the hopes

And fears of men, doth still remain unchanged)
In beauty exalted, as it is itself
Of substance and of fabric more divine.

> (*Prel.* XIII, 438–452)

It is on this prophetic note, this conviction that his was a mission to redeem and to teach a generation brought to despair by failed millennial hopes that Wordsworth concludes his masterpiece. It is, then, no more than doing justice to Wordsworth to take him seriously as a teacher of social truths meant to be adequate even to those spun round and confused by the might of revolution. And it is, in part, of the moral balm to a politically wounded generation that Matthew Arnold spoke in his "Memorial Verses" when he wrote of Wordsworth:

> He too upon a wintry clime
> Had fallen—on this iron time
> Of doubts, disputes, distractions, fears.
> He found us when the age had bound
> Our souls in its benumbing round;
> He spoke, and loos'd our heart in tears.
> He laid us as we lay at birth
> On the cool flowery lap of earth. . . .[4]

It is no dishonor to Wordsworth to question the adequacy of these restorative truths, or even to question whether or not he taught less disinterestedly than he knew. For it is in just such "obstinate questionings" (*P.W.* 4:283) that Wordsworth would have recognized the serious moral life to which he was committed.

NOTES

One: The Need for Community

1. William Blake, *Poetry and Prose*, p. 35.
2. Aristotle, *Politics*, p. 5.
3. Sigmund Freud, *Civilization and Its Discontents*, Joan Riviere, trans., in *The Complete Psychological Works of Sigmund Freud*, 21:64.
4. Sigmund Freud, "On Narcissism: An Introduction," C. M. Bains, trans., in *Works*, 14:67–102.
5. M. H. Abrams, "The Correspondent Breeze: A Romantic Metaphor," pp. 113–130.
6. Donald Woods Winnicott, *The Maturational Process and the Facilitating Environment*, pp. 29–36.
7. Charles Brenner, *An Elementary Textbook of Psychoanalysis*, p. 25.
8. F. W. Bateson, *Wordsworth: A Re-interpretation*, pp. 151–154.
9. Lionel Trilling, "Wordsworth and the Iron Time," in *Wordsworth Centenary Studies Presented at Cornell and Princeton Universities* (Princeton, N.J.: Princeton University Press, 1951), pp. 131–152.
10. John Milton, *Paradise Lost*, II, 151.
11. G. S. Kirk and J. E. Raven, *The Presocratic Philosophers*, pp. 226–227.
12. Raymond Williams, *The Country and the City*, p. 78.
13. William Wordsworth, "The Ruined Cottage," in Jonathan Wordsworth, *The Music of Humanity*, p. 37.
14. Lionel Trilling, *Sincerity and Authenticity*, pp. 90–91.
15. Williams, *The Country and the City*, p. 150.
16. E. P. Thompson, *The Making of the English Working Class*, p. 265.
17. Williams, *The Country and the City*, p. 295.

Two: The Search for Community

1. Blake, *Poetry and Prose*, p. 469.

2. I am indebted to Professor Lionel Trilling for identifying Samuel as the model dedicated spirit to whom Wordsworth alludes.

3. *The Prose Works of William Wordsworth*, A. Grosart, ed., 3:451.

4. Mary Moorman, *William Wordsworth: the Early Years*, p. 132.

5. *Ibid.*, p. 170.

6. *Ibid.*, p. 170.

7. Blake, *Poetry and Prose*, p. 35.

8. Elie Halévy, *England in 1815*, pp. 150–151.

9. *Ibid.*, p. 142.

10. Sigmund Freud, *Moses and Monotheism*, James Strachey, trans., in *Works*, 23:12.

11. *Ibid.*, p. 12.

12. Sigmund Freud, *The Interpretation of Dreams*, James Strachey, trans., in *Works*, 4:262.

13. Sigmund Freud, *The Ego and the Id*, Joan Riviere, trans., in *Works*, 19:32.

14. George Lefebvre, *The French Revolution*, 1:214.

15. Albert Soboul, *The French Revolution: 1787–1799*, pp. 237–238.

16. Christopher Caudwell, *Illusion and Reality*, p. 90.

17. Soboul, *The French Revolution*, p. 276.

18. Freud, *Interpretation of Dreams*, p. 245.

19. Edmund Burke, *Reflections on the Revoluion in France*, p. 53.

20. *Ibid.*, p. 89.

21. Blake, *Poetry and Prose*, p. 37.

22. *Ibid.*, p. 35.

23. Burke, *Reflections on the Revolution in France*, pp. 47–49.

24. Blake, *Poetry and Prose*, p. 27.

25. Karl Marx, *Capital*, 3:786.

26. *Ibid.*, pp. 814–815.

27. Carl Woodring, *Politics in English Romantic Poetry*, p. 33.

28. Karl Marx, *The Eighteenth Brumaire of Louis Bonaparte*, p. 48.

29. Moorman, *William Wordsworth: The Early Years*, p. 163.

30. *Ibid.*, p. 180.

31. *Ibid.*, p. 296.

32. *Ibid.*, p. 296.

33. Marx, *Eighteenth Brumaire*, p. 15.

Three: Community Found: Part I

1. Sigmund Freud, "Formulations Regarding the Two Principles of Mental Functioning," M. N. Searl, trans., in *Works*, 12:215–226.

2. Sigmund Freud, "Character and Anal Eroticism," R. C. McWalters, trans., in *Works*, 167–175.

3. Karl Marx and Friedrich Engels, "Manifesto of the Communist Party," in *Basic Writings on Politics and Philosophy*, pp. 9–10.

4. Freud, *Moses and Monotheism*, p. 12.

5. Sigmund Freud, "Fragment of an Analysis of a Case of Hysteria," Alix and James Strachey, trans., in *Works*, 9:35.

6. Sigmund Freud, "Family Romances," James Strachey, trans., in *Works*, 9:237–241.

7. *Ibid.*, p. 237.

8. Percy Bysshe Shelley, *Complete Works*, p. 265.

9. Wordsworth, "The Ruined Cottage," in *Music of Humanity*, p. 48.

10. Williams, *The Country and the City*, p. 131.

11. Burke, *Reflections on the Revolution in France*, p. 53.

12. Brenner, *An Elementary Textbook of Psychoanalysis*, pp. 118–119.

13. Peter Laslett, *The World We Have Lost*, p. 60.

14. *Ibid.*, pp. 78–79.

15. *Ibid.*, p. 178.

16. *Ibid.*, p. 130.

17. *Ibid.*, p. 13.

18. Thompson, *The Making of the English Working Class*, p. 334.

19. *Ibid.*, p. 333.

20. *Ibid.*, p. 334.

21. Milton, *Paradise Lost*, i, 26.

22. Thompson, *The Making of the English Working Class*, p. 80.

23. *Ibid.*, p. 81.

24. Halévy, *England in 1815*, p. 451.

25. Percy Bysshe Shelley, A *Defense of Poetry*, pp. 74–75.

26. Milton, *Paradise Lost*, iii, 99.

Four: Community Found: Part II

1. Williams, *The Country and the City*, pp. 46–47.

2. *Ibid.*, p. 46.

3. *Ibid.*, p. 47.

4. *Ibid.*, p. 48.

5. I owe this formulation to Mr. Carl Woodring.

6. Ernest Jones, *The Life and Work of Sigmund Freud*, p. 212.

7. Samuel Taylor Coleridge, *Biographia Literaria*, p. 259.

8. Moorman, *William Wordsworth: The Early Years*, p. 378.

9. Laslett, *The World We Have Lost*, p. 31.

10. Blake, *Poetry and Prose*, p. 27.

11. Thompson, *The Making of the English Working Class*, p. 276.

12. Williams, *The Country and the City*, p. 98.

13. Blake, *Poetry and Prose*, p. 476.

14. M. H. Abrams, "English Romanticism: The Spirit of the Age," in *Romanticism Reconsidered*, Northrop Frye, ed., pp. 68–69.

15. Mary Moorman, *William Wordsworth: The Later Years*, p. 261.

16. Samuel Taylor Coleridge, *Table Talk*, in *Complete Works*, 6:425.

17. Walt Whitman, *The Complete Poetry and Prose*, p. 65.

18. Aristotle, *Politics*, pp. 9–10.

19. Marx, *Capital*, 3:807.

20. *Ibid.*, p. 807.

21. Williams, *The Country and the City*, p. 45.
22. William Hazlitt, *The Spirit of the Age*, in *Collected Works*, 4:271.
23. Thompson, *The Making of the English Working Class*, p. 56.

Five: A Challenge to Community

1. Thompson, *The Making of the English Working Class*, p. 197.
2. Trilling, "Wordsworth and the Iron Time," pp. 131–152.
3. Trilling, *Sincerity and Authenticity*, pp. 90–93.
4. Thompson, *The Making of the English Working Class*, p. 340.
5. Laslett, *The World We Have Lost*, pp. 17–18.
6. Thompson, *The Making of the English Working Class*, p. 416.
7. *Ibid.*, p. 445.
8. Karl Polanyi, *The Great Transformation*, p. 92.
9. T. S. Ashton, *The Industrial Revolution: 1760–1830*, p. 43.
10. Thompson, *The Making of the English Working Class*, p. 217.
11. Halévy, *England in 1815*, p. 240.
12. Marx and Engels, in *Basic Writings*, p. 9.
13. *Ibid.*, p. 10.
14. Thompson, *The Making of the English Working Class*, p. 203.
15. *Ibid.*, pp. 202–203.
16. *Ibid.*, p. 544.
17. *Ibid.*, p. 549.
18. *Ibid.*, p. 220.
19. Polanyi, *The Great Transformation*, p. 71.
20. Thompson, *The Making of the English Working Class*, p. 220.
21. *Ibid.*, p. 343.
22. *Ibid.*, p. 832.
23. *Ibid.*, p. 189.
24. Halévy, *England in 1815*, p. 133.
25. Thompson, *The Making of the English Working Class*, pp. 343–344.
26. Samuel Taylor Coleridge, *The Friend*, in *Collected Works*, I:II,160.
27. Thompson, *The Making of the English Working Class*, p. 330.
28. *Ibid.*, p. 329.
29. *Ibid.*, pp. 317–318.
30. Williams, *The Country and the City*, p. 49.
31. Thompson, *The Making of the English Working Class*, p. 341.
32. *Ibid.*, p. 402.
33. *Ibid.*, p. 76.
34. *Ibid.*, p. 736.
35. *Ibid.*, p. 57.
36. *Ibid.*, p. 402.
37. *Ibid.*, p. 403.
38. *Ibid.*, p. 405.
39. *Ibid.*, p. 197.
40. *Ibid.*, p. 57.
41. *Ibid.*, p. 403.
42. *Ibid.*, p. 79.

43. Milton, *Paradise Lost*, x, 508.

44. *Ibid.*, x, 505.

Six: Community Defended

* Future citations of Wordsworth's Cintra text will include the page number only.

1. Marx and Engels, in *Basic Writings*, p. 10.

2. Blake, *Poetry and Prose*, p. 35.

3. Marx, *Capital*, 1:609.

4. I owe this formulation of Wordsworth's ideas about democracy to Mr. Carl Woodring.

5. Milton, *Paradise Lost*, II, 666–670.

6. Coleridge, *Biographia Literaria*, p. 168.

Conclusion

1. Marx, *Capital*, 1:74.

2. *Ibid.*, p. 72.

3. *Ibid.*

4. Matthew Arnold, *Poetry and Prose*, p. 188.

BIBLIOGRAPHY

Works by Wordsworth

Wordsworth, William. *The Poetical Works of William Wordsworth*. 5 vols. Edited by Ernest de Selincourt and Helen Darbishire. Oxford: At the Clarendon Press, 1940–1949.

Wordsworth, William. *The Prelude or Growth of a Poet's Mind*. Edited by Ernest de Selincourt. 2d ed. rev. by Helen Darbishire. Oxford: At the Clarendon Press, 1959.

Wordsworth, William. *The Prose Works of William Wordsworth*. Vol. 3. Edited by A. Grosart. London: Edward Moxon, 1876.

Wordsworth, William. *The Prose Works of William Wordsworth*. 3 vols. Edited by W. J. B. Owen and Jane Worthington Smyser. Oxford: At the Clarendon Press, 1974.

Wordsworth, Dorothy and William Wordsworth. *The Letters of William and Dorothy Wordsworth: The Early Years, 1787–1805*. Edited by Ernest de Selincourt. 2d ed. rev. by Chester Shaver. Oxford: At the Clarendon Press, 1969.

Wordsworth, Dorothy and William Wordsworth. *The Letters of William and Dorothy Wordsworth: The Middle Years, 1806–1811*. Edited by Ernest de Selincourt. 2d ed. rev. by Mary Moorman. Oxford: At the Clarendon Press, 1969.

Wordsworth, Dorothy. *The Journals of Dorothy Wordsworth: The Alfoxden Journal, 1798; The Grasmere Journals, 1800–1803*. Edited by Mary Moorman. Oxford: Oxford University Press, 1971.

General References and Historical Studies

Abrams, M. H. "The Correspondent Breeze: A Romantic Metaphor." *Kenyon Review* (1957), 19:113–130.

—— *The Mirror and the Lamp: Romantic Theory and the Critical Tradition*. Oxford: Oxford University Press, 1953.

Abrams, M. H., ed. *English Romantic Poets: Modern Essays in Criticism*. New York: Oxford University Press, 1960.

—— *Wordsworth: A Collection of Critical Essays*. Englewood Cliffs, N.J.: Prentice-Hall, 1972.

Aristotle. *The Politics*. Ernest Barker, ed. and trans. New York: Oxford University Press, 1962.

Arnold, Matthew. *The Poetry and Prose of Matthew Arnold*. John Bryson, ed. Cambridge, Mass.: Harvard University Press, 1967.

Ashton, T. S. *The Industrial Revolution*. New York: Oxford University Press, 1948.

Barthes, Roland. *Mythologies*. Annette Lavers, ed. and trans. New York: Hill & Wang, 1972.

—— *Writing, Degree Zero and Elements of Semiology*. Annette Lavers and Colin Smith, eds. and trans. With a preface by Susan Sontag. New York: Hill & Wang, 1968.

Barzun, Jacques. *Classic Romantic and Modern*. 2d rev. ed. Boston: Little, Brown, 1961.

Bate, Walter Jackson. *From Classic to Romantic*. Cambridge, Mass.: Harvard University Press, 1946.

Bateson, F. W. *Wordsworth: A Re-Interpretation*. 2d rev. ed. London: Longmans, Green, 1956.

Batho, Edith C. *The Later Wordsworth*. New York: Macmillan, 1933.

Beatty, Arthur. *William Wordsworth: His Doctrine and Art in Their Historical Relations*. University of Wisconsin Studies in Language and Literature, No. 17. Madison: University of Wisconsin Press, 1922.

Blake, William. *The Poetry and Prose of William Blake*. David V. Erdman, ed., with commentary by Harold Bloom. Garden City, N.Y.: Doubleday, 1965.

Bloom, Harold. *The Visionary Company: A Reading of English Romantic Poetry*. Garden City, N.Y.: Doubleday, 1961.

Bouch, C. M. L., and C. P. Jones. *A Short Economic and Social History of the Lake Counties: 1500–1830*. Manchester: Manchester University Press, 1961.

Bradley, Andrew Cecil. *Oxford Lectures on Poetry*. London: Macmillan, 1920.

Brenner, Charles. *An Elementary Textbook of Psychoanalysis*. New York: International Universities Press, 1955.

Briggs, Asa. *The Making of Modern England (1784–1867): The Age of Improvement*. New York: Harper & Row, 1959.

Brooks, Cleanth. *The Well-Wrought Urn: Studies in the Structure of Poetry*. New York: Reynal & Hitchcock, 1947.

Brower, Reubin Arthur. *The Fields of Light: An Experiment in Critical Reading*. New York: Oxford University Press, 1951.

Burke, Edmond [sic]. "Appeal from the New to the Old Whigs." In *The Works of the Right Honorable Edmond Burke*, 4:57–215. Rev. ed. Boston: Little, Brown, 1866.

—— "Fourth Letter on the Proposals for Peace with the Regicide Directory of France." In *The Works of the Right Honorable Edmond Burke*, 6:1–112. Rev. ed. Boston: Little, Brown, 1866.

—— "Heads for Consideration on the Present State of Affairs." In *The Works of the Right Honorable Edmond Burke*, 4:379–402. Rev. ed. Boston: Little, Brown, 1866.

—— "Hints for a Memorial to be Delivered to Monsieur De M.M." In *The Works of the Right Honorable Edmond Burke*, 4:307–311. Rev. ed. Boston: Little, Brown, 1866.

—— "Letter to a Member of the National Assembly in Answer to Some Objections to His Book on French Affairs." In *The Works of the Right Honorable Edmond Burke*, 4:1–55. Rev. ed. Boston: Little, Brown, 1866.

—— "Letter to a Noble Lord on the Attacks Made Upon Mr. Burke and His Pension, in the House of Lords, by the Duke of Bedford and the Earl of Lauderdale." In *The Works of the Right Honorable Edmond Burke*, 5:171–279. Rev. ed. Boston: Little, Brown, 1866.

—— *Reflections on the Revolution in France*. Thomas H. D. Mahoney, ed. and introduction. With an analysis by Oscar Piest. Indianapolis: Bobbs-Merrill, 1955.

—— "Remarks on the Policy of the Allies with Respect to France." In *The Works of the Right Honorable Edmond Burke*, 4:403–482. Rev. ed. Boston: Little, Brown, 1866.

—— "Thoughts on French Affairs." In *The Works of the Right Honorable Edmond Burke*, 4:313–377. Rev. ed. Boston: Little, Brown, 1866.

—— "Three Letters to a Member of Parliament on the Proposals for a Peace with the Regicide Directory of France." In *The Works of the Right Honorable Edmond Burke*, 5:231–508. Rev. ed. Boston: Little, Brown, 1866.

Burra, Peter. *Wordsworth*. New York: Collier, 1962.

Caudwell, Christopher. *Illusion and Reality: A Study of the Sources of Poetry*. New York: International Publishers, 1937.

Chomsky, Noam. *Language and Mind*. Enlarged ed. New York: Harcourt Brace Jovanovich, 1972.

Clarke, C. C. *Romantic Paradox: An Essay on the Poetry of Wordsworth*. London: Routledge & Kegan Paul, 1962.

Cobb, Richard. *The Police and the People: French Popular Protest 1789–1820*. Oxford: At the Clarendon Press, 1970.

Coleridge, Samuel Taylor. *Biographia Literaria: Or Biographical Sketches of My Literary Life and Opinions*. George Watson, ed. 2d rev. ed. London: J. M. Dent, 1965.

—— *The Friend*. Barbara Rooke, ed. In *The Collected Works of Samuel Taylor Coleridge*. Kathleen Coburn, ed., with the assistance of Bart Winer. London: Princeton University Press, 1969.

—— *Table Talk*. Vol. 6 in *The Complete Works of Samuel Taylor Coleridge*. W. G. T. Shedd, ed. New York: Harper & Brothers, 1884.

Danby, John F. *The Simple Wordsworth: Studies in the Poems—1797–1807*. London: Routledge & Kegan Paul, 1962.

Darbishire, Helen. *The Poet Wordsworth*. Oxford: At the Clarendon Press, 1950.

Davis, Jack, ed. *Discussions of William Wordsworth*. Boston: D. C. Heath, 1964.

de Saussure, Ferdinand. *Course in General Linguistics*. Charles Bally and Albert Sechehaye, in collaboration with Albert Reidlinger, eds. Wade Baskin, trans. and introd. New York: Philosophical Library, 1959.

DeQuincey, Thomas. "The Lake Poets: William Wordsworth." In David Masson, ed., *The Complete Works of Thomas de Quincey*, 2:229–302. Edinburgh: Adam and Charles Black, 1889.
—— "On Wordsworth's Poetry." In David Masson, ed., *The Complete Works of Thomas de Quincey*, 11:294–325. Edinburgh: Adam and Charles Black, 1890.
Dobb, Maurice. *Studies in the Development of Capitalism*. New York: International Publishers, 1947.
Dobb, Maurice et al. *The Transition from Feudalism to Capitalism*. Reprint ed. New York: Science and Society Press, 1967.
Douglas, Wallace W. *Wordsworth: The Construction of a Personality*. Oberlin, Ohio: Kent State University Press, 1968.
Dunklin, Gilbert T., ed. *Wordsworth Centenary Studies Presented at Cornell and Princeton Universities*. Princeton, N.J.: Princeton University Press, 1951.

Ehrmann, Jacques, ed. *Structuralism*. With an introduction by Jacques Ehrmann. Garden City N.Y.: Anchor Books, 1970.

Ferry, David. *The Limits of Mortality: An Essay on Wordsworth's Major Poems*. Middletown, Conn.: Wesleyan University Press, 1959.
Foucault, Michel. *The Order of Things: An Archaeology of the Human Sciences*. A Translation of *Les Mots et les Choses*. New York: Pantheon, 1970.
Freud, Sigmund. *The Complete Psychological Works of Sigmund Freud*. James Strachey and Anna Freud, eds. 24 vols. London: The Hogarth Press, 1953–1968.
Frye, Northrop, ed. *Romanticism Reconsidered: Selected Papers from the English Institute*. With a foreword by Northrop Frye. New York: Columbia University Press, 1963.

George, Dorothy. *England in Transition: Life and Work in the Eighteenth Century*. London: G. Routledge, 1931.

Halévy, Elie. *England in 1815*. In *History of the English People in the Nineteenth Century*, vol. 1. E. I. Watkin and D. A. Barker, trans. New York: P. Smith, 1949.
—— *The Liberal Awakening: 1815–1830*. In *History of the English People in the Nineteenth Century*, Vol. 2. E. I. Watkin and D. A. Barker, trans. New York: P. Smith, 1949.
Hartman, Geoffry H. *Wordsworth's Poetry: 1787–1814*. New Haven, Conn.: Yale University Press, 1964.
Havens, Raymond Dexter. *The Mind of a Poet: A Study of Wordsworth's Thought with Particular Reference to The Prelude*. Baltimore: Johns Hopkins University Press, 1941.
Hazlitt, William. "Mr. Wordsworth," in *The Spirit of the Age: Or Contemporary Portraits*. In A. R. Waller and Arnold Glover, eds., *The Collected Works of William Hazlitt*, 4:270–279. London: J. M. Dent, 1902.
—— "Observations on Mr. Wordsworth's Poem *The Excursion*." In A. R. Waller and Arnold Glover, eds., *The Collected Works of William Hazlitt*, 1:11–125. London: J. M. Dent, 1902.

—— *Lectures on English Poets and The Spirit of the Age: Or Contemporary Portraits.* With an introduction by Catherine Macdonald Maclean. London: J. M. Dent, 1910; rpt. 1967.

Hill, Christopher. *Reformation to Industrial Revolution; The Making of Modern English Society (1530–1780).* New York: Pantheon, 1967.

Hobsbaum, E. J. *The Age of Revolution: 1789–1848.* Cleveland: Publishing, 1962.

—— *Industry and Empire: From 1750 to Present Day.* In *Pelican Economic History of England,* vol. 3. Baltimore: Penguin Books, 1968.

Jones, Ernest. *The Life and Work of Sigmund Freud.* Lionel Trilling and Steven Marcus, eds. and abr. New York: Basic Books, 1961.

—— "The Problem of Paul Morphy: A Contribution to the Psychology of Chess." In his *Psycho-Myth, Psycho-History: Essays in Applied Psychoanalysis,* pp. 165–196. New York: The Stonehill Publishing Company, 1974.

Jones, John. *The Egotistical Sublime: A History of Wordsworth's Imagination.* London: Chatto & Windus, 1964.

Kirk, A. G. S. and J. E. Raven, eds. *The Presocratic Philosophers.* Cambridge: Cambridge University Press, 1969.

Knight, G. Wilson. *The Starlit Dome: Studies in the Poetry of Vision.* London: Oxford University Press, 1941.

Kroeber, Karl. *Romantic Landscape Vision: Constable and Wordsworth.* Madison: University of Wisconsin Press, 1975.

Landes, David S. *The Unbound Prometheus: Technological Change and Industrial Development in Western Europe from 1750 to the Present.* Cambridge: Cambridge University Press, 1972.

Laslett, Peter. *The World We Have Lost.* New York: Scribner's, 1965.

Leach, Edmund, *Claude Lévi-Strauss.* New York: Viking Press, 1970.

Lefebvre, Georges. *The Coming of the French Revolution.* R. R. Palmer, trans. Princeton, N.J.: Princeton University Press, 1947.

—— *The Directory.* Robert Baldick, trans. New York: Vintage Books, 1964.

—— *The French Revolution.* Vol. 1: *From Its Origins to 1793.* Elizabeth Moss Evanston, trans. New York: Columbia University Press, 1962.

—— *The French Revolution.* Vol. 2: *From 1793 to 1799.* John Hall Stewart and James Friguglietti, trans. New York: Columbia University Press, 1964.

—— *The Thermidorians.* Robert Baldick, trans. New York: Vintage Books, 1964.

Lévi-Strauss, Claude. *The Savage Mind.* Chicago: University of Chicago Press, 1966.

—— *Structural Anthropology.* Claire Jacobson and Brooke Grundfest Schoepf, trans. New York: Basic Books, 1963.

—— *Tristes Tropiques.* John Russel, trans. New York: Criterion Books, 1961.

Lindenberger, Herbert. *On Wordsworth's Prelude.* Princeton, N.J.: Princeton University Press, 1963.

Lovejoy, Arthur O. *Essays in the History of Ideas.* Baltimore: Johns Hopkins University Press, 1948.

Marx, Karl. *Capital: A Critique of Political Economy*. Vol. 1: *A Critical Analysis of Capitalist Production*. Friedrich Engels, ed. Samuel Moore and Edward Aveling, trans. Moscow: Foreign Languages Publishing House.

—— *Capital: A Critique of Political Economy*. Vol. 2: *The Process of Circulation of Capital*. Friederich Engels, ed. I. Lasker, trans. Moscow: Progress Publishers, 1967.

—— *Capital:A Critique of Political Economy*. Vol. 3: *The Process of Capitalist Production as a Whole*. Friedrich Engels, ed. Moscow: Progress Publishers, 1971.

—— *The Civil War in France*. Friedrich Engels, introd. New York: International Publishers, 1940.

—— *Critique of the Gotha Program*. C. P. Dutt, ed. Rev. trans., with appendices by Marx, Engels, and Lenin. New York: International Publishers, 1938.

—— *The Eighteenth Brumaire of Louis Bonaparte*. C. P. Dutt, ed. New York: International Publishers, 1963.

—— *Pre-Capitalist Economic Formations*. E. J. Hobsbaum, ed. Jack Cohen, trans. New York: International Publishers, 1965.

Marx, Karl and Friedrich Engels. *Basic Writings on Politics and Philosophy: Karl Marx and Friedrich Engels*. Lewis S. Feuer, ed. Gardon City, N.Y.: Anchor Books, 1959.

—— *The German Ideology*. New York: International Publishers, 1947.

McConnell, Frank D. *The Confessional Imagination: A Reading of Wordsworth's Prelude*. Baltimore: Johns Hopkins University Press, 1974.

Miles, Josephine. *Wordsworth and the Vocabulary of Emotion*. Berkeley, Calif.: University of California Press, 1942.

Milton, John. *Paradise Lost. A Poem in Twelve Books*. Merritt Y. Hughes, ed. Indianapolis, Ind.: Odyssey Press, 1962.

Moorman, Mary. *William Wordsworth, A Biography: The Early Years, 1770–1803*. Oxford: At the Clarendon Press, 1957.

—— *William Wordsworth, A Biography: The Later Years, 1803–1850*. Oxford: At the Clarendon Press, 1965.

Morton, A. L. *A People's History of England*. London: Lawrence & Wishart, 1945.

Onorato, Richard J. *The Character of the Poet: Wordsworth in The Prelude*. Princeton, N.J.: Princeton University Press, 1971.

Paine, Thomas. *Rights of Man*. In William M. Van der Wede, ed., *The Life and Works of Thomas Paine*, vols. 6–7. New Rochelle, N.Y.: Thomas Paine Historical Association, 1925.

Palmer, R. R. *The Age of the Democratic Revolution*. Vol. 1: *The Challenge*. Princeton, N.J.: Princeton University Press, 1959.

—— *The Age of the Democratic Revolution*. Vol. 2: *The Struggle*. Princeton, N.J.: Princeton University Press, 1964.

—— *Twelve Who Ruled*. Princeton, N.J.: Princeton University Press, 1941.

—— *The World of the French Revolution*. New York: Harper & Row, 1971.

Parrish, Stephen Maxfield. *The Art of the Lyrical Ballads*. Cambridge, Mass.: Harvard University Press, 1973.

Perkins, David. *Wordsworth and the Poetry of Sincerity*. Cambridge, Mass.: Belknap Press of Harvard University Press, 1966.

Plumb, J. H. *England in the Eighteenth Century: 1714–1815*. In *Pelican History of England*, vol. 7. Baltimore: Penguin Books, 1950.

Polanyi, Karl. *The Great Transformation: The Political and Economic Origins of Our Time*. R. M. MacIver, intro. New York: Farrar & Rhinehart, 1944.

Potts, Abbie Findlay. *Wordsworth's Prelude: A Study of Its Literary Form*. Ithaca, N.Y.: Cornell University Press, 1953.

Price, Richard. "A Discourse on the Love of Our Country Delivered on Nov. 4, 1789 at the Meeting-House in the Old Jewry to the Society for Commemorating the Revolution in Great Britain." London: T. Cadell, in the Strand, 1789.

Priestly, Joseph. "An Appeal to the Public on the Subject of the Late Riots in Birmingham." Birmingham: J. Thompson, 1791.

Rader, Melvin. *Presiding Ideas in Wordsworth's Poetry*. Seattle, Wash.: University of Washington Press, 1931.

Reich, Wilhelm. *Character Analysis*. 3d ed. Vincent R. Carfagno, trans. New York: A Touchstone Book, 1972.

—— "Dialectical Materialism and Psychoanalysis." Anna Bostock, trans. In *New Left Review* (1966), 6(4):5–46.

Rudé, George. *The Crowd in the French Revolution*. Oxford: At the Clarendon Press, 1959.

—— *Revolutionary Europe: 1783–1815*. New York: Harper & Row, 1964.

Shelley, Percy Bysshe. *The Complete Poetical Works of Percy Bysshe Shelley*. George Edward Woodberry, ed. Boston: Houghton Mifflin, 1901.

Shelley, Percy Bysshe and Thomas Love Peacock. *A Defense of Poetry and The Four Ages of Poetry*. John E. Jordan, ed. and introd. Indianapolis, Ind.: The Library of Liberal Arts, 1965.

Soboul, Albert. *The French Revolution: 1787–1799 (From the Storming of the Bastille to Napoleon)*. Alan Forrest and Colin Jones, trans. New York: Vintage Books, 1975.

Stallknecht, Newton P. *Strange Seas of Thought: Studies in Wordsworth's Philosophy of Man and Nature*. 2d ed. Bloomington: Indiana University Press, 1958.

Thompson, Edward P. "Disenchantment or Default? A Lay Sermon." In Conor Cruise O'Brien and William Dean Vanech, eds., *Power and Consciousness*, pp. 149–181. London: University of London Press, 1969.

—— *The Making of the English Working Class*. New York: Vintage Books, 1963.

Thomson, David. *England in the Nineteenth Century: 1815–1914*. In *Pelican History of England*, vol. 8. Baltimore: Penguin Books, 1950.

Todd, F. M. *Politics and the Poet: A Study of Wordsworth*. London: Methuen, 1957.

Trawick, Leonard. *Backgrounds of Romanticism: English Philosophical Prose of the Eighteenth Century*. Bloomington: Indiana University Press, 1967.

Trevelyan, George Macaulay. *A History of England*. Enlarged ed. London: Longmans, Green, 1947.

Trilling, Lionel. "The Immortality Ode." In *The Liberal Imagination*, pp. 129–153. New York: Viking Press, 1942.
—— *Sincerity and Authenticity*. Cambridge, Mass.: Harvard University Press, 1972.

Venable, Vernon. *Human Nature: The Marxian View*. New York: Knopf, 1945.

Wellek, Rene, and Warren Austin. *Theory of Literature*. 3d rev. ed. New York: A Harvest Book, 1962.
Whitehead, Alfred North. *Science and the Modern World*. New York: Macmillan, 1925.
Whitman, Walt. *The Complete Poetry and Prose of Walt Whitman*. Malcolm Cowley, ed. New York: Pellegrini & Cudahy, 1948.
Whorf, Benjamin Lee. *Language, Thought and Reality*. John Carroll, ed. Cambridge: M.I.T. Press, 1956.
Willey, Basil. *The Eighteenth-Century Background: Studies in the Idea of Nature in the Thought of the Period*. London: Chatto & Windus, 1940.
Williams, Raymond. *The Country and the City*. New York: Oxford University Press, 1973.
—— *Culture and Society: 1780–1950*. New York: Columbia University Press, 1958.
—— *Keywords: A Vocabulary of Culture and Society*. New York: Oxford University Press, 1976.
—— *The Long Revolution*. London: Chatto & Windus, 1961.
—— *Marxism and Literature*. Oxford University Press, 1977.
Winnicott, Donald Woods. *The Maturational Process and the Facilitating Environment: Studies in the Theory of Emotional Development*. London: The Hogarth Press, 1965.
Woodring, Carl. *Politics in English Romantic Poetry*. Cambridge, Mass.: Harvard University Press, 1970.
—— *Wordsworth*. Riverside Studies in Literature. Boston: Houghton Mifflin, 1965.
Wordsworth, Jonathan. *The Music of Humanity: A Critical Study of Wordsworth's "Ruined Cottage," Incorporating Texts from a Manuscript of 1799–1800*. New York: Harper & Row, 1969.

INDEX

317